The Art of Angling

 **TINY BENNETT**

PRENTICE-HALL p OF CANADA, LTD.

Scarborough h Ontario

TO MY WIFE **Joy** WITH ALL MY LOVE

Preface

~~~~~~

This 'textbook' on how to catch fish is an expression of my philosophy of the joys and delights to be discovered in the true art of freshwater angling. It takes the beginner step by step through a study of fish and an inspection of tackle, with reference to different uses and specific localities, to the point not just of catching a fish, but of learning the skills and arts of taking big specimens.

Yet this is not simply a beginner's book.

The Art of Angling is a basic, general work on freshwater angling for North America, but does not follow what has gone before, as it often deals bluntly with those deeply implanted prejudices that are the bane of quality sports fishing for most people. I am a simple angler who likes to catch fish and who does not believe that certain fish are inferior because they are not deemed socially acceptable. I believe the sport to be a manifestation of man's deep-seated need to hunt and when people suggest — as they so often do — that trout is superior to carp, I want to know "In what way?" Carp are bigger, tougher, more cunning, and infinitely harder to hook and land. Some trout possess one advantage in that they are just a little bit more delicate to cook and eat. Yet a high status has been awarded the trout, while the carp is often contemptuously called a garbage fish.

I have not tried to establish individual preferences in this book, but simply to re-establish ideals that I feel are basic to the art of angling. I find it rather a pity that people will spend a great deal of money to fly north to hunt for big walleye, but are insulted by the suggestion that they fish the lake close to their homes for the monster carp that swim lazily around every bay. Saltwater fishermen usually evaluate sport on the basis of the fish's fight, cunning and ability to defeat angler and tackle. Although the fish pursued are most often inedible, no one would dare to suggest that the bonefish is a garbage fish or dream of talking down the capture of a bluefin tuna. So in this book I constantly challenge the attitude of anglers who become frantic with delight over the capture of small brook trout hauled straight into the bank, yet turn up their noses at the sight of an angler battling some cunning great carp that knows and uses every snag in the lake to retain his freedom.

To fit what I have to say into the available space I have had to cut down on the number of fish species covered — not, in my mind, a bad thing, for it avoids repetition and, in effect, broadens the coverage. An angler who thoroughly learns the art of catching a big pike, will find muskies on a par but just a little different. The fisherman who gets a solid grounding in the art of using light spinning tackle to take a white bass can take a walleye or a pickerel just as easily. The beginner who takes heed of the lessons in this book on how to fool the wily brown trout will discover that rainbows or brookies are easy to catch in comparison. For my purposes, I have selected the great central mass of the North American continent as the hunting ground and have taken the fish species that I know command the greatest attention of most anglers.

I believe that the fisherman who can consistently catch large carp is a thinking, expert angler, and in this book deal with the angling scene as it affects millions of such fishermen today. It's all very well to talk about big brook trout in some clean northern lake, but that's a long way off, while the local pond may be filled with big crappies and the nearby river boast big carp. Exciting fishing will be our reward if we pursue them after work on some fine summer evening.

Acknowledgments

It would be impossible to thank individually all who made this book possible, and many, such as the kindly advisors of my angling childhood, are not known to me by name. My greatest debt is to Bernard Venables who opened my eyes, and the eyes of an entire generation of anglers, to the thrill and joy of planned skills in catching fish in a sporting fashion. Bernard Venables — author, poet, artist, angler supreme and stout friend — gives us freely of beauty in all he says and does. Dick Walker, scientist and angler, brought a new dimension to freshwater angling that has created change and added to the art a depth of thought that can make catching fish an exciting challenge. A great deal of my angling techniques stem from roots planted by Walker and people such as Fred J. Taylor, Maurice Wiggin, Ken Sutton and Peter Brewster.

My thanks to Dr. W.B. Scott and Dr. E.J. Crossman of the Department of Ichthyology, Royal Ontario Museum, who were patient enough to listen to my theories and make useful comments, and who gave freely of their limited time. My thanks also in this regard to the scientists and biologists of the various branches of the Ontario Department of Lands and Forests.

Joe Brooks Jr., during a happy ten days light-tackle big-game fishing trip in Bermuda, taught me a new understanding of tackle that has been of value in my angling ever since. It was fun too, to fish with Joe Brooks from dawn to dusk, knowing that I had met at last a kindred spirit who would rather fish than eat, and who, with all his other fine qualities, possesses a spirit of sportsmanship I have never found excelled. My thanks also to four happy young anglers who allow me to take them fishing and who, by their fresh and excited attitudes to the art, renew afresh my youthful thrills in the game . . . these are not boys, but attractive young ladies named Tracy Bennett, Lynn Essex, Harriet Rantoul and Suzie Campbell. Finally, gratitude and thanks to Pete McGillen who held out the hand of friendship at a time when it was needed and through many unselfish acts of kindness smoothed the path in which I had chosen to walk.

Illustrations

~~~~~~

Grateful acknowledgment is made to the following for permission to reproduce their illustrations on the pages listed below:

Florida Development Commission, pages 37, 213, 217 and 224
Al Hill, page 283
Duncan Macpherson, page 117
Manitoba Department of Tourism and Recreation, pages 46 and 171
Michigan Tourist Council, page 237
National Film Board of Canada, by George Hunter, page 182
N. Carolina Wildlife Resources Commission, pages 98 and 193
Ontario Department of Lands and Forests, pages 25, 26, 27, 31, 82, 160 and 258
Ontario Department of Tourism and Information, pages 109, 127, 177, 184 and 201
Pennsylvania Fish Commission, pages 33, 113 and 230
S. Carolina Department of Parks, Recreation and Tourism, pages 126 and 167
U.S. Department of Commerce, pages 57 and 280
Zebco Manufacturing Co., pages 53 and 55

COLOR PLATES: Walter Coucill, facing page 33
Color sketches courtesy Loates Visual Arts
Eberhard Otto (from Miller Services), facing page 225
Miller Services, facing pages 17 and 241

Drawings by Loates Visual Arts

Contents

~~~~~~

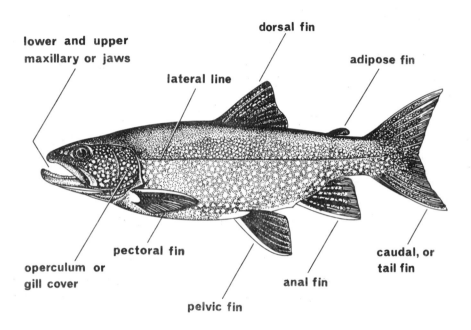

lower and upper
maxillary or jaws

dorsal fin

adipose fin

lateral line

pectoral fin

operculum or
gill cover

pelvic fin

anal fin

caudal, or
tail fin

The external parts of the fish. Above: *the lake trout.* Below: *the pike.*

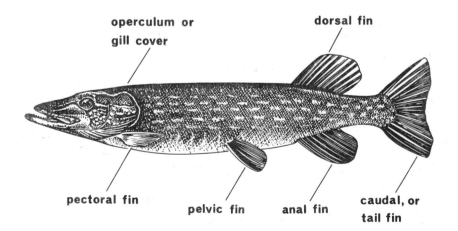

operculum or
gill cover

dorsal fin

pectoral fin

pelvic fin

anal fin

caudal, or
tail fin

1 🐟 About Fish

To be a successful angler, one must have a good knowledge of fish, for to understand the quarry is to defeat him.

The dead fish reclining on the slab at your food market may be quite lacking in positive personality, but when we meet with these creatures in their native element, we discover an excitingly different story.

This is not a simple animal, but a rich part of a complex family with an evolutionary history reaching back 400 million years. There are more than 20 thousand known species in a glorious range of shapes, sizes and diverse characteristics. Indeed, any study of fish can become of absorbing interest.

The largest fish known to man is the whale shark, a true fish and not a mammal, that cruises the open seas and is known to reach 60 feet long. Yet in the same family, we find the dogfish, a shark that matures at about a foot long, and may be full grown at only twice that length.

Some fish are superbly streamlined and actually beautiful in their wicked sleek lines. Some are flat like tea trays, others are round, and still others are long and ribbon shaped. The sharks have teeth that can sheer through bone and muscle with effortless ease, the carp and sucker have teeth, but in the throat, and they suck at food with thick rubbery lips. There are the speed stars such as the pike and salmon, the barracuda and the marlin which can travel at 45 mph. Yet there are also grotesque fish species, so clumsy that they can barely make forward progress in the water. The giant ocean sunfish, for example, is a huge globular creature that reaches weights up to 800 pounds and drifts helplessly through the seas at the whim of tides and currents.

It is usually correct to say that fish are cold-blooded animals living in water and taking oxygen into a complex blood system through the aid of gills. But be warned from the start: it is difficult to lay down guide rules for fish. No matter what you say, it is usually possible to find at least one species that fails to conform.

Certainly all fish dwell in water, even though there are species known to leave it for limited periods, but on the question of breathing with the aid of gills, we run into quite a few fish who have grown rudimentary lung systems that allow the creature to take in air from above the surface of the water. Usually this has evolved to allow species in dry countries to survive prolonged drought or oxygen-poor waters overheated by a tropical sun. Perhaps the best example of this is the African lungfish.

There are a number of species of lungfish, most of which are found in those lands where rainfall is sparse. The African lungfish has its home in regions where prolonged droughts will dry up streams and lake beds for periods lasting as long as three years.

The lungfish burrows into the mud of the stream and forms a nest which is lined with mucus extruded by the fish. It extends an opening to the surface, which forms a breathing hole rather similar to the snorkel sent up by submarines. In this prison, hard baked by the burning rays of the African sun, the lungfish exists by gulping down air through its breathing hole. The air is channelled down into twin pouches extending along each side of the gullet and these act as crude lungs by extracting the oxygen and passing it into the blood stream.

When at last the drought breaks, the waters wash away the walls of the mud ball, and the fish swims free once more. It may be nothing more than skin and bone, but it has survived.

In North America there are several species that can survive in a similar manner. The catfish and that strange relic of ancient days, the bowfin, often occupy waters that become overheated in summer with a consequent reduction of oxygen. When this happens these fish reach above the surface and gulp air. This goes into their swim bladder where blood vessels close to the surface extract the oxygen and feed the circulatory system of the fish. There is even a catfish in Florida that *walks* over dry land to new habitation. These adaptations to climatic variations are common factors in evolutionary development. Without them, fish species would die out, as did the great reptiles of the Mesozoic Age.

I observed a highly interesting illustration of this survival ability of catfish when a local conservation lake was treated with a gill-strangling poison to rid the waters of trash fish and allow the planting of game species. After the lake was dosed, great largemouth bass that nobody knew were present came up to the surface and died. For weeks the shoreline was littered with coarse fish and the experiment seemed highly successful. In due course rainbow trout and largemouth bass were stocked in the lake and everyone waited with keen anticipation for some very good fishing.

There was, however, a fly in the ointment, for three years after the original poisoning of the waters the lake showed a tremendous head of small catfish. Nets and traps were put in and ton after ton taken out. The logical explanation is that the cats had survived the gill-paralyzing poison by gulping oxygen from above the surface.

This ability to move along with a changing environment is a lengthy process usually spread over thousands of years of slow conditioning. If it is artificially speeded by man, the fish are unable to change in time and this results in their death, or migration to a more suitable habitat.

This has happened in many places with our lovely native brook trout. Where man has polluted the waters, cut down the forests and warmed up the streams, the brook trout has failed. For this is a cold water species needing oxygen-rich waters and shade. Where once there were fine brook trout to be found, we most often find none at all, or in a few of the fringe areas where they are holding on, the less delicate brown trout occupy all the best swims.

This points up the great difference between one species and another. Never make the mistake of believing that all fish are alike. Even under quite similar circumstances, there can be an amazing variation of ability and behavior, and it is this that makes our study of fish important.

One of the world's most magnificent game fishes is the giant bluefin tuna, a stout yet streamlined fish of the upper waters of the rich seas that reaches weights in excess of 1,000 pounds. These fish are tough and packed with massive muscles. Hook a bluefin of any size and you have taken on a tremendous fighter that can strain the heaviest tackle built. The line peels off a smoking reel, until the angler despairs of ever coming to grips with the fish. It gets down the tide and dogs away, shaking its massive head in jerks that often lift the angler clear of his fighting chair.

But when the wire leader is grasped by the guide and the gaff goes home, the bluefin usually becomes a docile hulk in the water. Its fight is spent and it seems to smother to death now that its forward speed is checked and the oxygen-rich waters have ceased to gush through its tremendous gills. At this point the only problem is to haul its ungainly and heavy body into the boat before a shark happens along and takes a great slice out of the quivering carcass.

It is of interest to compare this with another big upper-sea game fish, the mako shark, the finest fighter of what is often a dull and lethargic family. The mako, too, reaches 1,000 pounds, is streamlined and often makes great leaps when hooked. Like the tuna it can put up a grand battle, but when you get hold of the leader and sink home the gaff, unlike the bluefin, your troubles have just begun. For at this point, the mako, never a quiet fish, goes right out of its mind. Even when brought into the boat and lashed down with layers of rope, the mako is not finished. I remember on one occasion a mako lying quietly for several hours, until the sun bleached its beautiful cobalt-blue hide to a dirty grey. It had been given what we thought was the coup de grace with a hefty 4-pound hammer, yet that long after, it came to, burst the ropes and slithered around the boat's cockpit snapping those long teeth at any object it could reach.

Another one that we dragged behind the boat to drown rested quietly on the dock after being winched up from the boat. A commercial fisherman standing by remarked, "You caught a bottle-nosed shark, I see," and he poked the mako in the head with a handy piece of 2-by-4 timber. Our dead mako turned his head in a blur of speed, grabbed the end of the timber and happily bit it in two.

It is important that we realize differences, one species to another, and that what applies to one, may not apply to the other. But let's get down to a study of the senses that fish possess, as this will play an important part in our enjoyment of angling.

THE SENSES

Fish tend to dominate most life in the waters not only because they are bigger and more powerful than most other forms, but also because they have a highly developed range of senses, coupled to a large brain and a well-ordered central nervous system. It is essential that we understand these capabilities, in order to successfully pursue fish by angling.

Even highly skilled anglers at times have rather mixed up ideas of the important senses possessed by fish, often giving top marks to a limited sense, while tending to ignore highly developed senses.

Fish can see, hear, feel, taste, scent and judge distances. They also have a color awareness, as most experienced fly fishermen know through years of using specific shades in artificial flies. Science at one time felt that this color sightedness was limited, but recent work would appear to reveal that it is quite an important sense. The sense ability between one species and another often varies, but what we shall deal with here plays a part in most types of angling and is in essence general to most of the fish we shall cover in this book.

The eye of a fish resembles the human eye, as they both consist of a transparent lens focussing on a sheet of nerve cells that are sensitive to light. Unlike the human eye however, the eye of the fish changes the distance between lens and retina to alter focus, while the human eye changes the curvature of the lens.

The eyes of fish are large in proportion to their size and even the deep-dwelling species appear to use the sense of sight in a number of circumstances. Fish can not only see through water, but they can also see through water *and* air and many species are quite capable of spotting danger in the form of an unusual movement made by a human being walking close to the water.

It is my experience that sight warning of danger is more developed in heavily fished waters and I shall never forget the first time I fished on one of the chill and gin-clear streams that run through the chalk country of southern England. The trout grow very large on the rich feed, and the rental of one short length of some of the best rivers is usually only within the reach of the very wealthy. This is not my status, but I had been invited to fish an excellent stretch of one of the lesser waters.

As I wandered along with my fly rod set I saw the rings created by rising fish several times, but every time I got into position to make a cast, the fish stopped rising. I had been forewarned that it is a waste of effort to simply keep flogging the stream and anyway I wanted to take my first chalk-stream trout in the classic upstream dry-fly approach. So, on and on I wandered, until I spotted another angler resting on a rustic bench set well back from the river bank. In a well-used basket creel he had a pair of magnificent 2-pound brown trout, butter yellow and flecked with the most beautiful rosy spots.

He invited me to sit with him and when I confessed my lack of success in finding feeding fish he smiled and explained how tough chalk streams were to fish at first, and how even highly experienced fly fishermen from other waters often approached the angling in an incorrect manner. He told me of the extreme sophistication of the fish, and how they would go off feed at the slightest sign of activity on the bank. Then he showed me his fly rod, a delicate wand of slender bamboo, a full 12 feet long from butt to tip. He made it clear that the secret of fishing those waters was based on locating a feeding fish, making a careful approach, and then using the long rod well away from the bank, covering the fish with the fly. He told me that most regular anglers on this water made a habit of sitting quietly on one of the many benches along the river until a feeding fish was spotted. The approach was then worked out to get the angler into casting range without scaring the fish. Quite often this made crawling necessary, and my friend had a pair of elbow guards along for this purpose.

The long rod, which seemed out of proportion, was made so the angler could put out an accurate, long cast, while lying flat on the ground, several feet back from the bank. The rod length aided in keeping the line well up, to reduce the chances of snagging on the back cast.

I later saw my friend go into action on a feeding fish, and the extreme care he used to get into position showed how shy and wary the fish were. He threw his line from a kneeling position at least eighteen feet back from the water's edge, and when the fish rose and took his fly, it seemed to me a terribly long time before he lifted the tip and set the hook. I was told later that many fishermen on the English chalk streams have a formula that is said slowly, when a trout sips in their dry fly. They say, "God . . . save . . . the . . . Queen," and only then do they set the hook.

The importance of the sight sense in survival is not confined to the wary, hard-fished trout of an English chalk stream. It applies with equal force for brookies in our waters and for many other fish species.

I was walking with a friend along a river bank once where carp were busily spawning, when he suddenly threw up his arm to point out a lone wood duck winging down the river. This quick movement startled a huge carp lying unnoticed by us in the margin of the river beneath our feet. In sheer panic it thrust away, a huge scoop-like tail came out of the water and, lifting about a gallon of river water and mud, showered us from head to foot. This is not a rare occurrence, and I believe it is the sudden move that has the greatest effect upon the vision of a fish. Certainly we should always take great care to keep as well hidden as possible, and where practical, conduct an angling approach to the water as we would stalk a wild animal on a hunt.

My last word on the sense of sight in fish is that many a stream that is well stocked with good fish has gained the reputation of being fished out, because clumsy or unskilled anglers walk the bank in full view of their quarry. I see this happening all the time, with men wading in small clear streams where it is quite unnecessary to get into the water. Obviously a keen-sighted fish will go down at this gross disturbance, while an approach from behind bushes or trees might well reveal some fine lunkers.

The Lateral Line

Running down each side of all fish is a curious and faint line that appears at first glance to be nothing more than part of the pattern of the scales, or the coloration of the fish. This is the lateral line, a keenly sensitive organ that plays an important role in survival.

Found only in fish and some amphibians, the lateral line sensory equipment consists of a tube running the length of the body on each side and joining together at the head. These tubes are filled with mucus and are open to the water through minute canals that pierce through the scales.

Exactly how this sense system works is still being argued, but obviously some form of nerve cells here record such vital data for the fish as water temperature, currents, and, most important of all, vibrations and the movement of objects through the water.

The importance of this sensory system cannot be over-emphasized, for experiments appear to suggest that it is more critical to the fish than the sense of sight. In one experiment a batch of fish were blinded, yet still swam confidently through a maze of obstacles. When minnows were *moved* close to these blinded fish, they turned quickly and snapped them up. Since the lateral line plays an important role in the balance of the fish, it is doubtful that it could survive any severe damage to this system.

For anglers, the important factor in our study of the lateral line is that it acts as a sort of sonar system by picking up vibrations that can be interpreted as a warning of danger, or the presence of prey-food. A good hefty stomp on the bank will probably send a fish scurrying to safety, while the strum of a vibrating lure will bring the predator forward in an attack.

Primitive fishermen the world over are aware of this and make up lures to vibrate and produce strikes. In recent years there have been a number of gimmicky off-beat *vibrating* lures put on the market, with scads of publicity on what they will do. Some of the new lures are very good, some are silly. Vibrating lures have been around for a long time, and a great many old baits have been successful over the years simply because they were built on this principle.

The long slim Canoe Spoons used for lake trout strum and flicker through the green half-world deep beneath the surface, bringing in a great trout to the attack. A red and white spoon fluttering through a shallow weedy bay lures a pike out of hiding, the superb Mepps tap and shiver across a rainbow creek bringing a scarlet-sided fresh-run fish forward with a rush to engulf the bait. On the troll line for walleyes the almost purring action of a Flatfish or an Arbo-gaster put fillets in the skillet.

Predatory fish are attracted and drawn by all vibrations seeming to come from a creature struggling in the water. This effect is less known in freshwater than in the sea, probably because of the greater size and numbers of saltwater predators.

Fishing off Bermuda once, with light spinning gear, we baited up a big school of false albacore, by pouring quantities of bait off the stern. The false albacore resembles an overgrown mackerel; it is speedy, strong, and grand fun on light tackle. Indeed, my first two fish on this occasion stripped all the line from my spool in furious rushes down deep. The third fish took off down the tide and I was sure I was going to be stripped again, when he turned and came flying back, closely pursued by a motley bunch of sharks, a glorious wahoo, and assorted barracuda. There was a snick at the end of the line, and all I brought in was the head of what had been a fish of about 7 pounds.

Obviously the frightened flight of the first two fish I hooked, and lost, had sent out *struggle* vibrations that had drawn the predators. So when I hooked the third fish, they were ready for action. Note that they took the fish on my hook, and although there were many more false albacore around, they chased the one emitting unusual vibrations.

I have experienced similar incidents with pike and muskie and it is common for one of them to take a hooked panfish. Only once did I get into a situation where attack after attack was made on the fish I had hooked.

This occurred on a wild trail in Ontario on the way to Pickle Crow, a gold mining complex almost level with the south end of James Bay. Arriving at Rat Rapids, we pitched camp, I clipped a red and white spoon to my big baitcasting outfit, stepped to the edge of a boiling white-water chute and took a cast. A long lean pike of about 6 pounds took the bait almost as it hit the water and as cast after cast took similar fish, my two companions hurried down to get into the game.

In a two hour session during which we must have hooked around 100 hungry pike, giant pike came boiling in seven times to grab fish of 6 to 7 pounds while they were on the hook. The big pike simply wouldn't look at our lures, and I later kicked myself for not fixing up a hook rig on a 6- or 7-pound pike. If I had, one of those monsters would have taken it as it swam on the end of my line struggling and emitting unnatural vibrations.

Most anglers today are aware of the value of the vibrating lures, even if a few fail to understand the way they work, but less known and less observed is the warning effect on the lateral line system of some loud shock or noise. Water transmits sound and noise far more efficiently than does air; so the careless anchor heaved over to drop with a thud on a rocky bottom, the tackle box clanking against the hull of the boat, the incautious foot stomping against a rock, all send out waves of sound to create an area of disturbance.

Some fish, such as sharks, are attracted to underwater noise and it is well known that any explosion will quickly bring these giant predators to the scene. But for most freshwater fish, there is a point where vibration ceases to excite predatory instincts, and instead becomes a signal of danger.

← The brown trout is the smartest of the true game fish. Taken from European stock, the browns planted in North America survive conditions that quickly destroy native brook trout. Sought by specialist anglers, brown trout grow to huge sizes, even in small streams, and many a carefree fisher drifting a tiny bait down a creek has been shocked by a gentle bite turning out to be a tackle-smashing lunker brown.

↑ Well-concealed by a large rock, a fisherman angles for brown trout in the deep holes of a rushing stream. Little waters such as this can keep the brown trout angler happy for years, because when one large brown is taken from a hole another will take up residence within a few days.

Fish have ears and a sense of hearing, and for some reason I have never been able to fathom, most anglers pay more attention to this sense than to other and far more highly refined sensory factors.

The classic example of this attitude is when some oaf comes stomping happily into the pool where you are trying for a particular trout. He sends a great bow wave ahead of his waders, takes a couple of slashes at weeds with his landing net, kicks mud off his boot on a rock at the edge of the water, and then talks to you in a sibilant whisper . . . because he doesn't want to scare off the fish.

This drives me into a hysterical rage and I usually turn and ask in a loud voice why he is whispering, as there now isn't a fish for miles that will look at a bait or lure.

Fish simply do not have as refined a sense of hearing as do mammals. Fish have an inner ear, but lack the complicated snail-shaped cochlea found in mammals, which gives land predators and victims their vital sound sensitivity. However, ears in fish play a role in balance and are probably tied in with the lateral line and gas bladders for detecting low-frequency sounds.

Normal speech above water, even singing and loud shouts seem to leave fish unmoved and I don't care if a companion sings operatic arias at full blast, as long as he refrains from stomping on the bank, or kicking things around the boat. As a matter of fact, a friend and myself were once taken to task by some disapproving fishermen who heard us singing at full tilt all the old favorite hymns while enjoying a float fishing trip down a northern river. One man came over to our boat as we docked and said in a most disapproving voice, "You fellows will never catch fish making all that row while you are fishing." Then his eyes bulged as our French-Canadian guide Gerry lifted stringers of very nice fish from our stern. "Singin doan 'url," Gerry replied for us. "It is 'appy and I enjoy too, and dese guys move like de cat in de boat and dey never make de bang dat frighten de fish."

Taste and Scent

It is wrong to lump taste and scent together because these are separate senses, even in fish. But they are so closely associated in our minds when we think of fish senses that I have joined them for better explanation.

In both man and fish, the sense of taste covers limited situations, whereas the power of scent has a great impact in our daily living. Scents are highly stimulating to the human mind, to the point where a particular one can revive memories of things that happened many years previously.

The large barbels are an important feature of the channel catfish. They contain taste buds and enable the fish to locate prey or food in mud, or in deep waters. All the barbels point downwards for groping along the bottom.

Freshwater fish vary a great deal in their taste ability, some having quite inferior taste senses and others, usually bottom feeders, having them to a higher degree. The taste buds are located in different places according to need. The pike and muskie, who pursue their food, have little opportunity to taste before grabbing, so their taste buds are located in their throats where they can select, before sending the food down into the gullet. But make no mistake, these fish will reject an item of food if it has qualities of flavor that they find unacceptable.

Fish that locate food by grubbing on the bottom often have taste buds in their mouths, or in the case of catfish and sturgeon, in the barbels that hang from their mouths and are used as outside tasting feelers to locate food. Carp, one of the most selective fish when it comes to accepting a bait, have taste organs located all over their body surface. For these species the taste of the bait is a factor of capture and anyone with experience in carp fishing knows all too well that tobacco taint or the careless contamination of doughballs with insect repellent is a sure-fire way to get properly skunked.

The scenting capability of fish varies and yet may be of such power as to be almost incomprehensible to a human being. The salmon, it is thought, can detect the odor of its birth stream even when miles out to sea, where the scent is incredibly diluted. Catfish find most of their food by scent and it is always rather eerie to me when a channel catfish picks up my dead bait from the bottom of a deep and fast channel, in the middle of the darkest of nights.

Fish actually have noses, in the form of two pouches, one on each side of the head, although there is no connection to the mouth, as there is in mammals. Water flows through these nostrils meeting ultra-sensitive cells that fully line these orifices. It is these cells that are able to detect microscopic amounts of matter dissolved in the water.

Unlike taste, which plays a lesser part in the feeding patterns of predators, scent is important, far more so than most freshwater anglers imagine. I had a shattering experience of this once while fishing for lake trout and it left me much wiser. For years I had rejected the idea of placing dead minnows on the hooks of lures designed for fishing for lakers. It always struck me that this was nothing more than superstition and moreover I felt it interfered with the wobbling action of the spoon. I always refused to have minnows put on the hook, usually arguing that predators don't come along and take a sniff, they home in and hit. Since I usually got a good share of the catch, I never felt there might be a loophole in my argument.

Then out on a northern lake in Ontario with a highly skilled lake-trout fisherman who knew the water inside out, I met with a big debate. "OK," said the old fellow at last, with a disgusted snort, "you fish a bare bait, and I'll use a fish head mounted at the root of my gang hook."

At the end of the day, we had ten beautiful lakers nicely laid out for pictures, two limits of five fish each. But the old man had taken every fish! Not only had I not caught one, I hadn't had even a solitary hit. Since we had swapped tackle several times during the day, and the only difference was that I always had a bare lure while he had a fish head mounted, it did appear that he had a point.

The following day I too used the head of a river chub mounted on the root of the lure's gang hook. And that day the score was even, five fish each, and I was sold, even though this could not be called a serious test by any method of comparison. But since then, I have made a habit of wiping my lure down with cod-liver oil before it goes over the side, and this scent hangs to the lure even after it has been trolled for long periods. I would hesitate to suggest that this makes a difference in the number of strikes, but it only takes a second to do and does remove the taint of human odor from the lures.

For bottom-feeding fish, such as carp and catfish, the preparation of the bait can be important when it is realized that these fish have highly developed powers of scent. As some fish are frightened by unnatural odors, I feel it is important that hands that have touched tobacco should never touch bait. To keep my doughballs fresh I make a point of carefully washing my hands between smoking and baiting up. As well, additives of a highly scented nature can at times help improve baits intended for bottom-feeding fish.

Since time began, fishermen have used all kinds of wild materials in the manufacture of bait and some of those recipes that have survived from Walton's time are enough to curl the hair on a ghoul. We can read about adding the fat from a cat killed in the graveyard at midnight, mummy dust and a host of other enchanting ingredients. Strangely enough some of these are far more innocent than they might appear at first glance, because many of them are herbs that simply have horrific names.

Being a compulsive reader of all matters concerning the subject of angling since I was a small child, I often used to add substances to doughball baits. One great favorite of my youth was aniseed, which I would buy from a drug store in small glass vials. Believe me when I say that there is no vial small enough to hold an exact dose of aniseed, and when I was off on a fishing trip with bait treated with this oil, I enjoyed a similar popularity among nearby people as would a skunk at a tea party. Once again, I never found out if this scented bait was of value, but there is no doubt that there are many materials that can be added to bait to improve it, even if only through masking human scent, or some other odor unpleasant to fish.

Touch

To many people the act of sticking a hook into a fish is an act of cruelty. Approaching this from the point of human perception, they argue, "How would *you* like a sharp hook stuck in *your* mouth or throat?" They have a point that we should examine carefully, for if I felt that fish suffered the kind of pain that I would if I were hooked, then I would never fish again.

Fish are supplied with touch nerves in the form of small pits found all over their body. Nudge a fish with a stick, and he will respond by moving off, or possibly by turning and snapping at it. In addition to these touch-cell-pits, some species have touch nerves located in feelers, like the barbels of the catfish and the carp.

However, a sense of touch is one thing, pain is another. It is certain that fish do not experience pain in any way that relates to human experience. I honestly don't know why. All I have to go on is a great deal of personal observation that tends to prove that this is true. Let me cite an example.

While big game fishing, a friend was playing out a superb yellowfin tuna, when a big shark slid up to the scene of the battle, with the obvious intent of making a meal of the tiring tuna. I grabbed a heavy calibre rifle and from the upper bridge set high above the water, waited for the chance to take a shot at the shark. On a turn, close to the boat, this fish made the mistake of allowing his head and part of his back to come above the surface and I slammed a bullet home.

The shark shot off a short distance and then turned and came back in that curious questing and turning act they go into when on the track of something in trouble in the waters. I hit him again and then as he came by the boat, the mate gave him a tremendous thrust with a big harpoon, kept aboard for just this reason. Blood flowed freely from the shark as the razor sharp point of the harpoon slashed into his distended gill slits. The great predator wrenched free, shaking his head and almost without pausing, he shot forward in an attack and took a great hunk from the struggling tuna on the light-tackle rig in the hands of my companion. Again he turned, came back and ripped a huge mouthful of meat from the tuna, which had changed in seconds from a potential light-tackle record to a mangled wreck.

I do not think I am being foolish when I suggest to you that for this particular shark, hunger was a more powerful factor than pain. Yet this is not an isolated incident. There are many thousands of reports of similar happenings, even of sharks being gutted by the razor edge of a whaling flensing knife and with almost the entire stomach gone, continuing to feed on the floating carcass of a whale.

In terms of freshwater fish it is quite common for pike or muskie to feel the sting of a hook, shake loose, and then hit the lure again. Perch have been caught on one of their own eyes, torn off when it was foul-hooked and just accepted as food by the mutilated fish.

When we deal with pain and fish, we are in a field in which our own emotional outlook on the subject bears very little resemblance to how fish react to mutilation.

From this ramble through the various sensory powers possessed by fish, we should have learned that they are not exactly defenceless in terms of survival mechanisms rooted in their nervous system. But what of the brain? Are fish "intelligent" creatures?

FISH "INTELLIGENCE"

The fish brain, which is a specialized enlargement of the spinal cord, varies tremendously from one species to another, not only in size, but in the uses to which it is put.

Fish which feed mostly by scent will have one section of the brain enlarged to accommodate this needed sense, while others, each according to specialized situations, have other portions of their brains more dominant, to aid in the daily business of feeding and avoiding danger. In some fish, therefore, we might expect the mid-section of the brain —

which deals with vision — to be more highly developed if that species uses optic power in the pursuit of food.

Pike and muskies have binocular vision, with both eyes front and centre to allow them a greater degree of distance-judging efficiency in tackling prey. Both these fish species attack rather like a fighter pilot making a deflection shot at an enemy aircraft and it can be fascinating to watch their approach pattern. I was once casting spoons in a shallow, weedy and crystal-clear lake that was filled with medium-sized pike, and it was usually easy to see the pike hit the lure. They seemed to scull along, finning fairly easily and then, their minds made up, they would slightly curl their bodies and launch themselves in one sudden thrust. This action was so speedy that they turned into a blur. Still, I noticed with deep interest that they never hit the lure from the rear, but came out and slammed into the bait slightly from one side.

I am told, although I have never seen it happen, that very young pike and muskie appear to need to learn and indeed practice this sudden final attack. It appears that at first, the young fish often miss and can be seen to be at a loss as to where the chosen minnow has gone.

On the question of intelligence there is much nonsense bandied about, and anglers credit fish with a greater degree of brain power than they actually possess. Also, it is not uncommon for some species to be talked about in terms of human characteristics, such as the "brutal" shark, the "vicious" pike, the "dainty" trout and the "lordly" salmon. All these descriptions are human and have no true value in the evaluation of a group so low on the evolutionary totem pole. Fish are not vicious, or brutal, but are merely performing in a natural way according to what part they occupy in the scale of marine life.

You may have noticed my use of the words "wily," or "smart" in connection with carp. I make no apology for this as I know from experience that large, old carp are extremely difficult to hook. They have big brains and for my money are the most "intelligent" in terms of survival capacity.

Many fish can be conditioned to distinguish colors and to associate certain sounds with rewards and also punishment. It is my belief that some species have the ability to inherit wariness, especially those produced from stock that has been subject to constant angling pressure for a number of centuries. Possibly, fish dwelling in hard-fished waters are the product of parent strains that have escaped capture by sharpened senses, in which case we could expect to find the progeny owning many of the superior traits of the parent stock.

But one thing is clear in my mind. While it is not at all scientific to credit game fish with advanced powers of reasoning, it makes good sense for us to be aware that we are dealing with creatures having an excellent range of senses, and we should govern our approach accordingly. It is better to over-estimate the "intelligence" of our quarry, than to barrel in flat-footed and scare all the lunkers within casting distance.

SPECIES DISTRIBUTION IN NORTH AMERICA

Natural Distribution

A map of North America shows a climatic range from tropical, in the Gulf States, to pure arctic, in northern Canada.

The temperature difference through the year, between the hottest and the coldest places on this map, may be as great as 150° Fahrenheit. This is the difference between the 100° of a heat-wave day down south, to a frigid 50 below zero during a winter cold spell in northern Canada.

Through acquired skills and technology, man can work throughout this entire range of climate. I have often stepped from a house heated to 75° into 35 to 40 below zero, but suitable food and good clothing makes this sudden 110-degree drop quite acceptable.

Wild animals have their own zones. Great shaggy musk oxen browse the sparse lichen of the arctic with the thermometer dropped almost out of sight, while the alligator basks comfortably on a Florida mudbank as a heat wave goes on and on. Some animals have the ability to cover a wide range: for example, black bears are found in very cold and very hot locales. Some creatures, such as the beaver, once widespread, are now confined to places where the habitat has not been so changed by man that it is difficult to find food and acceptable living space.

The fish species found on our continent tend to follow the pattern set by the wild animals. Some are severely restricted by climate to narrow limits, such as the lake trout found mostly in Canada, and the great gars which roam the rich southern waters. Some fish are spread through a great swath of our continent; some, like the whitefish of Lake Erie, have gone from the places where man has changed the environment. Most important of all, man himself has taken a hand in introducing species into places far removed from their natural habitats. He has even imported certain species similar to native fish, but capable of accepting a larger scale of climatic conditions, or an inferior quality of water to that needed to sustain native stocks. Man pollutes and must then restock.

From this, it must be obvious that the distribution of game fish is affected by many conditions, both natural and man-made, and it is often possible to pinpoint on the map just where we can expect to obtain the finest sport with a certain species of fish.

The best and biggest largemouth black bass are to be found in southern waters where there is year round feed in rich, weedy waters preferred by this grand game fish. As we head north up our map, we come to areas where the largemouth bass start to taper off in size and numbers, until we reach a northern point beyond their range.

In similar manner, the chill, clear waters of the northern region are the home of the giant lake trout, a massive member of the char family known to exceed 100 pounds. These fish must have deep, clean waters for survival, conditions best found in the great pre-Cambrian shield scoring across half of Canada. Here in the quite limited zone of its range, the lake trout provides excellent sport.

Man-made flood control and water works often upset the natural distribution pattern of species. Quite often the building or damming up of a great waterway produces conditions not found naturally in the area and makes it possible for species from other zones to flourish. These works, and those that will surely follow in the future, will prove of tremendous value for all forms of outdoors recreation, with a special emphasis upon angling. More than just added facility, however, is the importance of the effect downstream from the big artificial lakes.

When a large-scale irrigation work is completed the water builds to a great height behind massive dams, flooding tremendous areas of often arid land that is infertile simply through lack of water. This creates a thriving situation for marine life and usually this is reflected in a tremendous growth of game-fish species.

Down below the main dam, when the waters are loosed, oxygen-rich and chill rivers sweep down old water courses that may in their original state have only possessed limited run-off during much of the hot weather. Instead of long dry stretches linked sadly by warm and dull pools, the waters from the chill depths of the deep water above the dam create new and exciting rivers. Instead of a few warm-water fishes, a new world of angling begins with the introduction of game fish such as rainbow trout, channel catfish, white bass, smallmouth black bass, and even muskellunge.

But this is not the end to this tale of delight. In the massive lakes above the dam, the deep waters provide a haven for even more fish, striper bass, coho salmon, kokanee, and — dare we hope? — lake trout!

Many more of these great works will rise in years to come, to make a mockery of any attempt to detail a map with the limiting zone of the species of fish in North America. For, given the right water of appropriate depth and temperature, fish can be taken from their natural range and made to flourish in the most exciting way.

Artificial Distribution

Moving fish from one place to another is not a new venture for man; it has been going on for hundreds of years. Indeed, the carp that now form a heavy menace on many a water in North America, origina-

An Ontario hatchery technician removes an infertile white egg from a batch of fertile Ontario Wendigo eggs which glow with life. These valuable eggs, in trays of water of calculated temperature and purity, receive constant attention by a watchful staff.

ted in Asia and were known in Europe as early as 350 B.C. Carp were introduced here in 1876, from Germany where they were — and still are — held to be a superb table fish. This attempt to enhance existing fish stocks backfired and this tough and largest of all the minnows has spread through great areas of the continent to become a violator of clean, cold game-fish waters.

In the years since that unfortunate entry into fish planting on a large scale, fishery management has made great progress and now it is common for species to be moved from one part of the continent to another; or even brought to freshwater from the sea. The actual movement of native fish, such as bass and walleye, has brought a new look to angling in places where they were not previously found. What must be regarded as the most exciting work has been done, and continues, in the Great Lakes region.

This gigantic collection of freshwater lakes covers an area of more than 75,000 square miles and has never provided the fish life that the rich waters could accommodate. In the 1930's an eel-like parasite, the sea lamprey, moved from Lake Ontario into the upper lakes through the Welland Canal, which gives seagoing ships access to the upper waters. These creatures, which are not true fish, fasten onto victims with their sucker mouths, and then rasp off scales to sear away the life

Trapped and held in nets, mature muskies are artificially spawned into special containers. They are set free, and the fertile eggs are raised in a hatchery. This system is held to produce better stock than that obtained from adult muskies kept in hatcheries – a difficult task, as the fish need lots of room, and also tend to attack each other.

of the host. They found rich territory for their deadly work and by the 1940's had devastated the stocks of game and predatory fish such as the lake trout, burbot and walleye.

This loss of valuable fish stocks was tragic, but even worse was the resulting population explosion of small fish that arose with the loss of balance when the predatory game fish were depleted. The prolific fish that started to dominate the waters was a small member of the herring family, the alewife. It thronged the lakes in billions, competing for food with better-class fish, and dying, clogged pleasure beaches and water intakes with stinking masses of useless dead fish. By the end of the 1960's the production of trash fish in these waters had reached the incredible level of 200 million pounds every year. These hardy little fish are useless for sport or commerce and at that time formed approximately 90 per cent of the total weight of fish in Lake Michigan.

When an efficient method of controlling the sea lamprey was put into effect, fishery management bodies around the Great Lakes were then faced with the problem of this dominating and expanding forage species. The solution was to convert the water to a game-fish water by adding a type of game fish that would prey on the masses of alewives.

The race to build new stocks of different species began. Rainbows planted as early as 1904 had shown an ability to withstand the attacks of the lamprey and also to feed hungrily on the massed shoals of alewife and smelt.

The kokanee salmon, a small freshwater form of the Pacific sockeye, was planted by the management units of the Province of Ontario and the State of Michigan. Michigan followed this by introducing coho salmon in a highly successful program. The first coho to be taken at the end of their three-year cycle in Lake Michigan were magnificent fish, grown to 20 pounds in eighteen months in the lake, following plants made when they were eighteen months old and weighed little more than an ounce.

This one species alone fired the imagination by the sheer magnificence of their growth, but a lesser-known program in Ontario began with the production of a fish that doesn't exist in nature — a hybrid — the wendigo, or splake (see illustration below).

This hybrid has been known since the turn of the nineteenth century, so the fish itself was not new, but the work of the Ontario fish-management scientists broke new ground. They took male brook trout and crossed them with female lake trout to come up with a fertile fish capable of wild spawning. Then the real work began.

The lake trout is a deep-dwelling fish of slow growth and slow maturing rate. The brook trout mature quickly, and the first batch of wendigo was culled ruthlessly to select the fastest-growing, quickest-maturing individuals. These chosen aristocrats were then tested for the ability to adapt to water levels regarded as suitable. The fish that successfully passed this test were given the prosaic title of F.1. hybrid, and formed the brood stock. On maturing, these fish were spawned artificially and again the ruthless culling went on to select the top fish

The Ontario Wendigo, a small but mature fish from the final selection of brood stock. This hybrid lake/brook trout is the hope for the Great Lakes and other waters where native lake trout stocks have failed because of some form of predation. Designed to foil the destructive attacks of the marine lamprey, the wendigo looks most like a lake trout, the only give-away being its square tail, inherited from its brook trout lines.

in terms of what was needed for the final product. Year after year this process took place in the main scientific stations of the Ontario Department of Lands and Forests, until F.5. and F.6. hybrids were developed. At this point, the brood fish were stripped, the eggs set out and the stock grown for planting in the upper lakes.

The important factor behind this careful work was a knowledge that the sea lamprey has a prey preference for fish 17 inches and bigger. Since lake trout are not mature at this length, they had all too often been destroyed well before they had spawned even once.

The faster-maturing wendigo is capable of spawning in its second year, which means that the fish spawn possibly twice before reaching the prey-preference size of 17 inches. Since it adapts to depths used by lake trout and is composed of the best qualities of two members of the char family, it is thought to be an outstanding fish to aid in the creation of the world's finest freshwater fishery in the vastness of the Great Lakes.

Only the future will tell how this will work out. The coho is an exciting fish, but since it dies at the end of a three year period at its first spawning, it presents problems.

It may be necessary to keep this fish going through continuous hatchery raising, although it is felt that this is well worth the value of the fish. A distressing factor may enter if they take too well for, since these fish spawn once and die, streams and rivers near a number of built-up areas may be affected by waters choked with dead and putrifying fish. But the work will go on and expand. Other fish will be grown and planted, possibly the freshwater-adapted striper bass, the chinook salmon, the zander, or the pike perch from Europe, which is a faster-growing cousin of the native walleye. And, as with the Great Lakes, so with other waters of this vast continent.

In this book, we shall deal with a great many fish, with the black bass, the walleye, pike, muskie, trouts, panfish, and the whole range of sporting species to be found in this great continent between the east coast and the Rockies, the Canadian arctic islands and the fertile waters of Florida. This area affords some of the greatest angling for freshwater fish to be found in the world.

We have looked at the wonder that is a fish. Now let us see what it takes to catch one of these exciting creatures.

A truly amazing fish, this 102-pound lake trout caught in Lake Athabaska in Saskatchewan was a sexual freak, in that it possessed no gonads. Caught in August, 1961 in commercial fishing nets, this lake trout was 50 inches long and had a girth of 44 inches. Alive, it outweighed the 98-pound girl standing by its case in Toronto's Royal Ontario Museum. It is probable that the fish grew to such a weight through not spawning. It can be readily seen that the body is grotesque in comparison to its normal-sized head.

2 To Catch a Fish

This book is going to cover a lot of territory. We shall be going fishing for bass at the edge of the lily beds, trolling for giant muskies in the big northern lakes, and casting for walleye by the light of the moon over some shoal where the lunkers gather. But I want to make it clear at the outset that, since angling is a sport of universal interest and practice, there is little room in it for any rigid adherence to one style rather than another, and even though one method may be used more in one place than another, when we deal with angling we are getting down to the simple proposition of catching a fish.

Angling has travelled many paths since it came to be a sport, and fishing tackle has become complex. A visit to a tackle store can be an ordeal for the beginner when he sees that glittering array of goods placed so temptingly at hand. By dealing with simple matters before getting down to serious discussions of tackle, I am saying again what I have said so many times in the past: the first important consideration in angling is the capture of a fish.

The great range of specialist tackle used often blinds people to the truth of angling — that it is a simple pleasure of a peaceful nature. Few tackle outfits reflect this as well as does the common cane-pole outfit with a bobber. Many people start off with something like it and in quite a few places this basic gear is known to be effective tackle. But for most people the outfit first chosen is usually quite a good set based upon certain regional preferences. It might be spinning gear, fly tackle or baitcasting rod and reel.

We live in an age of specialization where it doesn't seem enough just to be an angler. I wish I had a dollar for everytime someone has told me he is an angler . . . for trout of course . . . on the fly, naturally.

I don't think there's anything wrong with this, for I also enjoy many specialist forms of fishing. But it is often a form of snobbery in a sport where there is no room for such nonsense. It is a modern phenomenon, unknown to such wonderful fishermen as Izaak Walton. Old Father Izaak fished for all species in due season and dwelt with almost equal love on the chub as on the trout.

In a way, we have lost some of the delightful and pure innocence in angling that Walton knew, but then, this carries over in modern living to many other things, for example to our over-organization of the play of small boys who are put into miniature baseball uniforms and taught how to warm a bench, instead of being allowed to shout and yell and even get mad and make off for home, taking the ball . . . "It's *my* ball!"

KID STYLE

Let us then revert to how it was when I was five years old and fished in the old way, with simple gear, in a simple manner, where the fish were small, but the fun was terrific.

My first set of tackle was free, consisting of a bamboo cane about six feet long — one of the bundle my grandfather kept in his garden shed to support his raspberries in growing season.

Using the simplest tackle, these youngsters are contendedly fishing a nice-looking hole below a small dam. The lad on the left has a standard baitcasting rig; the boy on the right is fishing with the most basic of all tackle — a switch cut from a nearby tree.

The line was sewing thread, a coarse khaki color from the never ending length on the big spool in my mother's work basket. For a bobber, a big thick kitchen match was laboriously hitched to the thread, one foot from the working end, and since we were not allowed a hook, or even a bent pin, we just tied a small red worm on the end — not the easiest object to tie and retain in the best wriggling style.

We had a small angling society of boys all of the same age and we had a lot of fun. Best of all, a member of the group actually had a real pond behind his house where we would take our home-made tackle and sit for hours, staring at the usually motionless match resting on the green and weedy surface.

A bite was registered when the match started to move with jerky twitching motions, and excitement would grow until the match was pulled an inch or more under as the projected victim pulled lustily on one of the free ends of the worm.

This was a trying situation, for without hooks, we were forced to wait until the worm end was gorged. Then, with a smooth swing, we would attempt to sweep tackle and critter out of the pond and onto the grass.

If it was a three-spined stickleback, our usual quarry, we often got it, because the sharp teeth of this tough little predator hung on the worm long enough for the swift flight through the air. Things were not as easy if our catch was one of the highly prized little salamanders of the pond, because not only did the end of the worm come sliding out of their mouths like greased lightning, but, if one of these fell short it waddled back to safety on swiftly pumping little legs.

Our successes were usually satisfying and we would all head for home wet and happy and with little fish and newts proudly displayed in lard cans fitted with bale handles of coarse string.

It was solid fun: there were no anxious fathers hovering at our backs to teach us a better method of swinging the fish out of the water, or to keep us at the sport until we had beaten all the rest of the gang. If the fishing palled, we played ball, or climbed a tree and played pirates, on the lookout for a fat and rich merchant ship on the horizon. Since we were left alone — except for meals and bath-night calls — we worked our own way up the ladder of angling techniques and tackle.

The next step was longer canes and more delicate line in the form of embroidery thread: we bent pins and stole the corks from medicine bottles for bobbers.

And as the years passed, we grew up a race of cane-pole fishermen tried and true, with pride, and no feeling of shame at our simple tackle.

We used this gear even when we were at last allowed to travel to some small lakes nearby, where we would go complete with bottle of

←*A fresh-run rainbow, newly arrived in a stream from a big lake, competes for minnows with a brilliantly hued Belted Kingfisher. Swift and powerful, these fish have been planted throughout the world, wherever there are chill, clean waters and anglers to fish them. In many of North America's larger lakes, the spring and fall runs of this species draw thousands of people to crystal clear streams and the broad edges of lakes.*

↑ *Surf fishing for giant migratory rainbows is popular along the rocky shoreline of Georgian Bay, the Ontario extension of Lake Huron. With baits cast well out and rods set high on special tripods, anglers await the slashing take that indicates a rainbow trout hit.*

A youngster armed with his first set of proper tackle begins to unravel the complexities of reel and line. At this stage, children often spend less time fishing than they do attempting to work the tackle properly, and it is a shame to see them caught up in techniques when they could be better off fishing happily with a basic cane-pole rig.

cold lemonade and a doorstep hunk of bread and jelly wrapped up in a piece of clean rag. But ambitions grew, for it was here that we fished alongside men armed with real tackle: with long rods and cunning reels, oiled silk lines and, of course, delicate little hooks whipped to the finest of natural-gut leaders. And we copied them, taking in their much lighter gear and substituting bird quills for our stubby bottle corks, and black, japanned eel-hooks for our bent pins. The men were patient with us, showing us how to tie the proper knots and where to cast our bait to entice the eager perch and panfish.

We caught fish. Not big ones, or even game species, but ones that were important to us, just as they would be to any kid today. For it is not the tackle but the sport that counts, and the sheer thrill and joy of holding in your hand a fish taken by personal effort.

PROPER TACKLE

I was twelve years old before I obtained my first real tackle, a massive vintage fly outfit — a wonderful relic of the 1880's — built from greenheart wood and as heavy as a bridge beam. With it there came a small brass fly reel filled with oiled silk line. The reel plates were bent and when the handles were turned it squealed like a nervous horse, no matter how much grease was forced between the plates. Over the years this old outfit had gathered dust in an attic; the line had congealed into one sticky mass that had to be cut out of the reel cage with a sharp knife and a good deal of patience. Yet no tackle outfit I have owned since has given such a shock of pleasure as the one I experienced when my uncle passed over that monstrous rig.

It would make a fitting end to this tale if I could relate how I caught some giant game fish with that old outfit, but I must admit that there were many years ahead before I could boast of a really big fish.

Since the reel was bent and wouldn't operate unless forced, I continued for some years as a cane-pole angler, while becoming more refined with the smaller items of gear. In a way this was valuable, for my being confined forced me to concentrate on the purer techniques. As casting was only possible as far as the taut line to the tip would permit, I learned cunning as well as the importance of recognizing the places where fish swim and feed in the different seasons of the year.

FIRST TACKLE

This background of how I became a dedicated angler may read strangely to those used to the array of tackle in the stores; it must seem like doing things the hard way. But the opposite is true and I'm now going to suggest that we catch our first fish by reverting to the cane-pole style. The cost will be low and it is a superb way of quickly rigging up to take a youngster out on that all-important first fishing effort.

For a basic rod the best item is a long, slender and light length of green bamboo, 7 to 9 feet long. I have cut my own when I have fished where this tough grass grows, but for most of us it means visiting a garden supply firm and spending about 50¢ to take our choice from the bundle they will have on hand. Get a really thin cane, and don't worry if it has nodules spoiling a smooth tip; we are not going to use a reel, but will tie the line directly to the top.

For our line we will need a 20-yard spool of 10-pound-test nylon monofilament which will supply many lines, since we will only need to use a length as long as our chosen cane. For a bobber, it is worth while spending 35¢ on one of the slim plastic clip-on models. We will need a small box of split-shot sinkers to carry the bait down, cock up the bobber, and give casting weight. And we can buy a dozen or so size-10 medium-length shank hooks, with eyes to which we will tie the line.

To rig, we tie the nylon monofilament to the tip of the cane and cut it from the spool so it is just 6 inches shorter than the rod. The hook is tied in any fashion to the end of the line, the bobber is clipped to the line 18 inches above the hook, and one, two, or three split shot (depending on the number it takes to make the slim bobber sit upright in the water) are clamped 9 inches above the hook.

Notice that there is no talk of wire leaders, or indeed of any kind of leader. The clear qualities of our single length of nylon permits it to act as line and leader. We do not need swivels, snaps, or any encumbrance: this is angling simple style, without any frills.

To complete our outfit, we will need a can with holes punched in the lid, and a supply of worms, either dug from the garden, collected by scraping aside wet leaves beneath a tree, or bought from a store. If the worms are large, we will need only a snippet at a time on the hook, so if you are squeamish, carry along something to cut off a section as needed. In the full-blown tradition of an angler who went through a youthful apprenticeship, I make out by nipping off the right length between thumbnail and forefinger.

You will decide where to fish according to the available waters, but don't be too fussy: we are after any type of fish and I've found that such fishing waters are legion, even in cities.

The best choice is any small and relatively unpolluted stream where there are fairly good pools, usually close to a road bridge. But it can be a shallow pond where there is at least a band of clean water-weeds, or even some large game-fish river where it is safe to operate with a kid in tow.

Most important of all, if you are taking out a youngster for that first fishing trip, leave your tackle at home and concentrate on the boy or girl catching the fish. Give full attention and it will pay off in great dividends over the years.

The adult reader may try this himself, and let me say right now that there is no shame in this. Take no notice of other people, enjoy your day, and if things go well you will be surprised at how many passers-by will take a keen interest in your simple but successful angling skills.

Find a nice little pool outside the main course of the running stream, where an eddy appears to go around in circles close to the bank. Do not get into the water, but stand back as far as possible while dropping the baited hook into your chosen swim.

Fish, even smaller species, usually prefer to be on the bottom in these little waters, so it is a good idea to raise or lower your bobber by sliding it up or down the line, until the hook swims just clear.

If the bobber keeps sliding under at one spot, there may be a snagging branch or shoal that is catching the hook. If it happens too often, lower the bobber on the line so it drifts past and doesn't snag.

Now we are ready. The hook is baited with no more than an inch of worm fragment, and if you like you can run it right up the hook to cover the metal. It really doesn't matter, but this way you will tend to lose less bait. Swing it out anyway you can and allow it to drift around the pool or to sit calmly by the edge of the water weeds.

On most waters it is seldom necessary to wait very long before the bobber starts to flick and dance as a fish bites at the worm. Don't be impatient. Allow the bobber to either dip right under, or to be pulled along the surface a few inches. At this point, bring the cane up firmly until the line is taut to the bobber and give a mere flick of the wrist to set the hook. Then, in a smooth flowing motion, firmly lift the cane. If there is no action, fish on for at least ten to fifteen minutes, and only then move off to another spot.

After a few attempts you will find setting the hook becomes easier and you will learn the correct point of the bite at which to set the hook. With luck you may even tie into a good fish. My small daughter often lands a decent brown trout while cane-pole fishing for minnows in the creek running through the back of our lot.

This is simple angling with plain tackle costing only a few cents and it can be a lot of fun. I use a fly rod dumped from my major armament in this way, tying the line directly to the tip, and using a slim bird-quill bobber to catch live bait for a game-fishing jaunt. I once introduced a whole gang of expert fishermen to this easy bait-catching method and they enjoyed taking the minnows so much that I had a tough time getting them to pack up so we could leave for the big water. In a healthy creek it is possible to catch several dozen minnows, such as chubs, dace and suckers, up to a foot long, in as short a time as one hour.

ADVANCED POLE TECHNIQUES

We have dealt with the cane pole as a weapon for the beginner, or as a method for quickly gathering in some live bait, but many expert anglers use this style in various refined versions.

Throughout most of Europe, competitions are held where competitors fish team and individual tourneys on slow-moving rivers and canals to see who can land the most fish in a given time. There are even

An angler fishes for bass and big sunfish in a Florida river, using a simple cane-pole and bobber outfit. In the hands of an expert, this type of rig can be extremely effective and is highly popular in many areas of the south for a variety of sports fishing.

international events with lines of legal bookmakers at the site offering incredible odds.

Most continental match fishermen use cane poles in lengths from 2 to 28 feet, with the most beautiful and delicate tackle for fooling the extremely wary fish. The fish they catch in this style are usually small, and purposely so, for a large fish tends to throw their style off. In an hour and a half, 300 to 400 fish is not considered out of the ordinary.

At one match I attended in Britain, the winner had a coach, a time-motion-study expert and two helpers at his back while he whipped out fish after fish from the ducal waters of Woburn Abbey, the seat of the Duke of Bedford. At the end of a four-hour match, the helpers came down to wrap up the gear, the coach and time-study man approached with clip boards and advice and the exhausted fisherman discussed where he had failed and what he could put right.

However, his formidable technique and preparations were not in vain, for he won the match with 38 pounds of small fish, gained a gigantic silver cup and around $2,400, and then walked up to collect about $2,600 from a bookmaker, having bet on himself at the odds of 750 to one.

In many parts of this continent cane poles are used for serious fishing. I was once on the Niagara river away below the Falls and spotted a family in action who seemed to have it down to an art.

On the Canadian side of the river, below the spidery span of the Lewiston Bridge, there is a narrow gravel road that runs beneath towering cliffs to end at the Sir Adam Beck power station. Here, in the boiling white water, white bass throng by the hundreds of thousands during the summer, and people come from miles to fish for these husky monsters in the fierce race. I was there one day spinning a lead-headed jig and taking fish almost every cast, when down trooped this wonderfully colorful family.

Six adults carried 20-foot-long cane poles and a horde of kids toted lunch baskets, bait buckets, empty sacks and all the materials for an old-fashioned picnic. Heading the assorted band was a huge woman, obviously the matriarch of the tribe. Arriving at the steep slope by the end of the pier where the white water foams out of the giant races, she grabbed one of the poles, unhitched a jig from the handle and with a flex of powerful muscles sent it out into the water about 38 feet from shore. She gentled the pole as the jig danced down along the bottom, all the while shouting orders to the rest of the group.

The tip bent over hard, and with one smooth and easy sweep she lifted the point and plucked a brawny white bass from the water and onto the shore.

Mom shook the butt of her pole and the white bass dropped off onto the bank, where it was quickly grabbed by one of the kids. Almost before he had the first fish safely in a sack, Mom had another wriggling on the grass. The other cane poles were brought into action and soon the kids were kept on the hop as, squealing with sheer delight, they ran back and forth picking up fine, fat fish that averaged 1½ pounds each.

What I have tried to convey here is that simple tackle can be effective, efficient, and fun. This is important. It is good for people starting out to catch fish (even if those caught are rather small) and this is most true for kids being introduced to the game.

There is no room in angling for a rigid adherence to snobbish forms. Be a specialist if you will, but never allow yourself to forget the delights of angling in simple fashion.

With that off my chest, I will next discuss more sophisticated tackle, for while I enjoy the simple things of life, I also delight in the challenge that sports fishing has to offer. Izaak Walton spoke eloquently of the pleasures of fooling some big and cunning old fish. To do this, we need a good understanding of the finer points of the game.

3 🐟 Tackle Talk

There is such a bewildering amount of tackle on sale, it might be easy to believe that it forms a study too complicated to be quickly learned.

This is not true. Many people buy a basic fishing-tackle outfit and use it with joy and pleasure all their lives. We must remember that much of what we find in sporting goods stores is designed for taking fish in a sporting, yet ritual way. A good example of this is fly-fishing gear. It is delightful to use and enchanting in action and appeal. Yet the truth is that a highly skilled fisherman, using balanced bottom-tackle and a gallon of maggots, could take ten fish for every one taken by a top-class fly fisherman using artificial bait.

Some tackle is specialized for use when after fish in unusual habitat. In this category I place the wire-line trolling gear used for lake trout in deep water. You can catch lakers on the surface, even in summer, but the use of the proper gear that takes the lures to the bottom of 100 feet of water makes catches more certain.

We must never forget that fishing tackle is designed for sport, for taking fish in a way that gives us pleasure. This is a very real part of angling, for if the sole idea is simply to catch fish, there are many more effective ways to do it than by rod and line.

People in societies where fish forms an important staple of life seldom bother to use angling gear. It is simply not efficient when food must be put on the table. A primitive uses a gill net, traps, spears or harpoons, and even vegetable poisons which he runs into the water and which bring great quantities of fish to the surface where they can be easily collected.

Some commercial systems are similar to sporting ways, and in these cases the anglers have usually adopted those methods that fall into a pattern which allows sport. School tuna are taken on massive cane-pole rigs in commercial quantities; South Sea islanders troll pearl lures behind canoes, as we troll for muskies and lake trout; the dory fisherman of the Grand Banks puts out his longline and then while it fishes, he uses a jig on a handline just as we might jig for a walleye over the side of our boat.

So don't be put off by the apparent mystery of tackle. Just remember that it has been designed for pleasure and you will find that tackle, while expensive, can come to be a study that is a joy in itself. In the making of an angler, tackle can become an obsession, and you will probably own before long a growing collection of different rods, reels and accessories. I'm no exception to this rule; I delight in good tackle and at the time of writing own twenty-two complete outfits of rods and reels in a range of weights, shapes and types. To these complete outfits, add spare rods, spools of line, boxes of hooks, swivels, snaps, leaders and bobbers, plus two portmanteau-sized cases filled to overflowing with plugs, lures, spoons, spinners and all kinds of cunningly devised accessories (some of them pretty, but useless).

As I say, many people select a good, all-purpose outfit and stick with it; others, of whom I am one, tend towards specialization.

This is all so easy to do, for it starts out in such an innocent fashion.

You may be fishing with a frog, a worm, or a minnow, when there is a sudden lunge and the bait is taken by a lusty, hard-fighting black bass. It hits and comes out of the water, gills rattling, mouth open and spray flying across the still surface. Startled out of your wits, you gaze almost with fear, at the great boil where the fish has gone back in and awaken when a tremendous slash at the rod tells you that you have actually hooked that monster fish.

You lose or land it, and it becomes a high point of your fishing that you recount until everyone is tired of hearing about it — especially if you lose it and can then add a couple of pounds to its weight. But it changes you; you are not content now with just catching a fish, you want a bass bigger and better than that first one and you find out all you can and you fish for them. At that point, my friend, *you* are hooked.

You are now a bass fisherman and you walk, talk, eat and sleep bass, catching enough to make you feel you know the game, until, one day while you fish in your full pride, someone comes along with baitcasting gear and, using it with a skill that makes your eyes pop, slams into a largemouth, on a surface plug, that makes all you have caught seem like minnows.

Now comes the push into a new style: you get rod and reel and the best line money can buy, and a great box with a whole row of spaces for plugs and you start to fill it. You get surface plugs, medium-diving plugs, deep-diving plugs and some lures that look like nothing on earth, yet amazingly enough do catch fish. Now all the effort is on expertise in casting, to land the bait just at the right spot and to give the lure life, the way you have seen the experts do it.

You get it licked and life takes on a fresh and rosy hue and your talk at this point is on thumbing the reel and how that big lunker by Old Charlie's dock looked at your bait twice in one evening. And what happens? You meet up with someone using a fly rod and bass bugs. Once again you are a lost soul, but believe me, it is still fun. I know, because I've been the course, and after forty-four years of fishing, it is still new and fresh and enchanting.

There are many paths by the waterside. A casual fishing trip to a northern Canadian lake can turn into the start of a lifetime of love for the mystery of the lake trout in the dark green of its habitat in the depths. A fisherman may see the capture of a migratory steelhead and from that time may date everything by the times of the fall and spring runs of his chosen fish.

There are those who always seek out the biggest fish, and they may work and plot the demise of some old and crafty lunker over many a happy year. Some people just fish for big brown trout, taking an hour at dusk and another at dawn, through the sweet of the year, when the old cannibals cruise out of their holes to feed in the pools. Others favor light tackle, delighting in the capture of quarry on a hairlike line and a dainty wand of a rod.

At least some degree of specialization comes to us all, but at this point it is in the future. Right now we are going to discuss that important set of tackle, the basic outfit, the one that will lead us to all the joys to come.

WHAT STYLE?

A fairly short while back people tended to buy a specific style of tackle, because of various factors usually based on local preference or regional needs. Potential anglers living in upland country with fast, bright trout streams dominating would tend to obtain fly tackle and after serving apprenticeships with bait, would move on to wet and then dry fly. This still happens, just as in some regions where bass are top quarry there will always be a liking for standard baitcasting gear.

This is less pronounced today. Not only is angling changing in many subtle ways, but we can take advantage of improved transportation and fish for a range of species in places far from home ground.

Fly-tackle and baitcasting rigs are very much in evidence today, but the style for beginners and for the greater range of angling is spinning. Far easier to learn than the other methods, spinning allows an angler to master casting and all handling techniques in a shorter time.

There are two basic spinning styles, both based on a casting system that allows the line to peel freely from the reel, with only a limited chance of a miscast. In either spinning or spincasting (the two basic styles) the line flows off the open end of the line spool. The spool does not revolve and when the bait or lure hits the water, the line stops running and thus should never tangle.

Since this action forms the basis of spincast fishing we should understand how it works, and this can best be illustrated with a spool of thread.

If we stick a pencil through the spool and pull on the loose end of the thread, the spool will revolve quickly and the thread will peel off for a while, then, getting caught in the momentum of the spool, will usually bunch back on the spool in a backlash. This is how a revolving-spool reel works, but we thumb the spool to prevent the tangle.

Take the same spool and this time hold one end in the fingers of one hand while your other hand grasps the loose end of thread and rips it off the free end. This way the thread peels off quickly, doesn't tangle, and stops flowing when you cease pulling. This is a highly simplified description of a spinning reel's action, and since there are many additional guards to ensure a steady, trouble-free line flow, it is easy to see how spinning gear allows for effortless casting with a minimum of instruction.

If it all ended there, spinning would still provide a valuable introduction to angling, but there is one more highly important factor built in — a drag system.

This is an adjustable mechanical device set to allow the spool to slip when a big fish is hooked and threatens to snap the line.

We will deal with this later at length. It is enough for now to know that this gear allows trouble-free casting and the safe playing of powerful fish on light tackle.

For these and other reasons, I believe spinning tackle forms the best outfit for the beginner and for the widest possible range of angling. Let us get down to the facts on spinning, compare styles and types, and attempt to put together an honest fishing outfit.

THE HISTORY OF SPINNING

For centuries, inventive anglers tried to perfect the casting of a bait or lure. At first there were no reels; the line was tied to the tip of the rod and the angler could reach only as far as the combined length of pole and line. The first reels — called winches — were crude, consisting of a simple line holder, and anglers continued to manipulate the line by hand.

Even when precision reels were devised, casting was difficult with all but the heaviest lures and this set the scene for work on a superior casting system for light weights.

Some of the methods used were complicated, some were simple and effective. Some years ago, I watched an old Frenchman casting a wooden, baited jig for octopus, off a rock to the east of Nice on the Côte d'Azure. He was using a primitive spinning system, his line wound tightly around a large wine bottle, with the turns starting from the base and ending near the mouth. To throw, he held the base of the bottle in his left hand, twirled the jig around his head and let go. Sure enough the line peeled superbly from the end of his bottle in a neat duplication of spinning action. He then retrieved the jig slowly, hand over hand, so it just swam over the rocky shoreline where the octopus lived.

An older and terribly bulky system for casting very light baits was used in Britain a couple of centuries ago. The angler carried a rod with a tip line guide, plus a large wooden tray hung by straps from his shoulders, similar to those used to vend food at a baseball game. The line was spread neatly out on this tray, and with a flip of the rod the fisher sent the bait flying out and the line whipped up from the tray and flew through the tip guide. Distance was controlled by stubbing off the line and the retrieve was carried out with the hand not holding the rod. There were many such systems, all devised for the one purpose of effortless casting of medium and light lures.

The Malloch

The first practical light-lure casting reel came from the inventive genius of a Scottish angler, Peter Malloch, who in the 1880's presented the reel that bears his name and who deserves credit as the father of spinning reels.

The Malloch was constructed like a single-action reel, with a revolving spool and handles for the retrieve, yet with a unique system for casting. The spool was set on a well-made turntable so that when the cast was to be made, the whole spool was turned end on to the line guides. This allowed the line to slip off unrestrained as in the second part of our experiment with the spool of thread. The cast made, the angler turned the spool back into line and reeled, as with a normal single-action reel. Since casting off the end and then retrieving and winding on the same side produced line kinking, the Malloch was made so that the angler could use the spool either on the left or right side when winding in. This helped keep kinking down.

These reels were and are practical units, well-made and precision-finished, and they remained popular for more than fifty years. Indeed, since there was rugged strength built in, many are in use today for various heavy-tackle fishing uses. There is little doubt that the inventor of the spinning reel proper knew of Malloch's work and had this design principle at hand when he made his first reel.

The Illingworth

Alfred Holden Illingworth, the designer of the first practical end-spool casting reel, was an English woolen manufacturer, with a passion for all kinds of angling. It has been said that his first reel, produced at the end of the nineteenth century, was prompted by the daily sight of the yarn spindles in his plant. But there is little doubt that it also owes a debt to Malloch.

The important thing is that Illingworth turned out the very first reel to use the principle of a stationary spool on which the retrieved line was wound by a flier that travelled around the spool. This then is the reel that forms the basic design we use today.

At first, spinning reels made in this style were crude and rather flimsy, but keen-sighted manufacturers could see the obvious value of the design, and tackle firms in Britain and France got to work to produce their own models. In Britain, Hardy Brothers, the famous tackle makers, and Pezon-Michel in France produced well-made reels that became popular by the end of World War 1 with a highly select band of angling specialists. As this group voiced approval of the new idea in angling, better and more precise reels were brought onto the market and spinning, as it is known in North America, began to boom. In Britain, the cradle of this design, these reels are today called fixed-spool reels; what we call spinning, refers there to an established form of rather heavy baitcasting.

The Growth of Spinning

By the early 1930's, spinning was well established throughout Europe, especially in Britain and France where light forms of angling have been very popular for many years. With the new reels came rods to match, and lines, and a whole series of baits suited to the style. High priced, they were the envy of many a European angler who, in those days of unemployment and depression, could not raise the money to add one to his tackle kit.

The first batch of spinning reels commercially imported into North America arrived from France in 1935 and found sales resistance among anglers used to baitcasting and fly-fishing techniques and tackle. And when war in Europe put an end to supplies in 1939, this hiatus further slowed the acceptance of spinning as a new force in the angling field.

It has been said that spinning owes a debt to returning servicemen who brought back to this continent reels and rods bought in Europe during service overseas. This is perhaps a slight exaggeration, as there seems little doubt that many people were aware of the new sport and were simply awaiting the end of the war for the opportunity to get an outfit.

Production in Europe turned from war materials to more peaceful products and by a strange coincidence, a purely American invention came along to offer powerful competition.

Based broadly on lines similar to the original open-face spinning reel, the American design, known as the spincast reel, combined spinning ease with a touch of baitcasting to present a valuable addition to North American tackle.

Since many people confuse the two, let us take a close look at each and see what advantages are to be found in the two designs. For ease, and in line with a well-established naming system, I shall call the European open-face end-spool reels *spinning reels*, and the North American closed-face end-spool reels *spincast reels*.

One or the other, in a range of types and shapes, will form the choice of reel for our basic fishing outfit.

THE SPINNING REEL

The spinning reel is an open-face, end-spool casting unit with a stationary spool around which the line is wound by a flier put in motion by turning a reel handle. It has a built-in drag system which allows the spool to slip and release line against the pull or run of a fish.

These reels are so closely associated with the use of light line that it is not generally known that they come in a range of sizes and weights that will accept line testing as light as ¾-pound test and as heavy as 30-pound test, with ample capacity for several hundred yards of line.

The smallest and the largest reels are for special use. The standard models of interest to us here weigh from 12 to 18 ounces, will accept line from 4- to 12-pound test and give superior performance with 8-pound-test line.

This happy angler caught his pike on light open-face spinning gear, with a small Mepps lure. The gear permits light lures and baits to be cast a considerable distance, and a slipping clutch system allows the use of light lines in the capture of large, hard-fighting fish. Note the angler's grip on his rod, his fingers around the reel post and his forefinger at the correct point to engage the line and make the cast.

All the better models are sold with a spare spool that can be alternated with the one in use to provide a change of line test. For this reason, most anglers tend to fill one spool with the standard 8-pound line and carry 6-pound line on the spare for lighter or more delicate angling. This increases the possible range with a single reel and does not add much to the weight of gear carried by the angler.

Spinning reels are designed for fishing *under* the rod, where they balance and operate efficiently during the cast and retrieve. This is important, for with this style of reel, when the cast is made, the line flows off the spool in a fairly wide series of spirals. Fished under the rod, these spirals of flowing line droop and stay clear of the rod; if turned over for the cast, those same spirals will sink down and slap against the rod, reducing casting length and possibly resulting in a snag against any projecting object.

It is not uncommon to see someone attempting to reel a spinning outfit with the unit on top of the rod and their right hand going backwards. This happens mostly when people have been used to handling casting reels using their right hand for line retrieve. This is a poor way to use a reel, and it is best for any rigidly right-handed person to buy one of the spinning models fitted with a right-hand wind. Myself, I use my right hand to wind a baitcasting reel and my left to handle spinning or fly reel handles.

The size of the spool is an important factor in a spinning reel. It should be wide, but not too wide, and deep from top to bottom. We can get a good understanding of this through the use of our spool-of-thread test. Select one spool as wide as possible, filled with thread; and another, narrower one of a smaller size, with the level of thread sunk below the lip. Tie lead sinkers of equal weight to the end of each and throw each away gently so that the thread slips off one end while the other end is held firmly by the thumb and forefinger of your other hand.

The well-filled, wide spool should allow for a longer cast than will the narrow, less-filled spool, for in the wide spool there is less friction. The same applies to the spool of a spinning reel (see illustration, page 75).

If the spool is too wide, however, the line will tend to fly off in over-sized spirals that will create constant friction at the point where the line is forced through the first line guide. Keep this in mind when choosing a reel, plus the fact that spinning-reel spools should always be kept filled with line to at least 3/16 inch from the lip, to reduce line friction and loss of casting distance.

Line Pickups

The line flier that travels around the spool and lays back on the line in the retrieve is called a pickup, and these come in three styles — *manual, bail* and *automatic*.

All, regardless of design, are fitted with a hard steel roller, or pulley, over which the line runs. This roller in turn is attached to the revolving base-cup of the spinning reel, which revolves when the handles are turned. With the revolving system of line recovery there is a matched up-and-down motion of the line spool to ensure that the line is spaced evenly across the face of the spool.

Manual

This is the original form of pickup, seldom seen now, except possibly on reels designed for the heaviest of spinning. It consists simply of a fixed-roller mount, set on the housing. To cast, the angler slips the line out of the pulley and holds it taut on his forefinger; the rod is snapped and the line released at the correct point in the cast.

At the end of the cast, the angler reaches out with his finger, pulls back the line, and turns the handles. As the pulley pickup swings around the spool, it engages the line, which is then released by the angler.

I used reels fitted with manual pickups for years and found them excellent. I have often felt manufacturers would be doing us a favor if they fitted the larger reels with this system as it is the strongest type, highly suitable for heavy work.

Bail

The bail pickup is the most common, coming in many styles that operate in the same way, but with degrees of mechanical difference. This is the type to be found on most reels and it consists of a hoop of metal attached at one end to the line roller with the other circling around to fix into a socket on the other side of the revolving-spool housing. The line is passed *under* this hoop of metal before being pushed through the line guides.

On the cast, the angler picks up the line with the tip of his forefinger and pushes the bail back and away until it locks into position out of the way of the line. The cast is made as before, but this time, as the reel handles turn, the bail strikes a stop, whips over across the face of the spool and flips down, hitting the line and sending it sliding into place under the pulley.

This excellent system, remarkably free of troubles, requires less handling movements than does the manual. In use, this bail pickup becomes easy and automatic.

There are, however, two mishaps that may occur. First — and this happens even with the best reel — it is not uncommon for the sudden snap of the bail to whip the line down and throw a loop over the base of the pulley. This registers as a tightening sensation as the angler reels and can be picked out quickly by the thumb and finger of his spare hand.

The second mishap occurs either with an inferior reel or when a good reel has been neglected in the oiling or lubricating of the pulley, the bail and the bail socket. In these cases, when the reel handles are turned the bail flies over, meets the resistance of the line, stays upright instead of clicking down and quickly twists the line into a dreadful tangle.

I might mention here that too few anglers oil their reels — and they should. I squirt a drop on the bail socket and the pulley about every twenty casts, and carefully lubricate all major moving parts several times a day.

Automatic

This system predates the bail and was standard on most good spinning reels for quite a few years. I only deal with it here because there are fine reels still being made that use the design, and also because I like it and regard it as a good strong fitting.

This is like the bail pickup, but instead of the metal hoop extending across and being fixed to the housing, it extends across the spool as a metal spur.

The automatic bail pickup allows for greater strength of construction and is suitable for use with heavier gear used for bigger fish. For this reason it is fairly common to see large surf and big-game spinning reels fitted with this system.

In use, the line is picked up by the forefinger and the spur pushed back and away from the spool. After the cast a turn of the reel handle brings it whipping back across the face of the spool where it shoves the line down into the pulley for retrieve.

The only problem I find with this type is a tendency on windy days for the line to get caught around the spur. When this happens during the cast, it usually means goodbye to the lure or bait, as it always seems to occur at a moment of power-drive at the start of the throw.

Anti-Reverse

All spinning reels are fitted with anti-reverse locking — a vital part of the mechanism. This is usually fixed in such a way that a lever or a button can be moved to put the reel in and out of lock.

For such an important functioning part of spinning, there is an amazing number of skilled fishermen who never seem to grasp what this device is intended to do. Yet with the drag system, which we will deal with next, the anti-reverse plays one of the more important roles in spinning techniques.

When on, this lock prevents the reel handles from being turned backward by a pull on the line. It is usually formed in a rachet/dog combination that operates against the revolving housing, although it can also be used against the main gear or the main gear-shaft.

I keep all my spinning reels in lock at all times, so that I never get caught and am always ready for immediate action. Let us take a look at the reason for this and why it is so necessary to fully understand the anti-reverse function.

Let us take as an example a fishing expedition for carp, those massive bronze battlers that can spend three to four hours making up their mind to take the bait, then in a snap decision, while you are relaxed and possibly not paying attention, will pick up the cornmeal ball and light up their after-burners.

Warned by the frantic slash-down of your rod tip, you make a grab, get hold of the rod handle, missing the reel completely, and stagger up slashing the tip back in a fast strike. The fish is hooked, he takes off and line purrs off the spool as the slipping drag allows it to peel off quickly.

On your feet, you tuck the butt in tightly, raise the rod into a fighting curve and place your right hand in the correct position on the rod butt, your fingers on each side of the reel post.

Since the anti-reverse lock was on, there is no problem at all; you met the fish on a taut line, set the hook, and the drag slipped perfectly, preventing a break. If the lock had not been set, if you grabbed without getting hold of the reel handles, the speeding carp would have socked his full strength against limp tackle. The reel handles would have galloped around, spilling line in shuddering coils, the fish would have felt the check, spat out the bait and hook, and left you with cuss words on your lips and a horrible tangle of line looped in a series of coils around the reel.

Now, because you did it correctly and had the lock set on, you stand with a bucking rod held firmly in your right hand, and, with your left hand resting lightly on the reel, you wait for the chance to start pumping against the flight of the bronze battler.

If the carp swings wide down the bank and must be followed, the matter can be handled easily with the reel in lock. You simply walk down with the rod point kept high, taking up the line as you close with the fish. In the final act, the lock frees your left hand from the reel handle to operate net or gaff. The rod is held upright and slightly back so that the line will run smoothly from pressure applied by the drag, in the event of a final despairing run.

For trolling, the lock allows the rod to be put into a carrier, thus freeing the angler from holding on all the time. It is useful and indeed necessary to work the bait a great deal of the time, but there are times when it is vital to be able to allow the rod to fish alone. The anti-reverse system is no gimmick, but forms, with the drag, an essential part of spinning-reel technique.

The Drag

Sometimes called the *slipping clutch*, sometimes the *brake*, the drag system allows the capture of big fish on light line by acting as a safety-slip mechanism.

Without the drag, spinning for larger fish would be impractical, for the design of these reels does not allow for a systematic reverse flow of line as with single-action models.

I once read with amusement an article in an English angling paper by a beach fisherman who suggested that the best way to play a big fish on a sea spinning outfit was to turn the reel handle steadily backwards as the fish ran, and then turn forward to take up line as he weakened. Since he was writing on catching cod, I suppose this would work, but it would be amusing to see that man try his technique with a bonefish speeding across a marl-flat in Bermuda, at speeds of up to 35 mph.

The drag applies pressure against a hooked fish within the strain limits of the tackle, and slips at a point before this strain becomes excessive, allowing the spool to revolve and more line to be taken by the fish. You can get away with not using the anti-reverse gear, but you will be in trouble and due for breakage if you attempt to play good fish with a drag that is not set just right.

Most drags are little more than a specially selected series of washers and discs pressed against the forward movement of the spool by adjustable fittings. This series must be capable of close tolerance to allow for smooth, even slippage without the jerks or jars which might impose sudden stress on the tackle. When you hit that once-in-a-lifetime lunker, you must have a perfectly functioning drag, for any hitch can mean the loss of the fish and your tackle.

In the thirty years that I have owned spinning tackle I have had many spinning reels. Some were of poor quality in the early days when I couldn't afford the better reels, but luckily that was before I got into the big-fish game, where quality counts.

There is nothing that tests tackle and angler more than ultralight spinning for fast marine game fish in the warmer waters of the world. I'm not writing about big fish now, but those speedy species of less than 10 pounds, such as the false albacore, the yellowtail snapper, the Spanish mackerel and the master of them all, the bonefish.

Some years back I tested out a new American spinning reel by fishing with freshwater tackle and 8-pound-test nylon line for the reef fish found offshore. On the famed Challenger Bank 20 miles off Bermuda, you anchor, toss out a handful of bait and see the clear waters at the stern become alive with the darting forms of fish.

On my first attempt there I baited with an anchovy, put it over the stern to drift back with the slight tide and got an immediate hit from a 5-pound false albacore. On the strike, I threw in the line flier and raised the rod into a deep curve as the fish fled for distant horizons. That flashy fighter simply stripped all my line to the bare spool, but the drag whined away and let line slip under strain without one jar or catch. I caught some and lost many, but that reel behaved superbly and I now use it with complete confidence.

Setting the Drag

Few anglers understand the importance of setting the drag and it is common to see people fishing without the slightest idea of how this should be done.

All too often, I see fish hooked and the angler cursing and fumbling with drag settings while the fish is playing games with the tackle. This is one cause of lost fish. You must set tackle at the start of an angling session, so that when rod and reel are assembled, with the leader and lure attached, the drag is fixed at its correct setting. Here is how this should be done:

1. Open the reel flyer and pull 20 feet of line clear of the top ring.
2. Close the flyer and unscrew the drag completely.
3. Check that the anti-reverse lock is on.
4. Set the hook into a fixed object that will not injure the barbs or the point, stand back to the full length of the line and lift the rod.
5. At first the reel spool will slip, so screw up the drag, testing by pulling with the rod, until the drag starts to take effect.
6. From this point, tighten the drag adjustment a fraction at a time until you reach the point where the spool will not give with the full strain imposed.
7. Now unscrew in fractions until the line peels off in an even movement when the rod is fully bent.

The common error is to select too light a setting at first, for the proper one seems to be far too hard. In practice, the first movement of the drag takes more pressure than when the drag is slipping during the run of a fish, so if it starts too easily, you won't be able to put on enough pressure.

If it should be set a little too tightly, it is a fairly simple matter to ease it off a fraction while playing the fish. However, in principle I am opposed to the setting being altered in action. It is worth while taking a little time to get things right first.

Once the drag is set, it shouldn't be necessary to make any changes during the day unless a spool must be changed, or a mishap occurs. But if this does happen, make sure that the drag is again set properly before making the first cast.

Reel Costs

There is a great difference in the prices asked for a medium sized spinning reel, for they range from a few dollars to $60 or $70. And I have handled reels in the upper bracket that I thought of less value than some of the more moderately priced models.

Since these are fairly complex items of workmanship, it pays to devote attention to innards, design and quality of materials used.

My rule of thumb is to pay more for my spinning reel than for my rod, to decide the maximum amount I can afford, and to buy the best reel available for that price. This means I pay between $45 and $50 for my reels, but I should add that I have a reel in the range of $50 that has been in use for seven years in some wild angling situations. It has never let me down, has no worn parts, has needed no replacements and I am sure that I could get around $15 for it now, used.

On the other hand, I have a friend who buys cheap reels and while I have owned the one mentioned, he has gone through three that were bought as bargains and thrown away when a part wore out or broke.

He has spent more money than I and has nothing to show for it.

Buying for a youngster is a different matter, and I can't see buying the best unless money is really no object. There are a number of moderately priced reels made by good manufacturers which will give excellent service. For example, a Mitchell CAP, which happens to be my wife's favorite, is a grand reel, and I consider this to be an excellent choice for a youngster, or even as a spare for lighter-tackle angling for the adult.

It is impossible to set hard and fast rules and the situation is subject to constant change as American makers turn more and more to licensing foreign firms to make reel series at greatly reduced labor costs. The highest priced reels are usually superior, so choose the best in your price range, by makers with good names.

There is an important point that I would like to make on the question of tackle costs, and this applies to the whole range of gear, from reels to landing nets.

On the tenth anniversary of Zebco, R.D. Hull, the father of the closed-face spinning reel, was presented with a range of reels showing developments over the years. At nine o'clock is the original 1949 standard model, with the advancing developments placed clockwise. On the tips of the rods behind Mr. Hull may be seen rubber casting sinkers. These practice sinkers can be invaluable in assisting the beginner to get accuracy in his casting.

Fishing gear forms by far the lesser part of the cost of angling, when you consider trips, gas, boat rental, bait, accommodation and guides. It seems foolish to me to attempt to save money by using cheap tackle, and I hate to see people using a $14.95 set of gear from a $3,000 boat. Get good gear, look after it, and it will be a joy throughout many years of good service.

SPINCAST REELS

This American development from the European open-face reel enjoys an important role on the modern angling scene. Built with a hood that covers and protects the line, spincast reels are simple to use and remarkably free of handling problems.

Spincasters are excellent for beginners, yet should not be dismissed as beginners' reels. They are invaluable for night fishing, as the almost automatic handling of the line results in fewer hitches and casting snags. However, it would be a mistake to suggest that they are perfect; in some ways, spincasters have limitations when compared to the spinning reels.

Let us take a closer look at their workings and how they can become the first choice as a basic outfit for the beginning angler.

Spincaster Principles

These reels, which vary in shape and design much more than the spinning reels, operate from a fixed spool, a revolving, separate line-retrieve system, and have anti-reverse locks and built-in adjustable drags.

The major difference is in the shroud or hood that covers the line spool. This has a small hole in the top through which the line runs on cast or retrieve. Since a wide spool is usual, this means that the line is forced early into a narrow cone with a considerable amount of friction, tending to reduce casting distance.

Once through this hole however, the line travels in a fairly straight line up the rod and through the guides and the danger of line-slap against the rod is efficiently reduced.

While it is doubtful that existing spincast reels will ever compete successfully against spinning reels in distance-casting events, the length that is obtained is perfectly effective for all practical angling purposes. Indeed, as I have said, it is this principle of design that makes them valuable and useful for some fishing styles where spinning reels may be at a disadvantage.

There are two major types of spincasters, those for use below the rod, and those designed to be fished on top in a baitcasting setup.

It may look like just a gag, but this reel works. When the spin-cast reel first came out, traditionalists sneered and likened it to a beer can. Ever-obliging, the Zebco people made this gag reel, that serves now as a reminder that yesterday's joke can often become today's technique.

To make a cast, a button or similar device is pressed at the start of the cast. This retracts a pin or set of pins mounted in a cup built to revolve around the line spool. At the same time, the cup is pushed against the spool to lock the line and prevent it from running free. The rod is powered, the button released and the cast is made, with no chance of an overrun, since the line-flow ceases with the finish of the cast.

When the reel handles are moved forward to start the retrieve, the line pins flick out to engage and, as the cup in which they are fitted revolves around the spool, the line is spooled on evenly and without slack.

The drag and anti-reverse lock operate under similar systems to those used in spinning reels.

Under-Rod Models

Spincast closed-face reels for use under the rod tend to be rather similar to spinning reels, with just the shroud over the spool and the push button setting them aside.

Some of these models have push buttons, others have levers and still others operate by unlocking the line by pressure on the rim of the shroud. One type has a triggering button in the rod butt, making the reel and butt a single unit. In this type, a selection of different rod tips can be used to allow for different weights in lures or baits.

There is a tremendous range of different models, accepting line testing from 6 pounds to 15 pounds, according to the power of the outfit.

Top-Mount Models

These reels form an angling class closer in use to the revolving-spool baitcasting reel. It would not be exaggerating to suggest they are a more simple form of baitcasting gear.

The first time I saw one of these in use I was shocked at the brute force used by the angler. Fishing a weedy lake filled with largemouth bass, he was throwing a noisy surface lure into holes close by snags and weeds, and when he got a strike, he really put the stick into the fish.

With his drag screwed almost all the way in, he walloped the fish out of their weedy homes and battled them across the surface into open water where he kept them on the move until ready for the net. It was brutal fishing, but really a highly successful method for that particular water. With his 15-pound-test braided line, and a powerful short rod, he boated fish that would have been goners on light tackle.

At first, I rather felt he would come a cropper if he latched onto one of the bigger fish present, but late one evening he did just that, and successfully landed a grand bass weighing 5½ pounds.

These top-mount reels are designed for use with crank-handled spincast rods up to 6 feet, 6 inches long. Without this crank in the handle the angler would have trouble, as the push-button line release would sit too high for comfort.

Line release for casting is effected by the pushing of the button when the mechanism comes into play, as with the other closed-face reels.

Line tests for this style have a limited range, because light lines tend to bunch up and catch at the hole set in the spool cover. This is of little angling importance, as this style, if used properly, tends to follow baitcasting rather than spinning, and so much baitcasting is best done with a line of from 10- to 15- pound test, that it would be wrong to suggests this as a serious limiting factor.

These, then, are the reels that will form our basic set of tackle, and the time has come to match our choice with a suitable rod.

THE ROD

It may appear strange to some readers that I have spent so much time on reels before getting to the rods, but I see this as the best order for the range of gear covered so far. In spinning or spincasting we choose the system first and since this depends upon the choice of reel type, it makes sense to deal with them first.

The rod acts as a spring to set the hook without snapping the line and then its limber tip forms a factor of safety between the pull of the fish and the breaking point of the line where it works in conjunction with the slip action of the reel. It is beautifully illustrated by this angler, fighting an obviously large and powerful fish.

The same is not true of other angling styles; in fly work, where the casting is done by the weight and taper of the line, we might well select the line first and then the rod. In true baitcasting with a revolving-spool reel, I'd start on the rods because most reels would match the final choice.

It would be a mistake, however, to believe rods less worthy of study. It is the spinning rod that develops the power in the cast, and forms the instrument that is the vital link in the playing of a fish. There are as many types, tapers, designs and styles as there are reels, and the wrong one applied to a good reel usually has a painful, distressing result.

Right now we must learn about the rod in order to form our basic outfit; we will delve into rod function, materials and fittings. Later in the book we will find it necessary to return to the subject, for when we deal with areas of specialization it will be essential to re-examine the gear we will use.

Rod Function

The rod forms an extension of the angler's arm to help him gain casting distance and accuracy, so an important design factor is gearing it to this end. While fishing the bait or lure, the rod is used to control action, direction and depth.

With its great delicacy and light touch, the rod is used as a spring to set the hook without snapping the line. It forms a safety factor between the pull of the fish and the breaking test of the tackle, where it works in conjunction with the slipping action of the reel drag.

I fear that too few anglers learn to appreciate these vital roles performed by the rod. It is certainly true that few people understand how the rod acts to prevent a strong fish getting a solid pull against light line.

When a fish hits, we sweep the rod up in a strike that should set the hook in its mouth. Bringing the rod up also acts as a safety play, because at that important point of contact with the fish, our rod is placed in the perfect position to form a curving spring to absorb the first shock if a big fish hits. Since we can call the shots on paper, let us say that it is a big fish and, feeling the sting of the hook, it turns and flees. Our rod's limber length dances down suddenly and as the pressure grows, the properly set drag snarls and releases line under steady pressure.

Now we have our rod set into a delightful curve, the line spool slipping and a fish speeding away or slugging hard against a system that won't give a taut effect on which it can show its power. The rod forms a spring and works in close co-operation with the drag. Unless the fish is fast enough and big enough to keep running to the end of the line, it will be unable to come to grips with the tackle.

Fishermen who are unaware of this simple matter tend to use heavy line, in the mistaken belief that a fish must be held by brute force. Many fish are lost through this misunderstanding. I see this happen every year at my favorite carp hole, a local lake where a warm water outlet from a power plant attracts some big bruisers. In the spring, before the game-fish seasons open, a group of us get along the bank and use ultralight spinning gear to fish for these carp, which grow to 35 pounds. The sport is excellent and is made more fun by those locals who sneer at our 6-pound-test lines and tell us we should use at least 30-pound test.

Since there is a minimum of current, we tie size 4 short-shank hooks to the end of our lines and with a big blob of cornmeal bait the size of a walnut on the hook, there is enough weight to do without sinkers.

Carp are smart fish and will bite much better on light line where they don't feel the resistance of the gear. So the line goes off and we stagger up with our rods bent into deep C's as the lusty golden fish head for the far shore. Being tough, heavy fighters, it often takes forty minutes or more to get one to the net.

The people with the heavy tackle who are always attempting to tell us how wrongly we fish don't get as many bites on their heavy lines, especially since most of them reel the line up hard against the rod point where the fish gets good warning on the bite.

When they do hook one there are real fireworks. With their standard heavy rods, star-drag sea reels and coarse line, they usually first attempt to reel these tough fish without giving an inch of line. If this fails, and it usually does, they often drop the rod and try hauling in on the line, hand over hand. We have seen those carp snap 40-pound-test line, and even shatter a powerful rod at the butt. All this, simply because the people involved do not understand the basic facts of how tackle is used in the playing of fish.

The amusing finale to these jaunts is that we finish up by giving our carp away to the same anglers who tell us we will never land one on such light tackle.

So write in words of fire across your heart: *One of the important functions of the rod is to act as a safety spring between the power of the fish and the breaking point of your tackle.*

Rod Materials

There are two major rod-making materials in common use today: fiberglass and split-bamboo cane. There are a few relics of past days around, but the field has now narrowed to these basic materials.

Those of us who were anglers forty years ago feel a romantic association with the old materials such as greenheart, hickory, lancewood, Spanish reed, and even steel. But this is simply nostalgia; a fisherman would be foolish to suggest that they were as good as glass or bamboo. I once had a rod custom-built by a top-notch craftsman. It was the joy of my life but, being built of greenheart, would be too heavy for comfort these days. Greenheart — a heavy, straight-grain tropical timber — also had the nasty habit of snapping if the wood was allowed to dry out.

Bamboo Rods

Split-bamboo rods are better than ever, owing to improvements in materials and manufacturing processes. The craft-built rods are among the finest fishing rods made and are sometimes beautiful enough to evoke an emotional response in the breast of a tackle-lover.

Bamboo is a form of grass, and the best type, which is in short supply, comes from the Chinese border. Chances are, as time goes on, that this valuable bamboo will be even harder to get, unless there is a drastic change in world politics. Bamboo is a steely, hard material that can rip apart all but the best tools, and the making of a split-bamboo rod calls for loving precision work. Yet for all its strength, light and delicate rods can be turned out.

The selected canes are split into splines which are then cut and tapered until the parts can be fitted together to form a hexagonal stick. A special bonding material is put on, the stick is allowed to harden and then the fittings, butt, and wrappings are applied.

This exacting work brings the costs up and the best rods are expensive. But as long as there are craftsmen to make them, there will be lovers of fine tackle ready to buy them.

I own a number of bamboo rods, but find I am using them less and less, and my glass rods more and more. It is a sign of the times.

Fiberglass Rods

Fiberglass marked an important point in the history of angling because, being synthetic, it allowed mass production of quality tackle with a marked reduction in the price of good rods. The best rods are tough, resilient sticks, available in a complete range of rod types and tapers. Being built largely by automated process, there is little room for error and standards are correspondingly high.

The *glass* part of the name of this material is deceptive, conjuring a mind picture of a brittle substance. This is far from being true. The fibers used are drawn from pure glass, but look rather like silk thread. In one system of rod-making this thread is woven into a heavy form of cloth. This allowed me to pull off a delightful gag in the early days of fiberglass rods.

While working for an angling paper, at a time when angling was held to be too serious for humor, I got hold of some fiberglass cloth and fashioned a wispy bikini. With a very pretty model, I turned out a luscious cheesecake picture that I used as a centre-spread illustration for an article on how much fiberglass was used in the making of a spinning rod. It shook many readers, but the majority enjoyed the gag and the picture which dramatized the material.

In the building of a fiberglass rod, the fibers are bonded together with a thermosetting resin and the whole is then cured by heat. For the better hollow-construction rods, the material, in either cloth or spun-fiber form, is wrapped or woven around a steel mandril of a correct length and taper to form a rod or a rod section.

Less accurate rods are made in solid form to produce an incredibly strong section. In this style, the fibers in the form of floss are lined along a central core. This is then cured and the stock is finished in taper and length by machining. Rods of this type are excellent for heavy-duty trolling with metal lines, as they possess power and, since they are not used for casting, can be built on simpler design lines.

This is a simplified explanation of a complex design and manufacturing process, but I believe it is sufficient at this stage in our study of tackle. Let us just realize that fiberglass is a material that provides rods of grand action for every form of fishing, and that it is tough, enduring and reliable. There is little doubt that many new ideas will come along to improve the use of this material, as well as superior designs to further gladden our hearts.

I suggest that you start off with a glass rod for your basic outfit. Then, at a later date with added skills, you might move to cane and put out the rather high price asked. I'll stick with glass.

Rod Length

I own spinning rods measuring from 10 feet down to a mere 5 feet, ultralight — and my preference is for longer sticks than those in general use. This is partly because I grew up using longish rods, but I am sold on the superior control possible with sticks of greater length than the average 7-foot model. This is a personal matter which may stem from the fact that I am 6 feet, 6 inches tall.

There is too easy an acceptance of *average* when choosing rod length and I am pleased to see longer rods coming into fashion. The setting of 7 feet as standard length was based upon early work in spinning and to a degree, upon comparison with the often quite stubby rods used in baitcasting. I have recently noticed the trend for the length to be extended, with several top rod-makers showing spinning rods in one model, but in a length range from 7 to 9 feet.

For our standard open-face or under-the-reel spinning rod I'd advise a length of 7½ feet, with maybe 8 feet as a better choice for larger waters. Spincast rods for top-action reels start at 5½ feet, which is too short. A 6-foot-6-inch or even 7-foot model is better than the stubby ones. For the angler who fishes stumpy, weedy waters for bass, a 6-foot spincaster may be long enough, but this is a matter of choice.

Most rods come in sections, which makes them easy to carry, but some long rods break down into lengths that are difficult to handle. I have often sat hunched in an airplane with my rod bundle angled between my feet and the ends poked over my shoulder; and in the bush, I have many times cursed my preference for the longer lengths. But I find it worth while, for when I am in some outstanding fishing spot I want to have all my favorite rods. The transportation problems become less important than my joy in being able to fish with the gear I prefer. The true fisherman wants to fish in the way he enjoys and this means for some of us that we must at times be prepared to stand foursquare at the hatch of a jet plane, smile, and ask if there is a nice safe place where our rods can be put.

Rod Fittings

The rod stick is the most important part of the rod, but there are factors we must examine in the fittings, such as line guides, butt, and reel attachment. Since we have discussed the need for sections in long rods, we really must take close look at the fittings that join them together: the ferrules. We need not spend too much time on this because the standard of accessories on North American rods is quite high; they may not be as well made, or as fancy as some fittings put on European rods, but they do a good job and are fitted on the basis of cutting costs for the buyer.

It took me a while to realize this last factor, for at first I rather felt that North American line guides were a little substandard when compared to the precision agate-centered units used in Europe. But after years of faithful service by rather plain line guides, I have come to know that the European adherence to the expensive materials is of a lesser value than this continent's mass production of good gear at a price that all can pay.

Ferrules

Ferrules are simply sockets and plugs to allow a long length to be pulled down into a transportable unit. If we desire the finest action in a rod, then we should buy a one-piece unit. However, this may be too long to carry. So remember that ferrules are a necessary evil, and that since we must accept them, we should ensure that our chosen rods are fitted with units that work well.

Ferrules place a stiff section into a rod stick, and since this stiff section is subjected to strain by the flexing action of the rod, it is essential that the male and female fittings be accurate to about .002 inch. Metal ferrules are extremely thin, so it becomes important in the choosing of a rod to make sure that they fit just right and that they do not need great pressure to put them together or to take them apart.

Because of the fragile nature of ferrules every angler should adopt a system of oiling the male and female fittings before closing them home. The easiest way of doing this is by rubbing the male ferrule in a twisting motion in the hollow beside the nose, or on the forehead. This act picks up a fine layer of natural oil which lubricates the ferrule and allows the two to be pulled apart with ease at the end of a day's fishing. And since the metal walls of the male and the female ferrule are extremely thin, they should always be put in and taken out with a straight pulling or pushing motion. When you twist rod joints to get them apart, you strain and put ridges in this extremely thin fitting.

Before too long, all fiberglass rods will come with built-in glass ferrules. These ferrules, formed in the manufacturing process, eliminate that ugly stiff portion of the stick found with metal ferrule fittings, and those I have used to date seem to have a superior feel in handling. Most important, moulding the ferrule in this way removes the danger of an edge forming a pressure point against the stick when it is flexed in a cast, or bent in fighting a fish.

Rod Butts and Reel Fittings

The butt of a rod forms the handle and, because it holds the reel, plays a part in balancing the tackle. The usual form is a series of cork rings put on over a wooden core, or fastened together directly over the rod stick. On the butt is some form of fitting to hold the reel in place and usually a butt cap protects the raw end of cork from wear.

Some people go into dreadful tizzies over the shape and thickness of butts, but I regard this as a rather wasteful study. I prefer a thickish butt, because I have big hands, but I have yet to find one butt, out of the thousands I have handled, that I would reject on this point. I find it of greater importance to study the actual reel fittings.

How and where the reel fitting is set on the butt is something that can affect a day's fishing, for here we are dealing with balance and with firm attachment.

It makes for difficult handling if the reel works loose when a fish is being played and it can be disastrous if it falls off. With standard spinning reels this is less of a problem, because by design the reel stem is held fast between the second and third fingers. But I have had failures and a shaky reel is a pesky affair, even if held in the fingers. Indeed, in view of the superb fittings now available this is a fault we should not accept.

Reel fittings vary in design from the simple and effective pair of tapered rings that lock on each end of the reel seat to fixed units built into the butt. These hold the reel in place with locking sockets worked by screwing home bands mounted on a threaded tube. Variations on these styles are available and a test in the store should quickly prove the efficiency of a selected unit.

I use the lighter, unattached, sliding-ring fittings for all light work and prefer the fixed system on the heavy-duty tackle. The important points to observe are the balance point and a rigid hold, but since most spinning reels sit in the middle of the rod butt, it is a simple matter for the fixed seats to be built into the correct position.

Spincast rods fitted with a cranked handle usually have some form of screw-locking system. Just check that it works and won't allow the reel to slip.

Line Guides

Line guides are rings of hard metal through which the line passes to provide ease in casting and to spread the strain of fighting a fish through the length of the rod. Their positioning is important, as is the number used on any specific length of rod. If there are not enough

Tackle Talk 63

rings, serious strain will be exerted at different points on the stick and the rod will not flex properly during the fight with a fish. A similar fault occurs if the rings are not placed correctly, but this is less common than the use of too few rings.

To test a rod, a reel is slipped onto the butt and the line run through all the rings, with the spare end tied to a fixed object. When the rod is flexed into a good bend the line should run almost parallel with the curve of the rod. There may be some straight lines seen running from the butt ring to the second ring, and maybe from the second ring to the third, but from this point to the tip guide the line should flow in a fairly even curve.

The average spinning rod will carry five line guides plus a tip guide in its 7 or 8 feet; shorter rods may have one less, longer rods one more. It is not the number that is critical, but the way in which they work. Reject any rod that shows pronounced angles in the line through the length of the rod when the test is applied.

The line-guide setup on spincaster units with the reel on top provides us with a different problem, for if the number of guides or their placement is at all wrong, the line will touch and even saw against the stick. A certain amount of this is inevitable, and although it is not practical to pile on guides, as it would ruin the action of the rod, the use of higher guides is permissible up to a point but must be used with discretion. For if we use high guides simply to keep the line from rubbing, the line might pull on the rings, applying torque stresses that are more harmful than the problem we are attempting to solve, since the twist given to the stick can make it fail.

Spincaster fishermen must compromise and seek the happy medium of guides of slightly greater height and with proper distribution. This means making a check with line and choosing the rod that shows up best.

Spinning Guides

Apart from obeying the rules of spreading the strain evenly during the fight, spinning guides used on rods with open-face reels need to be larger to accommodate the line, which flows off the reel during a cast, in a series of fairly wide curls.

If we were to use small line guides, the swirling curls of line would be forced into a narrow path at the first guide with a resulting error of friction that would reduce casting length and accuracy.

To deal with this it is usual for the butt guide to be quite large, as big as ¾ to 1¼ inches in diameter. The next ring is smaller in proportion and so on all the way up to the tip guide. This system funnels the line evenly up the rod and causes a minimum of friction. Since most spinning guides are lighter in construction than other rings, this does not add weight and causes no imbalance in the stick.

It is important to remember that these larger guides are designed for use *under* the rod. It is tough to use this tackle the other way, yet I do see it so handled, even though those very high guides place considerable torque on the stick. This doesn't matter quite so much with glass sticks, but with a cane rod of even top quality, it can cause the cane to kink up like a dog's hind leg.

Spincaster outfits have less need for oversized guides, as the line issues straight from the small hole in the reel shroud, and there is less chance of friction reducing casts. But sensible guides for this tackle can be a little bigger than those used on the older style of baitcasting rods and if good quality bridge guides are used, it makes the tackle look nicer and also, in my opinion, gives superior casting performance.

My final point on guides in this section is on the need for constant inspection for wear, especially when nylon line is used. It is most important to check the tip ring regularly during the fishing season. This is because nylon is extremely tough material that will cut deep furrows in soft metal. Since a tremendous amount of strain and friction takes place on the tip ring, and to a lesser degree on the butt guide, it is possible to finish up with razor edges at these points that will fray or even slash the line in two. I was once fishing with an excellent angler who lost three heavy pike in a row and cursed the quality of his nylon line which was made by a most reputable manufacturer. I took his rod to inspect the line, ran it between my fingers and found it to be rough and jagged. It took just a moment to check his rings and find that the tip and butt guides had been worn into saw edges. A quick lapping job with a smooth file and fine emery corrected the fault, but we found that his line was badly frayed for 100 feet back on his reel. He had to cut off and discard this line and, of course, he was upset at losing three good pike.

To combat this effect, manufacturers tend to use harder materials in tip and butt line guides, the most common being hard chrome plate, tungsten-carbide and Carbaloy. It pays to spend a little more to buy a rod so fitted, but inspection for this problem should become a regular habit.

Rod Action

It can be painful to watch people attempting to test the action of a rod in a tackle store, for it is obvious that few are aware of how to go about it.

Most people, even those who should know better, pick up a rod and wriggle it back and forth at high speed until it is flexing and unflexing so quickly that its true action is not allowed time to develop. This proves nothing and often has the effect of driving the expert salesclerk into a suppressed fury.

The experienced person, however, handles the rod as if fishing and imparts a single casting thrust to the stick. He allows it to settle to a stop and repeats this action until he has a picture of the rod's flexing ability, power and taper. I know this sounds like something that takes years to learn, but in fact, using the rod in this way can give an accurate idea of action even to the inexperienced.

Giving a series of casting thrusts to a spinning or spincasting rod should give an immediate clue to its nature. You can tell if it has a tip action, if it is soft, stiff, or medium. The best way I have found to do this is by placing the rod butt against the belly, holding it with both hands and thrusting it from side to side, while keeping the butt rigid. By allowing the rod to flex properly back and forth at the speed needed by the stick, you allow the action to develop before your eyes.

Medium Action

What I call a medium action develops a good curve in the top third of the rod which carries on down with less effect until you can actually feel the rod working beneath the butt corks. There is action throughout the rod with a developing curve in the top third, support in the middle third and firm control in the bottom third to impart a steely effect.

This is the best action for general spinning and most of my rods are chosen in this style. I would recommend the medium action for our basic spinning rod and for all spincasting work, except where heavy baits are to be used. Medium-action rods are highly efficient engines for playing fish and will usually accept a large range of casting weights.

Tip Action

This action became tremendously popular a few years back, for all the wrong reasons. I tried out a tip action in standard spinning and hated it right from the start. But I had a number of people tell me I was wrong and that the tip action was great for all kinds of angling and especially for the popular wrist-action-flip used to throw a light bait. I ignored them and carried on using other actions. The fad seemed to die on its own, but this again is wrong, for the tip-action stick has a proper place in angling, as I shall attempt to explain.

In our flexing test, as we move the rod from side to side, the tip action is shown by a sharp curve forming quickly in the top sixth of the rod. This develops down the length, but more slowly and the curve of the rod is dominated by that sharp action in the first sixth.

Used with a light bait, you get the strange feeling of loss on the cast, because as you drive the rod forward you lose touch with the bait. This action is best suited to throwing heavier baits.

I have a 6-foot spincaster rod with this action and stout fittings to complement the whole. Used with large spoons of up to 2 ounces, it works in dreamlike fashion. So, for the beginner seeking tackle to use in weedy waters with big plugs, this action has much to recommend it. But I don't like it at all in the longer spinning rods, or where medium-weight baits are to be thrown.

Soft Action

What we call soft action might better be described as *slow* action, for in this fully flexing type, we get a very different feel when we anchor the butt in our midriff and move it from side to side. For a start, it is necessary to thrust the rod much more slowly, as it takes longer for the full curve to work in an even movement from the tip to the butt.

People who have never handled this type of action could be forgiven for believing that there is something wrong with the stick, for if you don't slow down and give the rod time to start, curve and stop, you will over-run the action and then it simply feels like a wet noodle. Yet this slow movement is put in for a correct action to be used in the throwing of the smallest and lightest baits. And in this ultralight field, the slow/soft action is perfect.

The first rods I ever used in this action were dainty 5-foot long wands designed and built by a master angler and rod-builder in the Netherlands.

Frans Domhof created this special tackle because of an unusual angling problem he discovered in the slow-moving waters of his native Holland. The anglers in Holland, like anglers in most European countries, fish for minnow species that are usually not predatory. So for most of the year, baits such as bread doughballs, worms, or fly maggots form the standard baits. It is known that certain of these fish, including the carp, roach and bream, feed on small fry in the time of year when they are present in the shallows. It seemed only sporting to attempt to take them on spinning gear, using a bait lure about the size of the tiny fry.

However, when the baits were made, it was discovered that the normal spinning rods simply would not throw 1/64- or 1/32-ounce lures to any distance or with any accuracy. Domhof, a rod-builder, produced some wandlike rods of a different style because they curved slowly on a thrust, right down the length and into the butt corks.

On a fishing trip with this master angler I was introduced to what was for me a new style and, although I was used to slower rods than I use now, those fully flexing ultralights were a great surprise. The tiny lures had almost no casting weight, but when the slow rod was put into thrust the power developed through the length sent the little lures sailing far out.

I own two rods with this soft action today, small fragile spinning sticks for use with 1- and 2-pound-test line, and midget baits for low-water trout angling. For this work they are unbeatable, but let me stress again that it is the medium action that fits closest into the field of general angling and forms the best choice for a useful basic spinning and spincasting stick.

Rod Costs

Rods, in the range we have discussed, can vary in price from a couple of dollars for a piece of junk to a hundred dollars or more for the crafted bamboo stick. In the more reasonable and highly suitable range, we have a selection of first-class hollow-glass sticks running from $20 to $70. Most hollow-glass rods have a price differential based on their fittings, as well as the quality of the material used in creating the stick. One rod set at the top price level may be very similar in glass quality to cheaper models, but be different in the quality of the fittings used. The more you pay, the better gear you get, and that $10 extra on the price tag might bring in line guides of top quality that will just about last forever. My best advice on this is to deal with people who know what they are selling and with manufacturers who have a genuine stake in what is a billion-dollar business.

LINE

Angling line these days is made from a number of synthetic materials. It comes in a range of types and tests and is remarkably cheap. Let us treat it with great care, for this is an item that we shall be buying at regular intervals all our angling lives.

Before the advent of artificial fibers, angling line was produced from natural fibers such as linen, silk, cotton, flax and silkworm gut. They were fine for their time, but poor compared to the superb materials in use today.

From Izaak Walton's time in the seventeenth century to the middle of the nineteenth century, the popular angling line was horsehair. The long glossy hairs from selected horses' tails were knotted into a single strand, or woven to form a stronger line. In the first angling book in the English language, dated 1486, there are illustrations of how this can best be done. It is interesting to note that this work, *The Treatise of Fishing With An Angle,* from the *Book of St. Albans* is said to be the work of a woman, Dame Juliana Berners, the prioress of a nunnery close by St. Albans.

Horsehair was held in high regard right until around the end of the nineteenth century. One reason for this is because it was far less visible in the water than other available materials.

In my youth, lacking the few cents needed to buy leaders, I made my own from the long, glossy tail-hairs of the giant Belgian Black funeral horses owned by the local undertaker. I got the occasional thick ear from a groom and found the hairs difficult to knot, but my single-hair leaders worked well.

Silk Line

In freshwater angling, silk replaced horsehair as the main line around the start of the twentieth century. I used silk lines for years and in the very light tests they were difficult to handle, as the wind blew them around and any tangle had to be picked apart with extreme care. Since this line was rather expensive, few people would dream of cutting out a knot and throwing a short end away.

Silk was the first spinning line and this in turn was superceded by a brittle synthetic from Japan known as artificial gut This was manufactured to appear similar to the superior leader material, silkworm gut but being manufactured, was sold in various lengths wound around card or wooden spools. Silkworm gut, being a natural fiber, came only in short lengths and for most people the idea of using a reel line knotted every 3 feet or so was a bit too hard to take.

Japan gut was brittle when dry. It needed soaking before any knot could be tied and at the start of fishing it was common to see anglers with pursed lips, wetting the last 2 feet in their mouths until it was supple enough to knot. This was dreadful stuff when compared to modern synthetics, but it was cheap and of low visibility in water, so we all used it. It certainly helped make spinning practical in those early days.

Nylon Lines

The big break-through to top-quality synthetic lines came in after 1945, with the introduction of nylon to the angling scene. The first lines had many faults, but were so superior to the rest of the field that they won acceptance with a hard core of anglers. Some traditionalists rejected them at first, but as the quality improved, even these people took them up.

Nylon monofilament, the best type of line for spinning, is a clear, round, glossy material, rather like plastic. It is produced from coal, oil, air and water by manufacturing processes.

The raw material is heated in an autoclave and the melted product forced through holes in a steel plate. From this point it is drawn out to a predetermined length, cooled with blasts of cold air, and the resulting solidified filament stretched to around four times the original length. This rearranges the molecular structure and imparts strength and durability.

The early lines were almost wiry and if kept on a spool for any length of time would peel off on a cast in springy coils that defied straightening. They stretched like rubber, making it difficult to properly set the hook if a lot of line was out, and not only did the lines have the nasty habit of snapping, but they possessed the ability to writhe out of even the most carefully tied knot.

Research proved that special jam knots were needed and as the tying of these was learned and the lines improved, the early troubles were overcome.

Today, nylon monofilament lines are limp and are free of the excessive stretch of the early days, but the nature of the material calls for care in handling and the use of specific knots that retain the maximum amount of strength.

Monofilament is outstanding angling line for most uses because it is hard-surfaced, resistant to water and weather and possessed of great strength. The tensile strength is about the same as mild steel, at 70,000 to 100,000 pounds per square inch of cross section. Little wonder, then, that when we run it constantly through and over soft metal line guides, the constant friction can cut deep grooves in the metal.

Nylon is a generic term for a group of similar materials, and is the common name used by anglers. I use it when discussing the single-strand, glassy-looking line also called monofilament, and to separate it from the braided lines usually made from a superb material called Dacron.

Dacron

Dacron is the trade name given to a material made by the Dupont Company and this synthetic fiber, while approaching the strength of nylon, has additional qualities that make it highly suitable for use in the heavier tests, with closed-face reels. Lines made with Dacron are almost impervious to water, have less stretch than nylon and a tremendous degree of resistance to rot caused by direct sunlight.

Dacron lines are superb for all heavy-duty work, for trolling and big-game fishing and in my opinion are superior for accurate casting with the standard baitcasting reels. I select this material for all angling work where the line must exceed 50-pound test, and for baitcasting. For angling tasks requiring lower-test line I prefer nylon monofilament.

The reasons for my choices of line are as follows. Nylon, being limp and supple in all the lighter tests, is excellent for distance casting with both fixed-spool and revolving-spool reels. I have used lines as heavy as 25-pound test on revolving-spool surf-casting reels and apart from the normal overrun, have done so without trouble for years.

But in baitcasting, where distance is less important than being able to drop a plug or bait into a pinpoint location, braided line has several advantages. First it is nicer to handle on a revolving-spool reel. Second, after a cast or two, it picks up water which coats the outside of the line on the drum and forms a natural, yet light brake that aids in preventing overruns and subsequent tangles.

For the heavier spincast reel, braided line sits better on the spool, and being less springy than monofilament has better handling factors.

Line Tests

All modern angling lines are sold in a range of breaking tests based on their snapping point when wet. These test-weight figures indicate the weight at which the wet line will snap, as established by a slowly applied machine pull.

In practical terms for freshwater angling the range starts at 2-pound test and jumps 2 pounds at a time to 30-pound-test line. This enables the choice of a line test very close to any weight that we desire. Since some lines made in Europe are based upon different test standards, it is possible to refine this choice to even more exact limits. It wouldn't really be necessary, but if you felt that 10-pound test was too light, and 12-pound test too heavy, you might pick up a European line of 11-pound test. For practical angling, this narrowing down is a sign of affectation. For the building of tapered leaders, however, this tremendous choice range is indeed valuable.

For specialists in light-tackle spinning, lines are manufactured far lighter than the 2-pound test I have set as the light standard. Some European lines go as light as ¾-pound test and there are also lines of 1-pound and 1½-pound on the market. There might be fun in using one of the ultralights in clear water for trout, but I feel 2-pound-test nylon line sets an excellent standard for all practical light spinning for North American waters.

In the upper range of line tests, nylon monofilament is sold in standard 45-, 50- and 60-pound tests, and up to even heavier strengths intended for commercial fishing. When the reef fishermen off Bermuda have set their big fish traps, they sit at anchor over the end trap and drop down handlines with baited hooks for the giant snappers 200 feet down.

They think nothing of using nylon monofilament of 80- to 100-pound test and it is exciting to see them play out a monster amberjack, with that vicious line running through their horny hands as a big one bolts. But they are fishing for commerce, not sport and you wouldn't get me to use one of those lines: it would chop my city-soft palms to pieces.

The heaviest-test monofilament I ever saw used in angling was a leader length of 80-pound test knotted by a member of the Carribean team at the International Tuna Cup Match one year in Nova Scotia. Bermuda angler Joe Lindley tied up that steel-like nylon, using heavy-duty pliers and a pair of powerful cutting shears. His idea was for a less visible leader than the normal steel rig, for the tideless drift period when an attacking tuna has a good opportunity to inspect the bait and the bottom rig.

In the heavier-test sizes of nylon line we run into a strange situation where the stretch capacity of nylon may gain an explosive force that can actually blow a reel to pieces. This normally occurs only in heavy-line situations, but it is a part of the story of line that every angler should know. It happens when a big or powerful fish has been played for a long period and has made long runs that have stripped great lengths of line from the reel. This line is reeled back onto the spool under extreme pressure, which means that hundreds of turns of stretched-out line fill up the drum. When the fish is gaffed and the pull removed from the fish, all those turns of nylon sigh with relief and attempt to return to their original diameter. If the angler has been careless and has not spread the line widely across the spool while reeling, or if the reel is not designed to counteract this effect, the cruel power of the nylon will mangle the reel, warp the spool, or even explode and spread the drum.

Most modern spinning reels have a spreader that prevents the line falling into too close a series of turns, but I saw a cheap reel once that had been ruined when the angler hooked a log while trolling a long line. Instead of pumping and then reeling on a slack line, he had reeled that terrible weight all the way back to the boat without pause. When he stopped, his 10-pound-test line expanded in all directions and warped the spool to the point where the reel wouldn't turn.

For trolling with heavy nylon it is best to choose a suitable reel designed for the task, or to first spool on a core of soft line to act as a cushion. Dacron is not subjected to this extreme stretch, and is thus a superior line for heavy trolling work.

What Test Line?

If all things were equal and we wanted to be sure of landing every fish we hooked, it might appear sensible to buy heavy line.

Happily for the sport of angling it is not as simple as this. The use of heavy line calls for rod and reel to match and this means we can only handle heavier lures and casting weights.

Heavy line is more visible to fish, creates more friction, needs more casting power and, since it is a good deal thicker than light line, leaves us carrying less on a given spool size.

The lighter lines have shorter life, are more easily broken, handle a lower ratio of casting weight and pose problems if we wish to put pressure on a really big fish. But we lose a little and win a little, because the lighter lines have virtues of their own. They are less visible, create less friction and will allow a lighter bait to be cast to a greater distance.

So once again we come face to face with choice of selecting the *average* in tackle — lines that are neither heavy nor light, but correct for the greatest possible use.

Because nylon is stronger and yet thinner in cross section than natural-fiber lines, we can afford to use a thinner line that gives superior strength. To this factor we add the ability of spinning tackle to handle bigger fish with less trouble than standard tackle, and once more we can lower the test strength of our chosen line.

While it was once accepted that 15-pound test was the minimum size line to use on large pike, most spinfishermen today use 8-pound test and not only enjoy enhanced sport, but tend to hook more fish. This test line is capable of handling very big fish indeed and also has good durability. It is light enough to be suitable for throwing medium-weight baits, and strong enough for fairly heavy lures up to 5/8 ounce. This is a fair standard for our average-weight line. I carry spare spools rigged with 8- and 6-pound test, but to go lighter or heavier than that I move to lighter or heavier outfits.

On 8-pound line I have caught bonefish of 7 pounds, channel catfish of 30 pounds, carp of 38 pounds and steelhead trout of 9 pounds.

For a basic spincaster in weedy waters I would go heavier, using 15-pound-test braided line as the standard. This is too heavy for normal spincast work, but I believe it to be a mistake to go below 10-pound-test braided line. It doesn't seem to work as well in the closed-face units.

Loading the Reel

In the early days of spinning there were many theories on how to best load line onto a spinning reel. It was important to do this in a way that would cope with the unusual winding system, in which the line was carried around the spool by a flier that put kinks in it. One of the methods preferred was an involved system of allowing the line to peel off the end of the new spool of line, in a way that would allow it to put in kinks opposing those being put in by the flier. This meant that the line was free of kinking when the spool was filled. I always used this method, as it seemed to make sense to use a non-kinked line.

Then one day, when I was visiting a friend who is a research scientist as well as an outstanding angler and tackle-designer, he asked my aid in spooling line on a spinning reel. He got a spool of line, stuck a pencil through the holes and handing it to me, started happily to wind kinky line in as fast as he could turn the reel handles.

I was rather shocked and told him so, whereupon he gave a great snort of laughter. He then put things straight. "Winding on this way with the line spool revolving around the pencil and the flier going around the reel, I'm putting the line on kinked, right?" he said. I agreed. "Well, if you do it your way, you finish up with unkinked line, right?" And again I agreed. "Now then," he said, "when I cast, my kinked line unkinks as it slips off the spool, but yours will kink . . . so who should make the longest cast?"

These days we can buy pre-wound spools, and when we need a new line, simply exchange our old spool for a new one filled with fresh line. This is a great system, especially for spincast reels, which are a bit harder to load.

The final word on loading spinning reels with line has to do with the importance of filling the spool right up to the lip. With most open-face reels this takes more than 100 yards and so, it is one good reason for purchasing bulk spools holding several spool-lengths of line.

If the spool is not properly filled, but has the line at a low level, there is considerable friction during the cast, as the line rubs against the spool lip. I have spotted so many anglers troubled in this way, because they have bought a 50-yard spool and have only filled their reel to one-third capacity. I always carry bulk spools on fishing trips and can usually help out by tying in and filling their reel from my spare. The expressions I have seen when that first cast is made from a properly loaded reel is well worth the small cost of the line I have given away.

Remember that too much line is also a fault that will create tangles as loose line spills off the spool. So fill to within 3/16th inch of the spool lip and watch most of your casting problems go as efficiency and distance increase.

Line Costs

The cost of all types of modern synthetic lines is low because of mass manufacturing methods. Anyone who doubts this need only take a look at the going prices for line a few years ago and compare them with what we pay today. I have a rather nice collection of fishing-tackle catalogs that go back to 1920 and it is interesting to compare the prices in my old dog-eared 1926 Hardy Brothers' catalog with a more recent one. In 1926, an undressed silk spinning line sold for $2 per 100 yards of 12-pound test; a superior line of dressed silk cost $7.50 per 100 yards and there was half a page of instructions on how the buyer could prevent the line from going tacky and unusable. The 1968 catalog prices 12-pound-test nylon spinning line at 75¢ per 100 yards.

Since line today is so cheap, it pays to buy the very best and to change all lines of this type every year. There is no doubt that a good

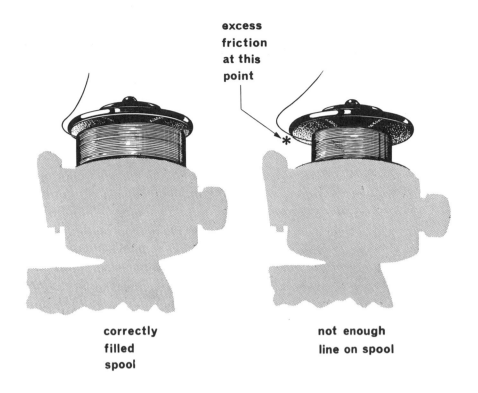

excess
friction
at this
point

correctly
filled
spool

not enough
line on spool

line will give excellent service for up to two seasons, but to use it that long is applying false economy to an item of low cost.

The new idea of selling nylon on bulk spools has further reduced the cost to the consumer. It is easy for several friends or club members to get together and buy a bulk spool of line with a tremendous saving over the standard 100- or 50-yard spool, and gain the added advantage of being able to properly load the reel to the exact point. I buy 1/8-pound spools which in 8-pound-test monofilament carry around 1,000 yards of line. This cuts the cost of the 100-yard spools by an average of 50 per cent.

BALANCED TACKLE

It is seldom realized that in a day's fishing the angler who does a great deal of casting exerts a considerable amount of physical effort. This can be tiring at the start of the season although we do tend to harden up as the days pass by. But this physical work is made easier if our tackle handles well and has a good balance in our hands. A properly balanced set of gear works superbly well with all parts in union, and all complementing one another.

Balancing a tackle outfit is an important part of angling skill and is far more subtle than most anglers would believe. It has become second nature for the experienced fisherman to match all items when choosing gear. A first-rate tackle salesman will sell you a balanced outfit if you simply ask him to fit you out, but this doesn't mean we should rely on others. During the life of an angler there will always be decisions to be made on this point and we must understand that this reel goes best with that rod, that this test line belongs with that weight bait, that this size lure is suitable for use with this specific set of tackle and this shape of hook is what is needed with that particular type of bait.

It is fortunate that most of us possess instinct for placing things in balance. It is a part of living that we accept without thought, for if our car needs a tow, we don't need a tensile strength expert to inform us that wrapping twine is too weak for the job, or that a big logging chain is over-doing the act. Given a choice of tow-lines for pulling our car, most of us would lay a finger at once on the correct item.

Balancing a tackle outfit is not quite as simple, for there are subtle factors to be observed and quite often we work to extremely close limits in obtaining the best match.

No one would dream of using a huge tuna reel on a 3-ounce fly rod, or a 3-ounce fly reel on a massive tuna rod, but when it comes to choosing between 8-pound-test line and 12-pound test, the beginner and even some experienced anglers find they have nothing to go on and would possibly select the heavier line as being more efficient and less liable to break with a big fish.

In our choice of rod and reel for a basic spinning or spincast outfit we have seen that 8-pound test is average for spinning, with up to 15-pound test advisable for work with heavy-duty plugs when spincasting in weedy waters. Using these guidelines we would have little problem in buying an outfit. Just by telling a salesman what we wanted, he could rig up a tackle outfit out of stock. By far, most gear in the stores falls into this field.

It is, however, an inevitable development of angling for us to spread out, to want to use heavier, or even lighter tackle, to perhaps throw a bigger or a smaller bait. If we believe our standard set of gear will handle this, we are due for a shock, for the main rule of the game is that all tackle used should be in balance.

I was once fly fishing a favorite trout stream when a fisherman showed up and started to set up his gear on the bank near where I was wading. I had just finished covering the pool, so I sloshed ashore, sat down on a rock and pulled out my lunch and chatted while I ate.

When he found that I had no fish he at once went into a happy dissertation upon the new fishing method for low-water trout. He'd read an article in a fishing magazine on ultralight spinning and was there, fully equipped with masses of tiny lures to clean out all the smart brown trout in that stream. Trouble was, because he was not aware of the need for a fully balanced set of gear, he had a standard spinning outfit with rather heavy line.

I took a dubious look at the midget lure he tied onto the end of his 12-pound-test nylon, and suggested gently that he would be hard put to throw it any distance with his tackle. This amused him — until he tried it.

When it became obvious to him that he could not throw such a light bait with basic spinning tackle, I suggested that his line was too heavy and he had the bright idea of using lighter line which he had on a spare spool. It still did not work. At that point I walked back to my car and got an ultralight outfit which I took back so he could see the difference. With my little slow-action rod and 2-pound-test line, he found he could cover the pool and joined me on my rock to seriously discuss the business of balanced gear.

The same thing would apply of course if this angler had attempted to toss out a big sucker minnow for muskies with his standard outfit. The rod would not have worked as it should and any snag during the cast would have snapped his line as the casting weight came up against the light line.

We must realize that while our basic balanced set of gear will perform many tasks, there does come a time when we must move outwards and obtain lighter, or heavier outfits built to perform the specialized tasks we require.

Efficiency fails when we attempt to convert our basic set of gear to heavier or lighter work by simply using lighter or heavier line. The heavier line will strain our rod and the rod will strain the lighter line. Better by far to stick to the standard, basic tackle outfit, for while you may meet up with trouble in the form of a giant fish, you stand a better chance with it on *balanced* gear.

In this respect I remember with lasting affection a party of anglers from South Dakota that I met up in the famous Rapid River Lodge on Rapid River, to the north of Lac La Ronge in northeastern Saskatchewan. This is big-fish country where the lake trout grow to more than 40 pounds, the pike to 30 pounds or more, and where the Indian guides tell you to throw back 10-pound walleye and just keep the 3- to 4-pounders for your shoreline lunch.

There were five men in that party, all keen fishermen on their first trip to northern Canada, and none of them had ever taken a hard-fighting fish in their lives. In fact, if what they told me was true, the biggest fish they had taken prior to this trip would not have bumped the scale over 3 pounds. Each of them had just one fishing outfit, plain spincaster rigs 6 feet, 6 inches long, with closed-face reels, all loaded with 15-pound-test line. These were similar and were all, I felt, in excellent balance.

With these basic spincast outfits, these keen anglers trolled big spoons for lake trout feeding on the surface. They cast red and white spoons for the giant pike in the shallow bays, and stillfished with cheap plastic bobbers and salted minnows for the huge walleye that hung around the quiet parts of the pools on each side of the many white-water rapids close to Rapid River Lodge. And they had a magnificent time.

By the third day of their stay they each had the current limit of 90 pounds of fish fillets and had caught some grand fish. They lost a few of course, but apart from running short of line, which I was able to supply with pleasure, because I always take miles of spare up north, they did not have one major problem with their tackle. This was, of course, because they were using balanced gear. Oh yes; one hooked a pike of about 35 pounds that streaked away and tangled the line on a cedar stump, snapping it as if it were cotton thread.

"Oh hell," said the excited angler, "if I'd been using stronger line I'd have got him."

Maybe he would at that. But I'm prepared to bet that that fish, if stubbed up short on heavier line, on that outfit, would have snapped the rod. It was just one of those things that happen to us all.

To sum up on balanced tackle, it can mean 8-pound test on average gear, 15-pound test on spincasters used in heavy water, 1-pound test on an ultralight, or 30-pound-test line used with a heavy muskie trolling outfit in big waters. But *our average* and *our choice* in balanced gear is a matter of personal judgment. I would suggest 8-pound-test nylon on a suitable rod and reel for our open-face set, and up to 15-pound-test line for our stumpy, weedy fishing with a balanced spincaster outfit.

We have now covered the basic outfit and have a fair knowledge of rods, reels and lines. We shall return to them later when we deal with specialized gear, but now we must get down to a neglected and largely ignored subject — the all-important matter of terminal tackle: the hooks, sinkers, leaders and other accessories that help complete an angler's kit.

4 🐟 Terminal Tackle

Terminal tackle is the gear that goes onto the end of the line and thus comes in close contact with the fish. It includes hooks, swivels, sinkers and a variety of small accessory items. Lures we will deal with in the next chapter, because they are quite secondary to the somewhat neglected little odds and ends that can make or mar a day's fishing.

Some readers may feel at this stage that I am giving undue emphasis to what is often regarded as a simple and straightforward tackle grouping. I disagree. I would say that 85 per cent of the lack of success in angling is because terminal tackle is not properly understood. It has often been said that 90 per cent of the fish, are caught by 10 per cent of the anglers and I'll bet that that 10 per cent has a thorough knowledge of how and with what to rig terminal gear.

I remember once arriving at a favorite fishing hole to see a tremendous shoal of white bass boiling in the gut between two big lakes. As I walked down the slope to the side of the bridge, I could not only see them hitting minnows, but could quite plainly hear the slurping noise they made as they nailed the frightened bait fish on the surface.

With a whoop of delight I slapped together my light rod and hurried to select a size O Mepps spinner to throw into the middle of the hungry school.

While tying this midget-sized spinner to the end of my 4-pound-test line, I noticed two fishermen sitting glumly on the bank a few yards down and I asked the usual question as to how they were making out. "They won't bite," said one of the men. "We've been here two days and haven't caught a fish."

Shaken by this starvation in the midst of plenty, I walked up to them and asked what they were using. If their tackle were right, they should have been taking a fish on every throw. To my surprise, the man who had first answered became abusive and snarled something to the effect that he didn't think some dude could tell *him* how to catch fish. "Let's see what you can do, before you start giving out unwanted advice," he sneered.

Rather upset at this most unusual rudeness from one angler to another, I looked at him for a moment and then whipped my spinner out into the middle of the gut without even looking, threw in the bail arm, raised the rod tip to run the lure shallow across the surface and hooked a fish before I had made six turns of the reel handles.

On my ultralight spinning rig, that 1-pound white bass boiled all over the surface before I slid him over the edge of the landing net, took out the hook and strung him. I threw again, and in that frenzy of white bass, nailed another, around the same size. Ten minutes and seven fish later I realized that the two men were on their feet, watching bug-eyed as the little wand of a rod bounced and danced to the tune of a frantically fighting white bass.

"Mister," said the second man, "I don't know your secret, but I sure wish you'd show me. What is that — some special killer lure? I ain't never seen fish caught like that before, and as my friend says, we've been here two days and haven't had a bite."

His friend agreed. "Yeah, I'm sorry for the words," he said. "But you were so damn confident that you were going to catch fish, it made me mad. But hell, you sure do know how to do it."

I put down my rod and told them to haul out so I could see what sort of rig they were using. I told them plainly that when the white bass were in a frenzy with bait minnows trapped in the gut, it was almost impossible not to catch them if the tackle was made up right.

When they pulled in I almost fainted at the sight of the awful terminal gear they had mounted on the ends of their 30-pound-test line.

On the end of their heavy lines — they were using big baitcasting outfits — they had tied solid steel leaders with massive snaps and swivels. On the bottom of each leader was a metal spoon at least three inches long, with small minnows impaled on each of the points of heavy gang hooks.

Three feet above this mass of hardware they had clipped plastic bobbers the size of oranges to hold the outrageous terminal monstrosity afloat. I am serious when I say that I have seen lighter gear used to take a shark; so there was little wonder they had not had a hit in two days.

I pulled my stringer out of the water, and picking the largest fish

— about 1½ pounds — opened its mouth and asked them how they expected it to get that mass of metal into such a limited place. In the first place, white bass have rather small mouths, and anyway why should a predatory fish feeding on massed fry bother to look at 3 inches of inert metal simply dangling in the water.

"Can we use one of those small lures you are using?" one asked. So then I had to gently explain that their heavy gear could never cast a bait as light as mine, and I asked if I could alter their tackle to make it suitable. Naturally, at this stage of the game they agreed.

I cut off their hardware and tied to the end of their heavy line a 6-foot length of 6-pound-test nylon. I tied a size 8 short-shank hook on the end, added a clinch sinker to give casting weight and put their plastic bobbers back on to allow the hook to sit 3 feet down. I showed them how to bait a small, live minnow so that it would stay alive and told them to sling out carefully into the middle of the gut. The first man cast, the bobber at once started to slide sideways, and before the second man got his bait in, there was a shout of joy as the first tied into a lively white bass. For the next twenty minutes the fun was fast and furious and we piled into those frantically feeding and wild-eyed fish. Then the school of minnows fled the gut and while we waited for another attack to occur, I took the opportunity to tell my now attentive audience some of the important facts about terminal gear.

Let us now get down to basics and examine hooks, leaders, bobbers, swivels and a few more of the highly important items that can make the difference between angling success and failure.

HOOKS

Hooks are recurved lengths of steel with sharp points, that are fitted to the end of the line to catch and hold a fish. The hook is not as simple an object as this makes it sound. It would be easy to write a book twice the size of this on hooks alone and at that it would still only skim the subject.

There are hundreds of shapes and patterns of hooks and a range of sizes from 1/8 inch all the way up to a 2-foot-long shark hook. This is one of man's oldest tools, and one common to every society from the island primitive using a wooden gorge to the arctic Eskimo who makes superb hooks — almost masterpieces — out of bone and walrus ivory.

But whether the hook comes from a modern factory where an automatic machine chomps them out in an endless stream, or is a root trained into hook-shape during growth on some tropical isle, it has several parts that play an important role in its efficiency. And it is the variation among these parts that separates the many hundreds of patterns. Here are the parts of a hook:

This recently made fish hook of wood, caribou bone, and caribou hide and thongs is a masterpiece of its type. It was made in about an hour by an Ontario Indian, and when baited with caribou meat can be fished through the ice for lake trout. It has all the major parts of a hook except for the barb, unlike many primitive Indian/Eskimo hooks, which do possess barbs (1½ x actual size).

Point. The sharpened end of the hook that pierces the mouth of the fish.

Barb. This sliced projection slants back from the inside of the point. It forms a holding unit to assist in keeping the hook point firmly fastened in the fish.

Bend. This curved portion at the lower end of the hook has the effect of creating a holding area for the hook. Being bent it gains in strength.

Shank. The long straight part of the hook. It runs from the finish of the bend opposite the point, right to the eye.

Eye. This is the line attachment part of the hook, on the opposite end to the bend, formed as part of the hook wire into a neat, small, round eye that should be completely closed.

Gap. The distance between the point and the shank forming the strong holding part of the hook.

Bite. This measures the distance from the apex of the bend to its intersection with the gap.

Hooks go back many thousands of years before the start of general manufacturing. And it is certain that the first appliance used to take a hold in the mouth of a fish was not a hook but a gorge. This is simply a short length of tough material — a bone, sliver of flint, a piece of wood, or some similar material — sharpened at each end, and with a recess ring in the middle around which the angling line is firmly tied.

The gorge was embedded in bait and when taken, the pull on the line forced it across the throat, or gullet of the fish, holding it fast. The gorge dates back to the Middle Stone Age, but I have used them and seen them used by African tribesmen and European gypsies. They are not as good as a 1¢ steel hook — but they work.

Copper hooks similar in shape to those used today came into use around 5,000 B.C.; bronze hooks arrived around 3,500 B.C. and steel hooks at some point prior to 1,000 years before the Christian Era.

The first major manufacturing centre for hooks was at Redditch in the English Midlands where Protestant refugees from the continent brought over needle-making skills that converted easily to the making of hooks.

Redditch today is still a major fishing-tackle centre but hooks are no longer a British monopoly. Possibly the most productive centre is Oslo, where the firm of O. Mustad & Son, founded in 1832, produces most of the world's commercial sea hooks. In addition, this Norwegian company sells a total of 60,000 separate fish-hook items, which will give you an idea of the complexity and range of the modern hook. Every country in the world buys their products — especially for commercial fishing.

Hook Making

Angling hooks were made by hand for centuries and it is perhaps surprising to learn that there are still some special lines today made with hand-tool methods.

Extremely small hooks of the highest quality are often finished by hand-tool work. Some of the best salmon fly hooks are made completely by hand with the points filed, the barbs sliced by a special tool and the bend and the eye formed by an operator on a hand-press machine.

Most hooks — millions every day — are turned out by mass production machine systems. And while there are those that leave me less than happy, the majority are very good indeed.

The usual hook-making material is 80 to 85 per cent carbon steel formed into wire of a size suited to the make and designation of the run. For saltwater use, special alloys and stainless steel have become popular and I find the stainless steel hooks highly suitable for heavier freshwater angling, such as the pursuit of the bruising channel catfish.

The hook is formed with the wire in a softened state. On completion of the mechanical stages, the hook is hardened and tempered for strength and flexibility and finally cleaned, plated, bronzed, or given some similar type of finish.

It is fascinating to watch row upon row of squat noisy machines spewing a steady stream of hooks into a hopper, knowing that those made by good manufacturers are so high in quality.

It is seldom the quality of hooks that gives us a headache, but more the selecting of what we want from the incredible range of shapes, varieties and designs available. I have at times walked into a sporting goods store and been unable to purchase what I want. When I discovered an outlet that carried what I felt was best, its owners got all my business, on the understanding that they would carry, or obtain for me, the hooks that I preferred. An interesting result of this occurred once when I mentioned in a column that I had obtained a specific type of hook from a particular store and one of my readers drove 75 miles there and back in order to lay in a year's supply. Now *there's* a fellow who appreciates the value of good hooks.

This sort of thing is sometimes necessary if you want to get the exact type of hook that you think is best although, if you know what's what, most storekeepers will order in a special supply for your needs. No store can carry 60,000 different hooks, so make up your mind that it is important to be able to pick the most suitable types.

In this discussion I will only cover loose hooks, because snelled hooks (those attached to a leader when bought), although useful, are expensive and far less versatile than the vastly superior individually chosen, and tied units.

Choosing the Hook

Hooks for freshwater angling vary in the thickness of the wire, shank length, length of point, length and placement of barb and in straight or offset characteristics. Let us run right through these variations and I'll give my hard-nosed choice on what I believe to be best — and why.

Wire Size

The weight of wire used in hook making has a complicated designation based on X used with the words Stout or Fine. There is a standard gauge for each specific hook size and the term 1-X Stout is used to describe a hook made up with the wire used as standard gauge for the next-size larger hook. 1-X Fine, therefore, tells us that the hook is made with the standard gauge wire used for the next-size smaller hook.

This isn't the type of thing we use when we buy on a personal visit to a store, but it is invaluable to know for any time that we might wish to order hooks by mail.

For most angling, the standard gauge performs in suitable style, and the finer or stouter categories belong properly in specialist fields where it may be necessary to reduce or increase hook weight to get a better balance. It is common to use X Fine for dry flies where floatation is needed and X Stout for wet flies where we want the lure to sink quickly. For use with fragile baits such as small red worms, the 1-X Fine can be a good choice, as fine wire does less damage to the worm, has good penetration power and the strength to handle very big fish. Apart from this, however, I use standard gauge hooks for general work.

Shank Length

There is a standard length of shank for each hook size and an X classification with the words Long and Short that closely follows the system describing the wire. Thus 1-X Long denotes a hook with a shank as long as the next-size larger hook, 1-X Short then is used to tabulate a hook with a shank length of the next-size smaller hook.

In this way we get a standard shank length that is always in proportion according to the size of the hook, and a range of shorter- and longer-shanked hooks for special purposes.

For most general freshwater angling the standard-length shank is easily the best choice, but it is also useful to possess a supply of shorter and longer shank hooks. You may have noticed that I have previously suggested the use of short-shank hooks at different times. This is because I believe that the shorter shanks hold better in a soft-mouthed fish, providing less leverage for him to work it loose during a fight. Also, extremely short shanks, such as the 5-X Short, are essential when using single salmon eggs as bait, as it allows for a more natural presentation when there is little or no shank projecting.

The long-shank hooks I find less useful, and I feel they are out of place for most freshwater angling. About the only value they have is for a youngster fishing with a worm for eager-biting little fish. Since kids tend to let fish take the hook down too far, the long shank makes it easier to unhook the fish without killing it. I have often felt that long-shank hooks are designed for *unhooking*, and standard- and short-shank hooks for *hooking* the fish.

There are certain jobs where long-shank hooks are useful, for example in tying a long streamer fly where room is needed to wind on the necessary dressing. There is also less chance of a sharp-toothed fish cutting the line when the long shank is used, but the ugly size and lack of delicacy are not worth this small advantage.

Hook Points

There are a number of different types of hook points, with most of them designed for specialist use. It is not of any great value to go into these; it will be better to examine what makes a good choice from the standpoint of utility.

The ideal hook has a very small, short and sharp point with a small barb set close to the point. Many poor hooks come with overlong points and coarse barbs that are tough to hit home and tend to wear a hole in the mouth of a fish. The short point with the small barb slides in easily and is less likely to come out during a scrap with the fish.

One night, fishing for large channel catfish, I lost three in a row after feeling them on the end of my line. Each time I lost one I checked the hook and at last came to the conclusion that the fault rested in an overlong point and a coarse barb. I switched to a better hook and didn't miss a fish for the rest of the night.

An interesting fact then came to light when I found it extremely difficult to remove the short-point, small-barb hook from some of the fish. The hooks had taken such a good hold, especially in the lips, that I had to leave them in and recover them when I cleaned my catch next morning.

I rather feel that when you encounter an unhooking problem you are using a good hook, and I have strong reservations about any hook that happens to fall out of the mouth of a fish when it is netted or gaffed and the line is slackened.

Hook Bends

There are a number of different bends applied to hooks, with varying degrees of roundness. Few people realize it, but the way the bend is formed affects the hook-setting ability and has a bearing on the actual strength of the hook.

A fully round-bend hook needs more force to penetrate than one that angles across from the shank, but since any sharp-bend point in a hook is a weak spot, the fully round-bend hook is stronger.

The bottom of the bend is the place where the strain falls when a fish is hooked properly. At times though, the point may hit bone, there is no penetration and all the weight comes on the point. When this fairly common incident occurs, the hook either pulls out straight or snaps in half, to the vast indignation of the fisherman. I had it happen once with a powerful seafish, and a big hand-forged hook came back straightened right out.

For this reason, and because constant use has sold me on round bends, I go for all the strength I can get. I find that a round-bend hook combined with a short, sharp point and a fine barb has excellent penetration power and baits seem to sit better too.

There are a number of different types of hook eyes, but for us there is less interest in the types than in the way they are positioned.

Since the eye forms the attachment point for our line it is important that it be well formed, with no gap to let our line slide off. Some cheap hooks are poor in this respect and I suggest that, rather than take the trouble of closing the eye with pliers, you should reject any hooks with gaping eyes.

There are three common eye position used for freshwater angling: the *Ringed Eye* (R.E.), the *Turned Up Eye* (T.U.E.), and the *Turned Down Eye* (T.D.E.)

The *Ringed Eye* is formed parallel to the hook shank and is commonly used in cheap, mass-produced hooks for commercial sea fishing. But when a hook is needed to form part of a spinner, its style is usually R.E. for more effective travel in tandem with the lure. This is not an efficient eye position for general work, as the line of pull is less effective than that achieved with the T.D.E.

The *Turned Up Eye* is used on small or short-shank fly hooks. Having the eye face up allows more space between the hook shank and the point and makes it easier to put on the fly dressing and to tie the leader tippet to the hook.

The *Turned Down Eye* forms the standard position for all general freshwater angling uses. This eye places the pull of the line in its most effective position for setting the hook and playing a fish. The eye is bent down towards the hook point, and in a well-made hook this eye should be quite small and have the end closed up hard so that there is no gap at all.

Forged Hooks

Some of the best hooks, when inspected carefully, show a flattened face on each side. These faces are hammered in after the hook is bent and before it is tempered. This forging increases the tensile strength of the whole hook, and is usually the mark of a superior product.

Hook Roundup

There are a number of other variations to be found in hooks, such as sliced segments on the hook shank to hold bait more firmly in place, and offsets either to the left or the right. The latter are known as offset or reversed hooks. A dead straight hook with no reverse twist is, of course, a *straight* hook.

For most angling the straight hook has it over the offsets because the offset hook spins and kinks the line, takes more force to penetrate the jaws of a fish, and when used with live bait has an unfortunate tendency to allow the point to be buried and masked in the bait. On the other hand, some anglers, of whom I am not one, believe that the offset hooks take a better hold and are harder for a fish to reject.

Hook sizes are a difficult matter to lay down in print as there are often variations in standard sizes, plus another set of variations for dry-fly hooks, another for salmon-fly hooks. For this reason I believe that it is much more important to get used to looking at hooks visually. Naturally, when I suggest the use of a hook in these pages, I'll give the size, but I believe that it is far more important to have standards based on what *forms* a good hook than to dig into the differences between one size and another.

From our examination of what makes a good hook, it should not be hard to arrive at a clear understanding of what to buy.

The kits of hooks in a range of sizes and shapes that come in plastic, see-through cases, are of less value than a set bought by a careful angler who knows what to seek in a top quality hook.

Hooks are cheap, with the most expensive costing just a little more than the cheapest and it makes sense to take the trouble to sort out a good set based on what we have covered here.

Add up what we have dealt with and it boils down to a hook that is close to the following description: a standard length, round bend, T.D.E., short point, small barb, hand forged, straight hook in standard or 1-X Fine wire.

Having found a hook range that is as close as possible to this, we should then start making a collection. There are many useful plastic containers available with a mass of compartments to hold our hook selection and it is an easy matter to get a fine paint brush and mark off the sizes on the top of the lid to make the selection of a hook easy.

Now what do we want?

I'd suggest for minimum needs a couple of dozen of each of the following sizes, remembering that the larger numbers denote the smaller hooks with 16 as our smallest and 1/0 as the biggest. So we pick 16's, 14's, 12's, 10's, 8's, 6's, 4's, 2's, 1's and 1/0's.

To this selection we can add a few with shorter shanks and maybe some with longer shanks in the medium-size range.

This set will cover most freshwater angling needs, although it will be necessary to add a few gang hooks for pike and muskie, and a few of a specialist type such as the effective weedless hooks that will carry a pork-rind bait through a tangle of stumps or lilies in largemouth-bass habitat. At this point, however, all that is needed to round out the kit is a fine carborundum stone to keep the points effectively sharp.

Sinkers are terminal-tackle accessories moulded from lead and used to add casting weight, or to hold a baited hook down where the fish may be feeding. A sinker in one circumstance may be no more than a single buckshot clinched to the line, or it may be a hunk of lead weighing an ounce or two for fishing in a rapid current.

Where possible, it is best to dispose of sinkers completely, as their weight on a line can often scare off a shy-biting fish, or impart an unnatural movement to a lively bait. In still water, or when fishing over heavy weed, the use of a sinker often becomes more of a nuisance than an aid. In a fast current, on the other hand, we can seldom get the bait to fishing depth without adding extra weight to the terminal gear.

Since it is best to streamline sinker use I carry three types for freshwater fishing, each in a range of weights; thus, I can select one sinker to balance the gear. This is essential, because when two or three small sinkers are used to make up the weight there is more chance of them catching or picking up floating weed.

Clinch Sinkers

These are quite simple sinkers designed so that they can be quickly attached and taken off the line without undoing terminal gear. There are several types with different methods of attachment and while various patent designs work very well, I prefer to use the basic type which costs less and works just as well.

This basic clinch sinker is a streamlined cylinder of lead with a slot for the line running the whole length and soft lead ears on each end formed in the moulding. To attach it, the line is slipped into one end of the slot, taken three times around the body of the sinker and then passed out through the other end of the slot. The ears are then bent down to hold the line in place. To improve this simple system, bend the whole sinker when this process is complete, so that the soft lead forms a crescent moon. This bend brings the line up taut, holds it better and allows the sinker to swim better when the tackle is being retrieved.

The clinch sinker is used to add additional weight when trolling to take the lure deeper. For this it can be attached just above the leader, or put on 3 feet up from the lure if you are using a plug or spoon that has a diving or fluttering action. Another use is to add weight just above the leader when fishing a lively bait minnow below a fairly large bobber. For this work, the sinker will aid in keeping the minnow down where it belongs, and also it tends to sink the bobber slightly and thus help reduce bouyancy so that a striking fish meets with less resistance.

A little-known but highly valuable use of the clinch sinker is in trolling with a spinner that revolves. A revolving lure has a strong tendency to throw twists into the line that can in time ruin a day's fishing and even destroy the usefulness of the line. To deal with this it is a good idea to place a clinch sinker right up against the line swivel at the top of the leader. This is then bent into a crescent moon, and in this shape and position, it will either force the swivel to work, or will prevent the twist imparted by the spinner from running up the main line.

Since this type of sinker has a strong tendency to snag or catch in rocks, it is not the best one to use right on the bottom. For this we go to the dipsey sinker, or a split-shot rig.

Dipsey Sinkers

These streamlined, bomb-shaped sinkers cover a great range of fishing uses, and the best ones come with a fine eye fitted in the pointed end of the lead. This eye should not be a rigid fitting, but a swivel unit moulded right into the lead.

The dipsey sinker, in its most common rigging, is tied to the bottom end of the line and hook units are tied at different points above it, for fishing close to the bottom and at various high levels, both at the same time. This is fine for eager-biting fish such as perch and schooling sunfish, but of considerably less value when shy biters are met, or when the tackle is intended for use in a current. Under these circumstances we should adopt what in England is called a *sliding leger*, a simple but outstanding system for bottom fishing.

To make a sliding leger the line is first passed through the end ring of the sinker and then the hook is tied on. The dipsey is now moved 3 feet back up the line, and two big split shot clamped below so that it cannot slide down to the hook. In this position the weight forms a stopper point to allow for casting, with the baited hook streaming free below.

When a fish takes hold of the bait with this rig, the bite travels up the line, pulls freely through the eye of the sinker and registers on the rod point, without the fish feeling any tug from the lead. The line simply slides through the eye.

I was happily catching carp on a rig like this, in a river with just too much of a current for fishing in the best style without a sinker. Nearby, on that day, was an obviously experienced angler who was also taking fish, but wasn't doing as well.

He landed a small carp of about 8 pounds, shook his head and walked up to visit for a while. "There is something different in what we are doing," he said. "Not only are all your fish bigger than mine, but you seldom seem to be bothered with false bites."

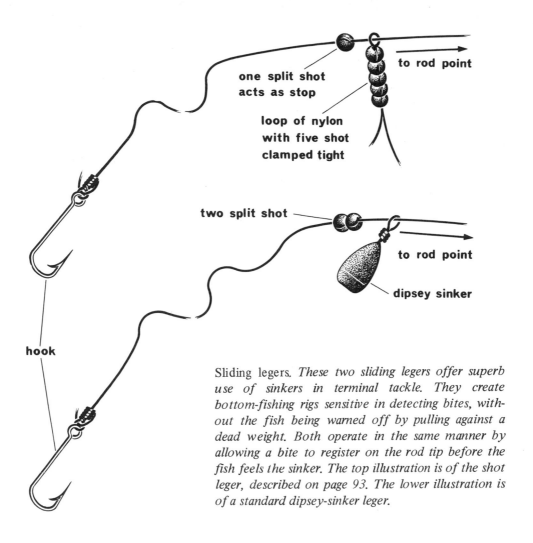

one split shot
acts as stop

loop of nylon
with five shot
clamped tight

to rod point

two split shot

to rod point

dipsey sinker

hook

Sliding legers. *These two sliding legers offer superb use of sinkers in terminal tackle. They create bottom-fishing rigs sensitive in detecting bites, without the fish being warned off by pulling against a dead weight. Both operate in the same manner by allowing a bite to register on the rod tip before the fish feels the sinker. The top illustration is of the shot leger, described on page 93. The lower illustration is of a standard dipsey-sinker leger.*

Comparing tackle, the sole difference was in our bottom gear. I was set up with a sliding leger. He had a dipsey sinker of the same size as mine, but it was fixed. Fascinated at the idea of the line running free when the fish took, this thinking angler pulled his tackle apart and made it up again into a sliding leger. Just ten minutes later he had a bite, reared back his rod and socked his hook home into his largest carp, a superb beauty of 29 pounds.

"It gives you an edge with the older, smarter fish," he remarked. "They were probably biting, but spitting out the bait when they felt the tug of the sinker."

Of course they were, and so do many other lunkers of all fresh-water species, when they come up against gear which signals that some-thing is not natural. That strong pull direct to the rod point lets the angler know the score *first* and adds to his chances of success.

When you wish to fish a hole in waters with a powerful current, simply use a lead heavy enough to stay in place. With the rod point taut to the hook, you still get the first warning before the fish is aware of the tackle.

Using a sinker just a little too light to hold the line still, it is possible to bump a bait downstream and cover lots of territory. The swivel eye of the dipsey seems to allow for less catching on the bottom and seldom causes the line to snag around the sinker.

I use this same system for drift fishing, where the boat wanders down before the wind and a bait is allowed to flow along just off the bottom. This is done by allowing the sinker to touch, at which point a couple of turns of the reel bring it up out of danger of snagging, while leaving the hook bait down to flow over the bottom. If the length of line below the sinker is increased, it is possible to come up with a rig that really allows for a natural presentation of the bait. I used this once on a snapper-fishing trip off South Carolina and hauled in some great fish. Our bait was small squid, used whole and with a 9-foot saltwater spinning outfit and a 9-foot leader flowing from the 2-ounce sinker. There could be little doubt that it was a superior system of bait-offering. The rest of the gang thought so, for they all changed to this accurate and delicate contact system.

Split-Shot Sinkers

Split shot are small lead balls with a slice cut in one side so that they can be easily crimped onto the line. The common size range runs from No. 5 birdshot which is .12 inches in diameter, to No. 00 buck-shot at .33 inches.

The finest split shot is soft enough to be put on with a pressure of the fingers and flicked apart by a finger-nail. This quality is hard to find but is worth the search. Most shot sold for angling is too hard, needing pliers and a knife for attachment and removal, which could pinch or cut the line.

Most anglers take split shot so much for granted that they fail to understand the important role it can play in terminal gear. From a good range of sizes we can select a single shot, just right for taking a fine leader downstream so that the bait travels along the bottom in a natural way. In a heavy current a string of shot can be added one at a time until the tackle runs nicely. To obtain the exact balance of a sensitive bob-ber, we can again add one shot at a time, checking between each addition, until the float unit sits properly in the water.

There are many uses for split shot and the inventive angler can always find some new use. For example, I was shown a method of making a sliding leger with split shot, that is the final answer for angling in the rocky, fast rivers where the rainbow or steelhead trout run to spawn.

This shot leger was shown to me by an English angler I was hosting on a favorite fast current swim. I was content to keep my terminal tackle (a 1-ounce sliding leger made with a dipsey sinker) anchored to the bottom, but my companion didn't want to sit pat. He wanted to run his dew-worm bait right down the stream. When I told him that it was a mass of snags, he pulled out a can filled with beautifully soft English-made shot.

First he cut off a foot length of 8-pound-test nylon monofilament, bent it in two and started to clamp shot over both ends, leaving a small loop of nylon at the top. When he had six No. 1 buckshot attached, he put his line through the top loop of the shot leger, and pushing it up three feet from the hook, clamped on a single shot to hold it in place. He then pushed up his six shot to close up the loop, so the leger would slide on the line in normal sliding-leger style (see page 91).

Baiting up with a whole dew worm, he dropped the rig over the side of the boat, allowing it to sink and flow down with the stream. When he found he couldn't stay in touch-contact with bottom, he hauled out and added one more shot to the tail, and tried again. This time it was just right and near the end of our fishing hole, his worm was grabbed by a beautiful smallmouth black bass. "That's it," said Fred. "I bet there's a whole bunch of them down there."

He was right, and for about seven hours I sat there watching with increasing enjoyment as Fred hit fish while bumping his bait down the bottom in that fast current.

He had four on the stringer before he got snagged and when he found that he was really caught, he simply snapped back his rod, gave slack and bumped it, in an effort to bounce it loose. When that failed, he got hold of the line, gave a slow, steady pull and sure enough, it came away. On reeling up, Fred showed me that he was missing four shot.

"That's how it works," he said. "It's usually the sinker that gets trapped and with most legers when you try to pull it free, you lose the sinker, hook and bait. In this style, all I lost was the last four shot which must have been caught between a couple of rocks. A steady strain just pulls the doubled nylon out of the soft shot. They come off the end, because there is nothing holding them."

The part I liked was that since he knew how many shot it took to work his tackle, all he needed to do was count what was left and make up the number with spare shot. At the end of the day, with the boat full of fish, he was still using the original shot leger, although he had added 25 to 30 by replacing ones lost when snagged.

That fall, when I went rainbow fishing in my usual place I used a shot leger balanced to run down through the very rocky stream, and it worked with outstanding success.

The shot leger is now part of my angling technique and the only problem is getting a supply of suitable shot. All the domestic sources offer steely hard shot in silly little plastic boxes holding little more than a dozen. I solved this by bringing in several pounds of superb split shot from England where what we would call a No. 1 buckshot size is known as swan shot. In England, this is carefully made for a discerning angling trade and is sold sensibly by the pound in quantities up to 50 pounds.

This swan shot, or No. 1 buck, is the best size for putting together a split-shot leger, and indeed for many other sinker uses better served by split shot.

LEADERS

Leaders are wire or nylon accessories used to protect the end of the line from damage by sharp-toothed fish or abrasive snags. They come in a variety of lengths and are fitted with snaps and swivels.

A quite different form of leader used in fly fishing will be dealt with later.

Leaders are often overrated, being accepted all too often as a normal part of the basic tackle. This is wrong, for while they are invaluable at times, in most angling they are quite likely to reduce one's chances of taking fish.

It is difficult to state rules in the use of leaders, because it is mostly a matter of common sense. This doesn't help the reader just starting out, so let us examine what I do, and why.

A long leader from 2 to 3 feet in length is my usual standard for trolling, for this length protects the fragile line end from snags and weeds, aids in preventing line twist and soaks up abuse handed out by a fighting pike or muskie.

For casting plugs and lures that are designed for underwater work I rig a 6-inch-long, fine-wire leader. This little leader protects the line and is short enough not to interfere with efficient casting.

When surface fishing with plug or popper bugs I tie the line directly to the lure, because for this work the rigid nature of the leader interferes with the action, and because it seems that I constantly get even the shortest leader tangled up in the gang hooks of the lures. This, of course, may be a reflection on my casting technique. The only time I

This good-sized lake trout was caught on a standard baitcasting outfit with a plain wire leader and a small wobbling spoon. The angler has rigged simply and sensibly with a light wire leader attached to the end of his line, and a spoon lure fastened on with a simple snap.

do use a short leader with a surface plug is when I am after pike or muskies, using some of the excellent lures designed for this work. But the casting here is less precise than that for the bass in weedy waters.

Leaders, I feel, are out of place in all forms of stillfishing. There are better methods for rigging live bait for pike than by putting a leader on the end of the line and using a gang hook dangling from the end snap; that's too much hardware. Instead of using a leader, I use bulk-steel leader wire to make up a pike tackle by attaching one end to my usual gang hook, and the other to a small swivel. This is neater and far more effective. Best of all, it is much cheaper than using a bought leader.

Wire Leaders

Wire leaders used in freshwater are usually made from twisted steel that is often plastic-coated. They come with a lure snap on one end and a swivel on the other.

In this material, leaders are obtainable from a very useful 8-pound test for ultralight spinning, to a most formidable 50-pound strength for use against the monster muskies of the Great Lakes and the St. Lawrence River. In these locales, the muskies are known to reach weights of 100 pounds, and the tackle used is often medium saltwater-trolling gear.

Standard lengths run from 3 inches, which I feel is too short, through 6 inches, 9 inches and up to 3 feet long. A selection of 6-inch, 1-foot and 2- and 3-foot lengths will cover every fishing task, and all these should match with the line test used. It is poor balance to tie a 45-pound-test leader on an 8-pound line. The better choice would be 10-pound test or, at the most, 15-pound. Twisted-steel wire leaders are quite thin and are not easily spotted by the fish.

The best leaders obtainable are quite inexpensive and are better than the cheaper items because of the use of superior hardware. The swivel plays an important role in reducing line twist and the snap is a major link between the main tackle and the lure, which is often an expensive one. Check them both before buying, and pay a little more money to obtain better quality accessories.

Nylon Leaders

The nylon leader, built in similar fashion to the wire leader, is a product of the increasing popularity of light spinning. Since they are usually fitted with stronger nylon than is used as the main line, they can perform a useful function in protecting the terminal end from wear and from the teeth of predators.

Whether nylon leaders are less visible than wire leaders is a moot point, as modern wire leaders are so fine in the lower range of test strengths. Generally, I don't use nylon leaders, having a marked preference for those made in steel wire. However, I do use nylon as terminal gear in the form of a shock leader.

Shock Leaders

This is a sensible saltwater-fishing development that can improve the efficiency of spinning tackle for all branches of angling. I learned it while fishing in the annual Light Tackle Big Game Tournament in Bermuda a few years back, and have used it ever since. The magnificent all-round angler, Joe Brooks, Jr., passed it on when we were out having fun with some medium-sized speedy reef fish.

We were 20 miles offshore and I had my big outfits set up. Knowing the thrill of taking on some of the smaller school species with ultralight gear, I had rigged up a 9-foot steelhead spinning rod, complete with 8-pound-test nylon. I was about to tie a hook directly to the end of the line, when Joe suggested I use a shock leader.

The shock leader is made up of two or three shortish lengths of heavy nylon fastened together by the blood knot (see page 249). Thus, when using an 8-pound-test line with a 9-foot rod, you would fasten a 4-foot length of 10-pound-test line with a blood knot to the 8-pound; a 4-foot length of 12-pound-test to the end of the 10-pound; then a 4-foot length of 15-pound-test to the end of the 12-pound nylon. This gives you a 12-foot tapered leader that runs well through the line guides on a cast, and yet offers increasing strength down towards the fish. You need a length at least 3 feet longer than the rod's length.

This type of leader can be made in any number of styles, including a short shock-tip, 3 feet long, for use with the lightest nylon used in ultralight spinning. Here is an example: using 2-pound-test main line tie a 1-foot length of 4-pound nylon by blood knot to the end, to the end of the 4-pound, tie a 1-foot length of 6-pound nylon; and to the end of this, a 1-foot length of 8-pound-test nylon. This gives a beautifully tapered yard-long leader that cushions the light line against the thrust of the cast, runs easily through the tip guide, and offers a stronger test point to withstand sharp teeth and abrasion by snags.

The thinking angler will see the value of this system and will no doubt come up with a number of variations and combinations to suit other situations.

Snaps and Swivels

Loose snaps and swivels are useful accessories for a number of terminal-gear tasks. Every tackle box should have a selection in different sizes, all of them the best available, because the work they do is important, and a poor link in the tackle can cause the loss of a fish or of an expensive lure.

Snaps come in a limited number of designs since their function is simply to introduce to our terminal gear a swift and efficient system for changing lures or leaders. The best type is rather like a safety pin, with the open point locking into a fold of metal. You can get plain snaps and also snaps that are fitted to the ends of swivels. Both are useful, although for the end of the gear the plain snap is best as it puts less hardware next to the lure.

Swivels, as the name suggests, are link attachments with a swivelling function that aids in removing line twist put on during fishing. Most are barrel-shaped with wire eyes on each end for attaching to the

For fish lacking sharp teeth in their mouths, such as this fine largemouth bass, a simple snap and swivel tied to the end of the line is preferable to a wire leader. Lures can be changed without constant knotting, and as can be seen in this picture, the swivel-snap unit added to the loop attachment of the spinner provides a reasonable length of protective metal should a pike, pickerel or muskie take the bait.

line, and some form of swivel mechanism, often very simple, built under the main part. In some of the most expensive swivels a ball-bearing system allows for a swivel effect under minimum pressure from the line, but it is seldom necessary in freshwater fishing to go this far. Most of the better class swivels will do a good job and they should be bought in a range of sizes and color finishes that will cover all angling needs.

BOBBERS

Bobbers act as a support for bottom-fishing tackle to hold the gear at a set height in the water and to be an easily seen indicator of a biting fish. They have never been held in high esteem in North America, being generally regarded as part of a most simple form of angling.

It is a different story in Europe where bobbers, called *floats* in England, have produced a delicate and superbly skilled form of angling called *float fishing*. Used there as a bite indicator, the float also performs many functions in the artistic presentation of baits to a large range of very shy fish. The round, plastic bobber common in North America is not used in England, where the skilled float fisherman will carry scores of beautifully made and carefully designed bobbers, each with a specific use.

The English floats are usually slim, with a stem of light material — such as reed, cane, or quill — fitted into a streamlined body made of cork, balsa wood, or some similar material. One type that has proven to be valuable for certain North American angling is the slider float, in which there is a rigged system that allows the line to run through rings until a set depth is attained. This is brought to a stop when a twist of nylon fastened on the line reachs the float, at which point the float cocks up and the hook is allowed to swim down stream at the desired depth.

Using one of these one day, I nearly sent a friend out of his mind as I kept on hooking smallmouth bass while drifting across a deep bay. This happened on Lake Erie in one of the large bays where, if the wind is right, you can drop a bait over the side, get it down to the bottom and allow the boat to drift while you work to keep your bait down so that it comes in contact with the bottom-feeding smallmouths.

My friend, and guide for the day, rigged up a modified sliding leger, baited with a live minnow and dropped it down. I slid a slider float up my line, tied on a hook, added four big split shot to balance the float, crimping them 2 feet above the hook, and dropped the end gear down until they touched bottom. I had the float in my hand, so the line ran through it, and when I had the depth, I tied in a twist of nylon *above* the top ring of the float. At this point I reeled up, baited the hook with a minnow and dropped the complete tackle over.

The line slid down through the float as the big shot sank swiftly, and at the right depth the stop hit the top of the float, which jerked upright and swam after the boat in fine style. I let out line until it was 20 feet behind the boat, and putting down the rod, allowed it to follow our drift. This bobber float was 10 inches high and, although streamlined, was quite heavily built with a hefty cork body mounted on a slim centre stick.

Out of the corner of my eye I noticed my friend do a double-take at the float, but he didn't say anything, even though I knew what he was thinking. You see the water was 20 feet deep over small rock and patches of sand and short weed, and since he had never seen a slider float before and had been busy while I was setting it up, he simply thought that I had a regular fixed bobber and was fishing my bait a maximum of 6 feet below the surface — and he was fully aware that the bass were right down on the bottom at that time.

After a few minutes there was a swift jab and my float shot under and came up again. I picked up the rod, gave slack line and told him that I had a bite. He shot his eyes towards my float in time to see it really shoot down and after allowing the fish time to turn the minnow, I threw over the line flier and set the hook. It was a dandy smallmouth and Joe just couldn't see how I had hooked it. Being unused to this type of gear, he had failed to notice that the float slid down as I reeled up the fish.

I landed three fish before he cottoned on to my specialist gear, and since the advantages were obvious he accepted some slider floats, rigged one up, and has used them ever since.

A similar slider system built into a large streamlined bobber makes an outstanding rig for fishing live bait for big pike in deep water. In fact, many of the deeper waters can be fished more efficiently with a slider-style float supporting the bait.

It would be easy to go on and on extolling the virtues of these crafted floats, and the different tasks they can perform, but let us just settle for a couple more techniques.

When the migratory rainbows come into my local river, I use a strangely shaped English float called a *trotter*. This is designed so the angler can set the depth to allow his bait, in this case salmon eggs or red worm, to swim downstream tumbling along the bottom, while the float shows where the bait is running. This trotting float is shaped so that it stays upright and doesn't flatten in the pull of the stream. By manipulating the rod, you can direct the bait into all the best spots, or hold it fixed in a place where the big rainbows are known to rest and feed.

Using this same float, I trot a small red worm under road bridges harboring shy brown trout, and because you can work it from 30 yards upstream, this system fools even the wise lunkers.

The lightest possible float, a slender quill which takes one tiny shot to balance in the water, makes it an easy matter to collect a big can full of husky bait minnow from any small, fertile stream I tie on a size 12 hook, bait with a snippet of worm, and allow the rig to roam around in any eddy curling close to the bank. One day, demonstrating this easy light-tackle technique, I caught 400-odd fish one after the other. On another occasion in a public demonstration, I landed over 200 brook trout, all of which, I hasten to add, were returned to the water. For the brook trout, I used a tiny size 18 hook with a fragile live nymph as the hook bait.

To most readers this is probably a new idea in angling and one that opens up all kinds of interesting possibilities. I hope people see it this way, because it's a shame when we settle down to the same old thing all the time. There's lots of room in this great sport for different ideas and I hope this will start something whereby float fishing may come to mean expert bobbing-tackle use, and not just floating down a river in a boat.

We now seem to have a pretty good basic tackle outfit, but before we tackle up, maybe we had better get some lures so we shall be ready for just about every branch of the sport.

5 🐟 About Lures

A lure is an artificial bait, either resembling the natural prey of predatory fish or capable, through movement, of provoking them to attack; or it may be a combination of both.

This is a delightful part of angling tackle because the tremendous variety of lures available brings out the collecting urge present in us all. It is fun to be able to open a tackle box and show off a glittering array of spoons, jigs, spinners and worms, and row upon row of gaily colored plugs. But it can also be expensive.

The majority of anglers purchase lures based on the human's visual response, forgetting that the prime objective of the game is how *fish* will respond. Many tackle boxes are filled with pretty lures — and some of the finest — yet plain lures are passed over in favor of fancy or highly lauded lures that have been given a false value through some big advertising campaign.

I well remember one of these that took place some years back. For week after weeks, magazines and newspapers carried full-page advertisements for a European spinning lure that was quite inferior. The claims included a boast that the grandson of the advertiser could outfish any angler with this lure, with the angler using his own choice of bait. Since I knew the lure to be less than useful, I wrote and accepted the challenge.

When this was ignored I sent, in turn, two registered letters and finally went in person to challenge this six-year-old master angler. It was, of course, nothing more than a slick deal, for I found my man in a small back-room office, up to his ears in mail and dollar bills; he was too young to have a six-year-old son, let alone a grandson. I told him to put up or shut up and he attempted to buy me off with a dozen of his useless lures. I answered that I had tried them fifteen years before and had come to the conclusion that they were worthless. All this I wrote up in a column, but with little result, for the advertising blurb was so powerful that suckers continued to send in money for these "new" surefire baits, at triple the list price.

This type of confidence trick bears no relationship to the advertising campaigns conducted by reputable lure manufacturers. These people conduct extensive field trials with all new lures, and only when they have something of value do they offer it to the public. I want to make this quite plain, because it is my opinion that North American lures for freshwater angling are the best in the world. There are, in addition, a number of outstanding baits made in Europe by equally reputable firms.

I want to condemn the attitude that suggests that all new lures are better than old ones. Modern production methods allow for a number of improvements, and the more we learn about fish the better chance there is of coming up with lures that are improved fish-getters. But some of the oldest designs are still among the best, such as the Canadian Canoe Spoon, which is deadly on lake trout and pike, and was used hundreds of years ago by the Ojibway Indians. The common red and white spoon should be a standard in every tackle box, yet this basic pattern is probably a couple of thousand years old.

Once, rummaging around an old-style hardware store in a remote area of Ontario, I discovered a pair of shop-soiled Bass Oreno plugs that must have been at least twenty years old. I carried my find back to the storekeeper who glanced at them and said, "Well, if you want those old things, just gimme 50¢ for the pair. They've been stuck up on that shelf for years." I payed the money and carried them away with pure joy. They were the good old wooden models, and I would have payed two bucks each for them, for it has been rediscovered that the wooden plug has a better *feel* than plastic and some of the best models are being reissued today, but at premium prices.

There are good new baits and good old baits, and the only way to buy lures is with a knowledge of what they should do, and of what constitutes a worth-while set. Now let us separate the types and have a look at their values.

There are five major classifications of lures: *spinners*, *spoons*, *plugs*, *jigs* and *plastic baits*. A few good lures defy classification and at times we will use one type in combination with another, as is the case with a spinner or a jig carrying a plastic worm.

No single lure will successfully cover the whole range of angling no matter what boasts are made. The comprehensive tackle box carries lures from each of the five types, with a limited number of *different* models, the best ones in a range of sizes and colors.

The lure box of an experienced angler usually shows a limited number of different lures and a surprising duplication of certain models. But when you look more closely you can see that there is variation in size and in color. When a box is filled with all kinds of different lures it shows that the collection was put together in a haphazard manner and not carefully selected.

A useful spinner box filled with Mepps spinners from the smallest, size 0, for white bass, panfish and ultralight spinning gear, up to No. 5, for muskies and pike. Mepps are also available in different shapes from round blades to slim Willowleafs. The slim blades swim deeper than the slower-sinking round models. This is a double-layered box and there are further Mepps spinners, in an additional range of sizes and shapes in the compartments beneath.

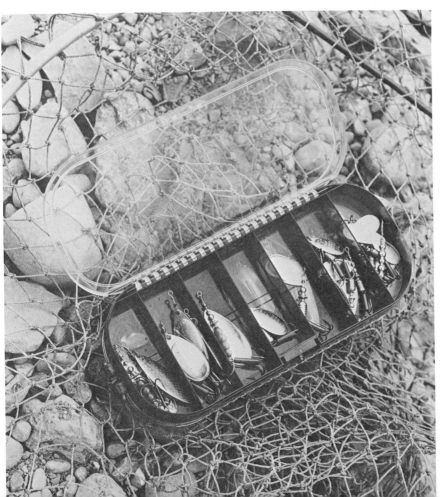

Spinners

These lures have a blade or similar part that revolves around a central stem. On some, the whole lure fishes by turning in a regular beat when pulled through the water. Most are made of metal, but quite a number have plastic blades. Spinners are generally smaller lures suited for spinning gear, but bigger sizes are also made, right up to the very large muskie baits. In the small- and medium-sized ranges they are valuable for a tremendous number of different types of angling.

Spinning lures go back many years, with such old favorites as Willowleaf spinners often used as a combination lure, with an artificial fly, a worm, or a plastic lure carried on the tail. These, and the modern lures that have developed from this principle, throb through the water when retrieved and since they offer strong water resistance with the blade, can be fished in slowly with maximum action. To do this work well the spinners must be balanced and so much in tune that the slightest pull through the water will set them going. It is the strumming vibration of the spinner that attracts predatory fish, probably because it resembles the twitching of an injured bait fish.

One of the finest of all spinners is the Mepps, a range developed in France. They were originally for trout, but are now made in sizes from the smallest 0-size (about an inch long), to sizes suitable for muskie and pike. Mepps are made in Willowleaf and oval-blade patterns, in gold, silver, black and other finishes. All the muskie models are fitted with bucktail dressings to add to their size effect. Hair and bucktail are the alternative dressings for lures through the small-size range also.

The blades of the Mepps spinners revolve around a central core on a D-ring mount that allows maximum action with a minimum of retrieve. They are so well-tuned that the majority will start spinning on completion of a cast, even when free-sinking. I have often taken smallmouth bass that have struck the sinking lure.

Because these spinners work so easily, they can be successfully fished shallow, medium deep, and deep, by manipulation of the rod point.

This fairly simple procedure is very useful when fishing for predators that are chasing bait. You might, for example, start off casting for white bass schooling on the surface, in which case you fish the retrieve with your rod held high to bring the lure back just a few inches below the surface. Since you can see the spinner, it is easy to regulate the speed of retrieve to run it through at the correct level. If the fish go down, it is a simple matter to reel more slowly with the rod point held level with your waist, so that the middle depths are searched. If this is unsuccessful, lower the rod point right to the water and turn the reel handles just fast enough to make the Mepps revolve, so that the lower depths are covered. With a certain amount of practice, it becomes possible to run a Mepps over the bottom, tapping the stones. For rainbows on their biannual run into the rivers, this is a highly successful technique.

There are a number of copies of the Mepps spinners on sale, some of them offering a useful series, but the genuine article is tough to beat, and I have a complete row of compartments in my tackle box filled from end to end with Mepps from the smallest to the largest sizes. Coming with a superb vibration retrieve factor and in a very wide range, this is definitely an outstanding spinner lure.

A series of lures sitting on the edge of the spinner range come in a lure/natural-bait combination that accounts for big catches of fish. This series includes the popular worm harness and is designed with a revolving blade and a long hook arrangement which allows some form of bait to be put on the end. Quite often this is nothing fancier than a big live dew worm, or it may be a plastic bait, or a dead fish or frog. This combination spinner can be cast but seems to be highly successful when trolled.

Once, on a northern river, I watched a woman angler throw a monster-sized spinner lure with a blade as big as a cigarette pack and a trailing bullfrog mounted on a double-single hook rig. The lady, a first-class angler, used a fairly strong baitcasting outfit, throwing her big lure setup out into the deeper holes by the rapids and bringing it back just fast enough to slowly turn the Willowleaf blade. She obviously knew the value of the deadly, slow retrieve, and caught a 19-pound pike.

I have often used a setup similar to her rig, cutting it down and using a smaller blade and a smaller dead frog to fish the deep edgings of the weedbeds for largemouth bass. It is an excellent system as the frog has a lightening effect on the tackle that allows the combination bait to be worked slowly and in deadly fashion at medium depth. However, the lure must be carefully tuned so that the leaf spinner works well at low retrieve rates.

I prefer not to use bait on the end hooks of throbbing spinners such as the Mepps. Any attachment outside of a bucktail dressing or hair dressing seems to detract from the effective action, and there are, anyway, many properly designed spinners built to take bait and work at full efficiency.

The one major disadvantage with spinners is their tendency to twist the line when trolled. This doesn't happen to the same degree when casting, as there are pauses to allow the line to straighten out. But the constant revolving behind a boat puts in horrible kinks, unless precautions are taken. These are to use a good leader with a first-class swivel and to put on a clinch lead above the swivel to make it work.

Spoons

These, along with plugs, form my favorite range of lures, possibly because I do a great deal of fishing for the bigger predators such as pike and muskies. Spoons have proven their ability to take fish over a period of a few thousand years. If chosen wisely, this style of lure offers a solid base on which angling techniques for a great many fish can be built. Also, since they wobble rather than revolve, there's no line twisting to ruin your tackle. As with spinning, the vibration of the spoon and the way it runs resemble a startled or hurt bait fish.

Spoons are so called because that is what they resemble. Sometimes they are broad and squat, sometimes slim and narrow. A few are built with fixtures to help them work, but most are shaped, curved, bent and tapered so that when pulled through the water, they flutter, strum and wriggle with complete abandon. The most important point to note is that when retrieved, spoons should create a definite vibration effect to attract fish and provoke an attack. The shape plays an important role and by carrying a wide range it becomes possible to select one suited to the purpose in mind, be it fishing deep down for lake trout, or casting in shallow, weedy waters for lurking pike. I prefer spoons made from thin metal of heavy density, that is to say, made from good copper plate, rather than the much lighter and cheaper alloys.

There are a number of reasons for choosing spoons built from *heavy* metal. For a start, being thinner at the same weight, they work better and are much more lively in action. With the concentrated weight they also have superior casting characteristics and in the long slim types I use when bottom bumping for lake trout their heaviness assists in getting the lure to the bottom.

While in a tackle store once, buying foot-long Canoe Spoons for lake trout, I found a selection of different makes, all identical in outward appearance and all the same price. I picked up two gold and two silver of one make and was about to take them to the cash desk, when it came to me that I should take a closer look at the different models. The shapes were about identical, all had well-made hooks with good attachment fittings and there seemed no essential factor that made one product better than the other. Then my better buying instincts came to the fore and I hefted one against another in my hands.

It came only as a slight surprise that one make out of the four was thinner yet heavier, and this valuable edge for a deep-running spoon decided my final choice.

The heaviest *thin* model usually costs a bit more, and in most tackle stores you will see a whole rack of common red and white spoons, ranging in cost from a few cents each to five times that cost for a lure of identical size. The cheaper lures represent no saving at all, since they seldom fish as well as the properly made spoon.

Wide spoons having a greater surface area sink more slowly than narrow lures and fish better in shallow waters. Once, on Lac La Ronge in Saskatchewan, I had an interesting demonstration of this, when a local angler beat me hollow on big pike that we found gathered in a bay averaging 3½ feet in depth. Using a Canadian-made Len Thompson spoon in red and white stripe, he harried the pike in water as shallow as 2 feet deep and seldom picked up weed or missed hooking a fish. Since the pike *averaged* 15 pounds and he was taking them every cast, I was frustrated to the point of fury by my own lack of success. I kept getting caught in weeds and, while shallow-running plugs also took fish, there was no doubt that the fish preferred the big spoons.

Comparing our largest spoons, I discovered this difference: his big Len Thompson had an overall length, including the hook, of 7 inches, and a width at the widest point of just under 1¾ inches. This spoon was also shaped wide for most of the length. My red and white spoon was 6 inches long overall and only 1¼ in width at its widest point. So that night, back at the lodge, I sent off a radio message for duplicates to his set and after the plane came in, I kept up with him when we hit that shallow water. It was the surface area of his spoon that had given him the edge.

The ability to swim at a particular depth, according to shape and width, allows for useful adjustment to conditions. When ultralight spinning with a spoon in a shallow stretch, a wider spoon, which sinks slowly, will work better than a slim one. Similarly, to get into deep holes, the best choice in a spoon is a slim model that will flash down and run deep. For shallow-water casting for pike or bass a wide spoon with a long, slow fluttering action will bring them out of the weeds. When after lake trout deep down, using wire or weighted line, a long narrow spoon such as the Canadian Canoe Spoon or the Williams Whitefish adds to the efficiency of our depth-seeking gear.

To get the best out of all spoons it is vitally important to have as much action as possible. All the best makes have terrific built-in wobble and flash that send throbbing vibrations through the water to attract an attack from a fish. This should be felt on the rod tip during a retrieve. The spoon and end-tackle should be carefully set to obtain all of this action, which means taking off swivels fitted to the end split ring. This swivel is a useless thing because good spoons don't revolve at all, but merely flutter. So, the first thing I do when I get a new batch of spoons is to remove the swivel, and sometimes the split ring too. With the leader snap fastened directly to the hole punched in the top end of the lure, the action is sharpened right away.

Some years back I made a mild protest to the maker of a fine lure range and received an honest and illuminating reply.

"We fit the swivels because the buying public demand them," he

This moderate-sized lake trout hit a large Len Thompson spoon. Note the fairly simple tackle used – a short steel trolling rod with a spring end to avoid kinking the metal line; a three-way swivel so that a bottom-bumping lead sinker can be attached; a spoon on a yard-long leader tied to the centre loop of the swivel with the metal line fastened to the top. The reel is a large, plain, single-action trolling unit – simple, but highly effective for this style.

said. "We once tried leaving them off but we ran into strong resistance and our sales suffered. You and I know that they cushion the sharp action and don't belong, and my firm is aware that people like you just take them off. We would like to put our wobbling spoons out so that everybody could enjoy the best action, but we can't afford to insist on it if our sales are going to suffer."

So, for those readers who want to get their money's worth from good spoons, here is how to rig the terminal gear for a wobbling lure. Remove the swivel and top split ring. When using light gear with nylon

The lure is removed from the formidable jaws of a fine muskie, using a sensible set of long-jawed hook removers. Note the simple snap arrangement used. The angler has removed the swivel and split-ring from the spoon and has attached the lure simply by the snap on the end of his wire leader. This rigid system makes the lure wobble with the sharp action that brings strikes. Note the pits on the under-jaw (see page 195).

line right to the spoon, first tie on a snap that has no swivel and use this as the connector. This is a sensible end-tackle, as it then becomes much easier to change from one lure to another by simply flipping open the snap. Generally, in the larger range, leaders are standard and you will have a snap ready for use. Don't just take my word for this increased action — get out and try two identical spoons, one fitted with a swivel, split ring and the snap of your leader, the other fastened on just by the leader snap. Most important, retrieve as slowly as possible. You will feel the improved action right away.

I should point out that the top-quality red and white spoons are always sold without fittings, which is one reason why they are so deadly.

Plugs

These lures usually imitate fish or another creature, or action that feels to a fish like that of a living creature. Plugs are delightful in every way and a pleasure to collect and use. The full range covers almost every type of angling.

Around the turn of the century standard-sized plugs were quite large and heavy, and were best for work with the rather stiff tackle then in use. Today we can get plugs as small as 1/16 ounce for ultralight work, and there is an excellent midget group at 1/4 ounce and 3/8 ounce. On the standard size for baitcasting we have 1/2 ounce and 5/8 ounce, and then the plug size range heads up until we come to the giants, built for muskies, that are 12 inches long and proportionately heavy.

The color of plugs can cause some hot disputes, but most anglers select them on the basis of what appeals to their fancy. Sometimes, too, an angler may hit a good bag on a specific color and ever after have greater confidence in that color than in others and will use it to obtain the best catch record. Who can blame that angler for holding strong views on what is the best color combination in his box? It is my conviction that a lure's action and the depth it is designed for are the most important considerations and I find color of secondary importance. But I still have my color preferences, most of which are based on values that would not stand up to a scientific test.

Among my favorite colors are red head with white body, perch finish, frog finish, and just about every shade of yellow. You know, it's funny — while writing this, I got up, opened my tackle boxes and took a good look. I was quite surprised to notice that I have a decided preference for yellow in the small and medium sizes and for perch finish in the larger plugs. So it is easy to see how personal color choice can be.

There is one color-type in my box that I find rather amusing. I call it the strawberry roan because it consists of a set of colored spots smothering a light background. I bought the first of these when after muskies in Ontario's Kawartha Lakes system. My guide looked into my tackle boxes, beamed with approval at what he saw and then tut-tutted and shook his head. He produced a Pal-O'-Mine minnow plug in this speckled finish and said, "You must have some of these. They are standard for these waters."

So I bought half a dozen and found them quite good. But the place where they first gave a great performance was in another lake system in Canada 1,500 miles away from the Kawarthas. In a lake which is unnamed on maps, but which the Cree call Iskwateegan, the strawberry plugs worked so well on walleyes that my Indian guide tried to buy them from me. I gave him all I had and I'll bet he now tells all his clients, "You must have some of these. They are standard for this water."

Local advice on lure color is often worthless but can be most valuable at times. The thinking angler will take a great deal of what he is told with a grain of salt, but will always be ready to test any suggestion based on local use and success.

However, when it comes to being told that only one make of lure will catch fish in any specific water, I dig in my heels and get ready to argue. If I am told that bass in a lake will only hit a frog-finish Hula Popper, I will stubbornly fish for them with a yellow Jitterbug. I had this happen with exactly these two lures and I caught limits of big bass on the Jitterbug. The man who had told me to use a frog-finish Hula Popper changed his tune and informed the anglers who came after that they *must* use a yellow Jitterbug — "*It is what the bass are now taking.*"

This attitude is pure nonsense, for I would probably have taken just as many bass on a frog Hula, or indeed, on any first-class surface plug. I was simply fishing in the right places, at the right time, with the right *type* of plug, using the correct technique.

Plugs are divided into separate groups according to the depth they reach and how much action they have. This has created an angling system allowing for coverage of fish from the surface to a depth of 30 feet or more. The angler who knows the value of this system and where and when to put it to work, has gone a long way towards understanding a joyful and effective angling style. Let us start from the surface and work down.

Surface Plugs

These are floating plugs designed to work on the surface, creating the impression of a wounded fish, a small mammal, or a frog, struggling or swimming across the water. Some have built-in action, others must be worked, but all of them are more effective when handled to produce an enhanced action. Among my favorites are the Jitterbug, the Hula Popper, and the Crazy Crawler. For some waters, a range of slim darter types or simple poppers work well.

Floater-Divers

This is one of the oldest types, usually of a straightforward shape. It floats at rest and, when pulled, dives by means of water action directed against a metal lip or a groove in the head of the plug. When the plugs are swimming just below the surface, the diving mechanism also creates a wriggling path that sends out exciting vibrations. My choice includes Pikie-Minnow, Vamp Spook, Pal-O'-Mine Minnow and Bass Oreno.

Sinker-Divers

Plugs in this class do not float, but sink slowly. Thus, they can be directed to a deeper level before the retrieve is begun. They are still moderate-depth plugs, with moderate action similar to the floater-divers. I own a few of this type — Pikie-Minnows for trolling — but the sinker-divers are less effective than those of the next class.

Deep-Divers

These floater plugs are fairly new and are fitted with long diver vanes that can send the plugs down to 20 feet or more. To make them come back along the bottom, the reel is pumped furiously for several turns. This tips the lure forward, creating heavy water-pressure against the diving vane. The plug zooms deep and touches bottom, at which point the reel is slowed to a normal speed. With the plug down deep, this slower rate of retrieve brings it back nicely along the bottom. If any snags are encountered they are first hit by the diving vane and this contact tips the lure up and over and flips the hooks away from the snag. Excellent for both casting and trolling, these plugs work extremely well in the correct type of water. They couldn't be used over weeds, as their diving action buries them deep. My favorites are the egg-shaped Arbo-Gaster, one of the deadliest of all plugs, closely followed by Heddon's Deep-Six.

A kit which includes a selection from each of these depth series enables an angler to cover the widest variety of water, and sometimes a change from one series to another will bring in fish right away. This happens quite often and I want to mention one make of larger plugs which incorporates a depth range — the Cisco Kid plugs, which are obtainable in models that dive to different depths. This permits carrying a range of identical plugs in which there are different depth values. according to the shape and size of the fitted diving vanes. If the lure runs too shallow, use a deeper-swimming model; if the deep-diving Cisco picks up weed, change to the medium-diver. The system really works well and is a helpful extra on a top quality lure.

Last, but very far from least, there is the Flatfish, an exciting range of banana-shaped plugs that look a bit ridiculous, yet are among the finest lures made. This twentieth century design by Charles Helin, a master fisherman and lure maker, comes in such a complete series that it would be possible to select a suitable model and color for almost every angling need. These really outstanding plugs have a built-in action that sends a massive spread of alluring vibrations through the water.

Jigs

Jigs are as old as hooks, and in their simplest form, consist of little more than a hook with a sinker head and some form of hair, feather, or nylon tail. It is indicative of the general lack of thought among freshwater anglers that this ancient lure has taken so long to be truly accepted. Sea fishermen have used the jig for centuries, but there are still a great many freshwater anglers who avoid it, because they lack the knowledge of how it is best used.

Far down, where the chill water is dark green and only a vestige of sunlight penetrates, the great lake trout feed. They are found throughout most of Canada, the biggest fish being taken in the larger lakes far to the north. To fish for the laker, you drop lures on metal lines well down into the depths, for this giant trout species can be taken in shallow waters only during the first few days after the break-up of the ice.

An angler fishes for lake trout in the harsh rocks of a rapids in northern Saskatchewan shortly after the ice has melted from the lakes. Spring comes to this northern land in late June, and the trout cram into the white water, feeding on the suckers and minnows that gather to spawn. In the foreground lies a partly eaten white sucker that was caught by a black bear which ran off when the angler climbed down to fish the pool.

Even with weeds masking the action, this banana-shaped Flatfish plug brought a strike and successfully hooked the hefty bass. This design, one of the best sellers throughout the world, offers an effective series that can cover just about every angling need from light work in a stream to heavy trolling on big waters.

Jigs have no action of their own. If reeled straight in, they simply slide through the water in lifeless fashion, with little to stir a fish to attack. However, they should not be used this way as they are a bottom-fishing lure, with the sinker head moulded to balance the hook point upwards. This allows a jig to be retrieved in a series of short hops, imitating the action of some small, lively creature flitting from one place of safety to another.

The art of jigging seems to work best on schooling fish, where an element of competition for food is present. When white bass are feeding heavily, they will race one another to hit a lively jig, and will even take it while it is being jerked through midwater. Schooling yellow perch wallop small jigs that are merely danced up and down under the rod point, and this simple technique will take many other fish too.

On one special occasion, a tiny 1/32-ounce jig with a flowing marabou tail helped me out of a tough situation and made a crippled child happy. It happened on a fishing day held by a service club for a group of crippled children, confined to wheel chairs and unable to take a trip into the country.

This service club had the excellent idea of cleaning out the swimming pool of a local hotel, filling it with sweet water and then dumping in about 500 large brook trout. I was invited along as an angling expert, to rig tackle and show the kids how to catch fish.

The trout, culled from hatchery stock, were as heavy as 2½ pounds, and being used to people, were not as shy as wild trout would have been. I showed the kids how to use a cane pole with bobber and small hook baited with a scrap of worm, caught three in a row (which I put back) and then invited them to have a go.

The kids started and as the uproar increased those lovely big brook trout were hauled out one after the other. I prowled around helping out the kids who showed a lack of success. I put my hand over theirs to hold the pole, manipulated the bait, set the hook and let go, screaming "You've got one!" Then I stood back to enjoy the wonder and excitement of a youngster with his first fish. I worked around steadily until, just before it was time for the kids to go back to the hospital, there was only one girl, about twelve years old, who had yet to take a fish. She was deeply disappointed, and with tears starting to her eyes, she told me that she had promised to take a trout back for her dinner and that her nurse was expecting it. So I told the organizer to hold the bus and I set to. By this time the remaining trout, terrified at the noise and splashing, were huddled in a corner at the deep end, so I made everybody stand back, got my big tackle box and tried every combination of trout lure I owned. At last I came upon the tiny marabou jig, tied it on, shot out a cast and, with my hand over the girl's trembling hands, started to flip it along the bottom past the huddled fish.

To my delight and indeed surprise, a dozen good fish shot out of the tightly packed school to chase the jig. There was a wallop, I let go, and an enchanted little girl put the stick to *her* trout. It was a big one of about 2 pounds, and since she had been left out till the end, I repeated my tactics until the youngster had four nice fish. She was wheeled out to the hospital bus with a plastic bag of trout in her lap and a look of great pride and happiness on her face.

With the kids gone, my wife and I, using marabou jigs on ultralight spinning rods, caught 40 fish in as many minutes for the adult barbecue thrown for the folks that had lent a hand.

Since then I have used similar little jigs on wild trout streams, and found them to be great fish-getters under many different circumstances. It certainly pays to carry a range of sizes and colors, for the jig, once it is mastered, is a valuable lure.

Plastic lures moulded to resemble fish, frogs, worms, snakes, eels, and leeches are made in a flexible vinyl. This is an old bait in a new form, for a rubber worm was put on the market as far back as 1860.

The success of plastic baits seems to vary with locale, being highly popular in Midwest and Southern lakes and less so in other regions. The plastic worm, snake or eel, work extremely well on spoon-bait, spinner-bait and jig-bait combination lures, especially for trolling or scratching bottom.

Another line of plastic baits includes a full rig, in which a worm is mounted on a lure with a weighted head and with weed-guards protecting the hook points. These are excellent for use in weedy waters, where they won't catch when slowly drawn over the weeds to bring strikes from bass hiding in the pools. In some Southern lakes, worm rigs are simply cast out to sit on the bottom without movement. When picked up by a bass, the strike is delayed to allow the fish to get the hook in its mouth. Apparently the soft feel of the lure allays suspicion.

The worm, eel, and slender leech styles of plastic baits are extremely useful in building combination tackles, or for use as units with some form of hook harness, perhaps with a small spinner at the head; but I am of the opinion that rubber fish and insects are of less value than a good spoon, plug, spinner, jig or even live bait. A tackle collection of the plastic worms should include a broad variety of colors, and yes, even some of the crazy patterns of spots, too. Once, in a northern lake, I saw a number of very large leeches colored pale green, with spots of a lighter color. I rigged a plastic worm with a color pattern that matched as closely as possible, and caught a big bag of meal-size walleye by allowing the spinner-worm combination to sink and hop close to the bottom.

Other Lures

Outside of the categories covered there are a number of excellent lures. Some, such as flies, we will deal with later; some defy classification owing to the variety resulting from man's never ending search for better baits. It is wrong to say that only the old baits are good and that all new baits are poor, because we are making new discoveries all the time. I would urge the collection of a kit of lures based on the factors we have discussed, always remembering that a well-made lure with good action is worth ten thousand gimmicks.

6 🐟 A Day's Fishing

It is time to gather together our beautiful new tackle, and head out for a day's fishing. We need to learn how to put the gear together with the proper knots, and to learn a few different angling techniques.

I have chosen a favorite fishing hole that has a good head of fish and conditions that are easy for the beginning angler. It is less than pastoral, being close to a busy highway, and most anglers sweep by it without a second look. But it is a good place to fish and has characteristics that may be found all over North America.

Picking a warm day in early summer, let's take all the gear, including the lures you have so carefully selected, for you never know what fish might happen along in this type of fishing hole. We will start with dew worms and live minnows for bait and these we will pick up at the site. While we do that, we can take a good look at the water and start learning how to recognize a good fishing spot.

Our fishing hole was once just a marsh, with a deep-water channel running through to connect a big lake with a smaller, weedy inland bay. It was an interesting place when wild, but a highway bridge built at a narrow point changed it into a hotspot.

When the traffic got too heavy for the old single-lane bridge, the makers of highways threw a massive broken-rock causeway across the marsh, covered this with fill, and put a four-lane highway on top. Across the deep, fast channel went a bridge with solid concrete piers set

This enchanting and amusing incident recorded by famed Canadian artist and car-
toonist Duncan Macpherson, will be familiar to all dedicated anglers. You are
driving along, and come across a stream with the fish jumping. The tackle comes
out of the trunk, the business jacket and shoes and socks come off, and for a few
enchanting moments the cares of the day are forgotten in the delight of angling.

fast in the current flowing back and forth in the gut, thus creating a
water race. The closing in of the channel speeded the flow, and this cut
deep holes and created massive eddies on each side of the bridge.

The deepened water attracted channel catfish, the eddies became
the feeding places of walleye and other species, and the various obstructions and covering spots brought along minnow shoals and a trailing tail
of resident and visiting predators. In fact, we now have a typical rich
fish-population because of works that provided suitable habitation for
all indigenous species.

We'll use bottom gear and a worm for our first attempt here, in
one of the big eddies below the downstream side of the bridge. The

water in these massive swirls is around 20 feet deep, and when the current swings to flow through the other way, we will still be able to fish in comfort, and hold bottom.

An early start lengthens the angling day, so here we are at 5 a.m., having coffee with the owner of the boat and bait livery, and chatting about conditions and learning which fish have shown recently. Advice from someone who lives right on the water is valuable indeed; and he tells us that the white bass are in, and that pike seem to have followed them and are being taken in the shallows on each side of the new bridge.

So, in addition to our worms we buy a couple of dozen small minnows. One dozen of these are less than 2 inches long, the right size for white bass, and the other dozen, for pike, are good-sized chub about 5 inches long. These go into our double-bait bucket and on reaching the point that we will fish from on the bank, the bucket liner is pulled out, sunk in the water and tied to a rock. It is going to get warm and this precaution will keep all the minnows lively.

At 20 feet the eddy is too deep for comfortable bobber fishing, even with a slider float, so we will use a sliding leger and, since the bottom is fairly clean, a dipsey sinker of 1 ounce.

The ferrule of the rod joint is rubbed between nose and cheek to add a little lubricating skin oil. The rod is pushed together, the reel screwed home and the line is threaded through the guides with about 10 feet pulled out of the tip ring so that we can build our terminal tackle. To make our sliding leger we need a dipsey sinker, two split shot and a size No. 6 standard hook. The sinker is slid up the line two feet and clamped in place. Now comes the important part — knotting the hook on the end of our nylon monofilament line.

Nylon can slip with a poor knot, and worse still be reduced in test strength. Some of the knots used with silk line hold well with nylon, but can drop the test strength by as much as 50 per cent. Since we are going to use 8-pound monofilament, it would be foolish to use a knot reducing its effective value to 4-pound test, so we will settle for the *clinch knot* which, under scientific testing, has been shown to retain as much as 87 per cent of the line strength.

The clinch is *the* knot to use in fastening the end of a length of nylon to a rigid eye, including those on the hook, the swivel, or the end of a leader. Since it is a knot that we will be using regularly in all branches of angling, it is just as well to learn how to tie it properly.

This can be awkward to tie at first, giving most beginners the idea that a third hand is needed. But a little practice quickly brings proficiency in tying and in as few as six practice ties, it becomes second nature.

The end of the line is brought to the hook eye and 6 inches are

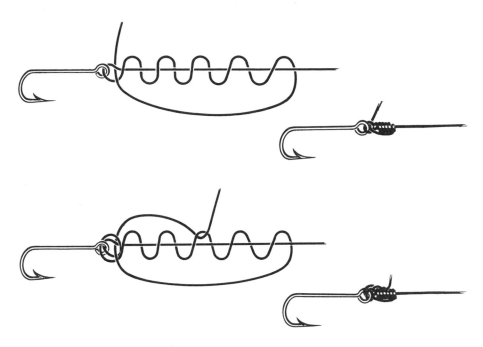

The clinch knot (above), *and the improved clinch knot* (below) *are the basic fastenings for attaching hooks, swivels, snaps, or leaders to the ends of lines. The important points to remember in tying them are that the proper number of turns should be made, and that they must be pulled taut with an even strain on the three ends — the main line, the end, and the hook or swivel.*

pulled through and doubled back on the main line. This short end is twisted five times around the main part, by holding onto both ends and twisting the hook. The end is now brought forward and passed through the eye formed above the hook eye in the nylon. This end, together with the main line, is carefully pulled taut against an even strain on the hook. The spare end is now burned off with a cigarette or snipped, leaving a small tag.

With light lines, many anglers, including myself, prefer to use the slightly more complex, but superior *improved* clinch knot. In fact, once mastered, this can be used all the time.

In the improved version, the line is passed twice through the eye of the hook, twisted five times as before, poked through both loops in the nylon above the hook eye and then through the next twist up the line. It is pulled taut on all three ends; the hook, the main line and the short end. Both of these knots form a neat wrap that allows the line and hook to be positioned at the best level for setting and holding a fish.

For clipping the end of the nylon, and for a score of other jobs, I always carry an over-sized pair of nail clippers in my tackle box. These are good for cutting anything from spare ends of nylon to the lighter-weight leader wires, and are available at drug stores. I keep mine tied with a length of strong line to a strut of my box, so that they are always ready.

Now that the hook is tied to the end of the line it is time to put the bait on, but since this is a first angling trip, it will be wise for a few practice casts to be made to make sure that we can plop the bait into the edge of the eddy. It is a pretty big target, less than 40 feet offshore, so it shouldn't take us long to pick up the necessary skills. But we had better take time out now for a few words on casting.

The best way to pick up casting skill is by practicing with a rubber sinker tied to the end of the line. Some level piece of ground, lawn or a local park is a good place, but most folks are more at ease and feel less conspicuous practicing over water.

Casting with spinning and spincast gear is a matter of *feel* and *timing*. It is more easily taught by a practical method than by a written description, so if you know someone willing to give a short lesson, that will be best. It is hard to explain in writing how much power to apply, or when to release the line, but I will take a stab at it, using the clock-face system to describe positions. So let's see what we can do.

When facing the water squarely, your head is at 12 o'clock, your feet at 6 o'clock. When you point your right arm forward, level with your shoulder, you mark 9 o'clock; with your arm behind, you mark 3 o'clock. All the other positions are relative to these.

Facing the water, reel the sinker to 18 inches below the rod tip and put the rod back over your shoulder until the tip is at 2 o'clock.

By moving your wrists slightly up and down you can get the feel of the weight of the tackle as the sinker draws the rod tip down. When you have done this, release the line and hold it either with your finger tip or with the spincaster button, so that it is set to flow when the pressure is released.

Next, dip the rod tip slightly, lift it to feel the sinker weight, and as it comes up taut, use wrist action to power it forward in a straight line over your shoulder towards the target. When the point hits 10 o'clock release the line and allow the rod to follow through until it is possible to sight the target over the tip.

If the direction is right and the correct amount of thrust is applied, the sinker will plop right in at the desired spot. Too much power and it flies over the mark, but can be reeled back into the proper spot. Too little power and it falls short, and will need to be thrown again.

If the line is released too soon, the sinker will fly almost straight up in the air, or at whatever angle the tip was at when the line was released. If freed too late, the sinker will crash into the water just in front, or wheel around in a full arc to smack painfully into your shins.

This is the overhead cast — quite simple really, and the one to be used 99 per cent of the time. It provides for the safety of others on the bank, and is mandatory for use in a boat holding other anglers.

After several practice casts and a couple of fair fumbles, you appear to have the range and the timing, so we will bait with a big dew worm and start fishing.

Since it is important to have a lively bait wriggling on the bottom to attract fish, it is a mistake to thread it up the hook, as this will confine it. The pointed end of the worm is the head, the flat end the tail. The hook is pushed through the thick collar ring, one-third down from the head. Bring it right out, hook eye as well, and stick it in again halfway down the worm. Don't push it through this time, but just far enough to allow the point and barb to show. This will sit the worm in the bend.

When using a worm on travelling-float gear I would only hook it once through the collar ring, as this allows the worm full movement and lets it swim like a small eel or live leech. But in our swim we can expect small fish, and the double hook-hold saves bait when the eager biters are around. A big fish will suck it straight in.

Now you make your cast and it is successful, landing the hook bait into the eddy, so sit down and make yourself comfortable. Put the end of your rod up on that forked stick left by another angler, allow the bait to settle on the bottom and when the line sinks slack, reel in until it is taut to the rod tip and then slack off a bit. This will allow bites to register, without a sudden pull warning off a fish. Sit tight on the rod, concentrate on the line and tip, and be ready to pick it up and offer slack when you see a bite.

Shut and lock the tackle box, so the gear won't be upset if it gets knocked over in the excitement of a fight with a lunker.

Yes, I saw that. It wasn't a fish, just a small piece of floating weed, or maybe a sunken stick washed against the line by the slow-moving current. The line tightened slowly to the rod and put a slight bend in the tip before it came loose and let the tackle go slack again. A number of small things like that happen in a day's fishing. When a true bite occurs, it will show itself as a definite *jag-jag-jag* or, in the case of a big fish, as a solid pull that will jerk hard at the rod. With experience, you can read what is going on below by the behaviour of the rod and line.

This is the moment of truth for the angler: waiting for something to happen. It is important to have quite a bit of confidence in what you are doing, to be able to say to yourself, "I'll give them time . . . I know there are fish here . . . my bait is still on . . . and I'll stick it out to give the fish a chance to find the bait."

The biggest problem is always the waiting. Not waiting all day without a bite: that's being dumb, not patient. But we must wait for a reasonable amount of time. Anglers too often give a bait just a few minutes, then pull it out to see if it is still on, or to move it a few feet in either direction. The truth is that it takes a little time for a fish to find the bait. Sometimes the starting technique is wrong, and we need to run through a few different plans to get into contact with the fish. But it never hurts to give the fish enough time to come around.

Your bait is settled where there *are* fish and it would show poor judgement to keep hauling it out. So leave it there. No, look! Quick! You've got a bite. Now pick up the rod gently without tightening the line and when you get a long pull or a heavy feeling, raise the rod to bring the line taut, and when you can actually feel the fish, jerk the rod up with a firm wrist movement to set the hook. Good. You have him. Now keep that rod point well up to act as a spring. Keep the line tight and reel slowly. Always take it easy at first. I once had a little bite here, set the hook, reeled easily for about 20 feet and suddenly a great boil erupted and a 27-pound channel catfish took off for the other side of the channel. I thought at first I'd set the hook into a small fish that had been taken by a big one, but in fact I'd hooked the cat right away and he had come along in docile fashion for the first stage. You must always be prepared for that type of reaction from a lunker.

Well, you've landed the fish and it's a rock bass. Now these fellows have a sharp dorsal fin (that's the one on top of the back) so fold down his fin, by bringing your half-closed hand over his head and down. Then grip him firmly behind the gills. You must have timed the strike perfectly, for the hook is right in the lip. Just take a firm hold of the shank, push the hook straight back and twist out. Fine. Now put him back to grow bigger — he's too small to keep.

Small fish such as the rock bass and sunfish are eager biters and often gulp the hook so that it finishes by sticking firmly in the throat. For this I carry a long pair of surgical forceps, the narrow kind with a long nose and a clip system in the handle that can lock the ends onto the shank of the hook for disgorging without damage. These are particularly good for use on a throat-hooked pike, as they keep fingers clear of the sharp teeth.

It is now 7 a.m. and you have taken eight fish: three small rock bass and two sunfish which you put back to grow, plus a nice-sized crappie and two brown bullheads of 1 pound which we have on the stringer in the water so that they will stay alive and fresh until we are ready to go home. I think it is about time to change to a large minnow for a while, to see if there are any decent walleye hanging around the swim. So, take off the small hook by cutting it close to the knot, and leave it to dry before putting it back into the box. Now, using the clinch knot, tie on a size 4 medium hook, and I'll get a minnow out of the bucket liner in the water.

You hear a lot of arguments over the best way to put a live fish on the hook as bait. Some people suggest a hook hold on the back, just in front of the dorsal fin, others stick it carefully through the side just in front of the tail.

Both these hook positions are useful and can be used for different circumstances, but for our purposes we'll use the one I believe best for leger fishing a live minnow. So hold the fish firmly, but not hard enough to hurt it, and gently push the point and barb through both lips, into the bottom and out of the top. I prefer this hook style because we are using 5-inch minnows which are fairly large for the job at hand, and since predators swallow prey head first, we give the biting fish time to turn the bait, so that when we strike, the hook should be well in its mouth.

A gentle overhead cast now, and check the line with your finger tip, just before the bait reaches the spot. This slows the bait and allows it to drop into the water softly, with less chance of being stunned. A *lively* bait tugging away at the tackle, will bring in predators from a considerable distance, and for this reason, let it sit there so that they have time to find it. Your cast was fine, so put the rod down on the rest. But this time allow more slack, for you may need to let the fish move off several feet before you set the hook. Any bite now will likely be a decent fighter, as the bait is really too big for small rock bass. You may need to wait longer for a take, but you have caught a few fish and it is worth-while spending an hour or so on the chance of a better size.

While we are waiting let us again run through what to do on a bite, as it will be too late to do so when a fish takes.

When your line and rod tip show action, pick up the rod, set the reel to give free line and let the fish move off. When he stops and then swims away again, flip in the line retrieve on the reel, put the rod point out towards the fish, and when the line comes tight, or a heavy pull is felt, reel to get the line taut, flip up the rod to set the hook and bring the rod up to take the strain on the limber tip. Got it? Now make yourself comfortable on that rock, sit over the rod and be ready for action. While you wait, I'll get out my rod and see if I can pick up something on float tackle. I'll fish right here where my bait can run down the edge where the fast stream and the slack water meet. It is 8 feet deep and I can handle that with a fixed-position float on my long steelhead spinning rod. There's no argument that a 9-foot light rod comes in mighty handy at times.

With the rod put together, and a spinning reel loaded with 8-pound nylon clamped on the butt, I thread the line through the guides and the rubber ring on top of the float and then through the metal eye on the bottom. Since I'm going to try with the small minnows first, I'll put on a size 10 standard shank hook, with three swan shot clamped 2 feet up from the hook to weigh down the minnow and balance the bobber so that it sits well, with just a couple of inches of the tip showing. My guess is that the water is 7 feet deep so the float is pushed up 8 feet, dropped into the water and allowed to swim down in the medium-speed current. Whoops! It's gone under — a slow shuddering sink. It's touched bottom. So out it comes and the float is pushed down 6 inches.

Drop it in again, and this time it runs the full length of the swim without catching. I will allow it to go down this straight length, then check it at the bottom, and by turning the rod over, will make it turn in and hang still in that tiny eddy 25 feet below where we are fishing. This will make the minnow swim along the bottom and into that little bit of slack water where fish often lie in wait for an item of food washed down by the current. Now the gear is running properly, so I put a small minnow hooked through both lips and, my line of swim assured, out it goes.

Since I have a long rod in full control of the tackle, the overhead cast is not applicable. My swim starts 10 feet out from the bank, and with the bobber gear hanging below the rod point, I flip over the flier and swing the terminal gear out gently. When the minnow reaches the chosen mark, I release the line as smoothly as possible and the bottom gear slides out and lands where I aimed. With the rod held high and a finger set on the lip of the spool, I allow the tug of the float to slowly pull line off the spool. The idea is to make the tackle swim down without a pause until it reaches the desired point, where it will be checked. With my finger on the spool, I can quickly clamp down on the line if I need to strike. Now it is in the little eddy, so the line flier is thrown in and the live bait allowed to wander around in that hotspot.

Hey! There it goes! Down in one smash. It's up again, but look now! It's going *bob-bob-bob*. That means the fish has it and is turning it. Since it's a small minnow, just give it a second . . . down again, right under this time, so it's up with the rod. I've got him — a nice white bass. There must be a school of them huddled in that swim, so I string the fish and start again. We're going to have a fish supper tonight.

By the time I string the fifth white bass I can see that you are looking uneasily at your still tackle and I know that you want to join in the fun. Then, as you open the tackle box to sort out a float, there is a clatter and your rod is pulled hard. Forgetting the advice about the time needed for a fish to take a big minnow, you rear back and to our mutual surprise and delight, meet the strong pull of a fair-sized fish. Come on, get your rod up. Don't panic. Sure, let him take line. If you try to stop him something's going to give. I wrap up my tackle and lean it against the bridge support. It looks as if we have a two-man fish on the line now.

Stand up straight, face the direction of the run of the fish, and keep that rod up to cushion his pull. Don't worry about the line peeling off, we set the drag to the rod and if you do everything right, the fish can't get a dead-weight pull on your 8-pound line. There are no snags at all, and lots of room for him to run and fight. Now look out! He's swimming back this way and your tackle is going slack.

There must never be slack line to a fish, so reel in to put that bend back into the rod and keep reeling as long as the fish keeps coming. But keep that rod up because your fish will turn away and bolt, and when that happens there's going to be a sudden strain on the tackle . . . you have to be ready with the rod point up where the slash of the fish will be cushioned by the steely bend of the rod. There he goes. He's turned and is running, so stop reeling at once. If you continue reeling while the fish is taking line, it will become strained, and worse, develop masses of twists. Wait till the fish stops. Pull very steadily and smoothly with the rod straight back, then reel the tip down the line gained. Keep repeating this procedure. It is known as pumping and is the only way to use tackle to fight a fish. Don't jerk − keep a steady strain and reel down smoothly without giving slack.

I am certain that you have tied into a fair-sized channel cat, for he's slugging away down deep and hasn't shown yet. If it was pike or bass it would have come up and tried to throw the hook by jumping, or by shaking its head out of the water. A walleye, unless it was a monster, would have started to weaken by now. I doubt that a carp would take a minnow as big as the one you used. By the process of elimination we can be almost certain that it is a channel catfish. So watch it; once you get him up near the surface where he meets the light, he's going to make one hell of a fast run. Be prepared for this to happen just when you start to believe that you have the fish licked.

Meanwhile I'll get the landing gear ready, for it is obvious that you have a fish that will give us trouble at the bankside. You won't be able to swing it ashore, as you did earlier with the smaller fish. So, as we have not yet studied landing techniques, I'll run through the basics, while you struggle on with your first big fish.

Landing Gear

I would just as soon go fishing without my pants as start off for the water without a complete set of gear to handle the landing of big fish. We know our 8-pound test line can successfully defeat large fish in the water, where the strain is not caused by a deadweight. But this happy situation stops at the point where the fish is played out and must be taken from the water. Any attempt to drag the fish out by grasping the line can only end in total failure, for even a 1-pound bass struggling as a deadweight on the end of an 8-pound test can snap the line.

Here is a fine, hefty catfish brought to the side of the boat, where a landing net is brought up to contain it. Big nets are essential for large fish and one like this, fitted with a heavy-duty twine, a wide and roomy opening and a long, strong handle, is ideal. Note that the angler's companion does not swing net and fish into the boat, but with the fish safely contained, untangles the tackle. He will grab the fish and then swing it aboard.

Because of this, landing gear, either a landing net or a gaff, is a vital part of angling equipment. It is possible to get away with just using a net, if it is big enough, but the skilled angler also regards a gaff as a necessary item of gear. Let us look at both and select what we will need.

Landing Nets

These are scoop nets forming a pocket, and are mounted on some form of handle. The top of the net may be a circle, a triangle, or even a square. The mesh is made of strong thin line and should be deep enough to allow a netted fish to rest easily in the bottom, with little chance of jumping out. The handle varies according to the style of fishing. For stream wading, folding nets that hang from the belt take up little room, stay out of the way and, being convenient to the landing hand, can be flipped open for the last stage of the fight. Where big fish are encountered from bank or boat, the best net handle is a substantial pole of at

Well-known outdoors writer Roger Latham shows the classic way to land a fish. Using light spinning gear, his rod held high, and his net sunk, he brings the fish over the net before raising it. If the fish attempts another escape, the poised rod will dip and act as a safety spring and the slipping drag of the reel will come into action. The length of line he allows from the rod tip to the fish will prevent breakage if the fish runs off.

least 4 feet, mounted rigidly on a very large, strong ring. Small nets, while convenient to carry, are less useful in dealing with a sizeable fish. Those trout-fishing landing nets, shaped like ping-pong bats, with a rubber connecting line to the angler's shoulder answer for small streams and small fish, but are worthless when a good trout is hooked.

I have two nets: one very big, the other bigger. My bigger net, an English salmon net measuring 23 inches across the ring, has a net 36 inches deep, and a handle 44 inches long, giving a total reach of 4 feet, 6 inches to the centre of the net. This is a salmon wading-net in which the ring slides down the handle and is then carried over the shoulder with a sling, ready for use. On one occasion I was after migratory rainbows on a crowded river, where lots of fish were being caught, some weighing as much as 10 pounds. All the anglers were carrying nets, most of them too small, and by the end of the day's fishing, I had been called in with my large net to land 12 big rainbows, the biggest banging the scale down to 16 ¾ pounds. This net has landed lake trout to 35 pounds, carp to 38 pounds, and channel catfish to 25 pounds. The net is heavy to carry but worth every ounce when a good fish is hooked.

Good, strong landing nets are quite reasonable in price and the buyer should look for good quality twine, knotted evenly so that the strain of a fish is taken by the whole mesh. The best are waterproofed with boiled oil, which imparts a yellow glossy effect and a stale smell. Since any landing net is only as strong as its mesh, this should be inspected regularly and replaced at the slightest sign of wear. It may make for exciting reading when a tale includes the common incident of the fish falling through a rotted net, but it is poor angling.

Gaffs

These landing instruments are little more than steel hooks mounted on the ends of poles, and are used to hook out the largest or most rampageous fish. Many freshwater anglers seem afraid to use them, although no saltwater fisher would dream of heading offshore without one, and often two or three. The gaff is essential for landing really big pike and muskie, and is excellent for dealing with the bigger catfish.

I use two types of gaffs, one a simple gaff hook lashed to the end of a five-foot-long hockey stick, with the head cut off; and the other a special wading gaff beautifully made, with a handle that slides together to half the length of the gaff for easy carrying. It has a spring clip so that it can be carried on a belt, and a protector locks over the needle-sharp point when the gaff is not in use.

I go through a couple of my hockey-stick gaffs every year, by giving them away to guides who, having seen them in action, are eager to own one. This is no problem, as the gaff heads cost around 40¢ and I pick up all the hockey sticks I need from those broken at the head during games at the local ice arena.

A third item of landing gear is the tailer, a steel-coil, buggy-whip device which opens on a taut spring principle to form a big loop. This loop is carefully brought over the tail of a tired fish, and a nudge against the body of the fish whips the loop shut over the root of the tail. The fish is then hauled out tail first. Tailers are effective and are used mostly by the Atlantic salmon-fishing guides when there are spawned fish around that must be put back in the water unharmed. Being rather expensive, they are less popular than a big net or a sharp gaff.

But now I see that your fish is tiring and as we have yet to see it, I have taken out the big net and removed the wine-bottle cork from the point of the hockey-stick gaff. Put on pressure — you've eased up. And

The lean and savage pike brings a touch of fear to angling. Swift to attack, furious in its fight, this northern fish grows to great size and weight. Lunging out from ambush, the water wolf, as the pike was once known, seldom misses its prey, be it a startled minnow or an angler's brightly colored plug.

A husky pike rolls on the surface and puts a sharp bend into the author's nine-foot glass spinning rod, before making one last desperate run for freedom. It is in this type of habitat — weeds, reeds, old stumps and tangled shoreline — that the best pike fishing is found. However, the biggest fish are out deep, lurking beside rocky shoals, or concealed in the shade of sunken logs.

don't have a full bend in your rod. When you do that the fish rests and it prolongs the fight. Look out for the run when he sees the light.

There he goes, just as I thought. Whoops! Get that rod up and keep it up. There'll be a couple more runs like that before he's ready for netting. He's stopped again, so pump him back. There he is just below the surface — a nice channel about 9 or 10 pounds. Easy does it now, I'll use the net on this fish, and because I don't want to scare him off I'll squat down in front of you with the net well out and under the water. You must now bring the fish over the net: we never use the net as a scoop, because it scares the fish and is likely to catch the hook and free him.

See that white flash? That was his belly showing. He's tired and beginning to turn over — that's a good sign. Okay. I can see that the fish has edged away down the bank but don't follow him. I'm not going to move from this spot, so you will have to bring him back. Swing your rod over so that it is level with the water covering the net, and put on some strain. This is known as side-strain and it has the same effect as reins have on a horse. To make a tired fish change direction, apply strain to his mouth on the desired side. This turns his head and he'll swim back and around to ease the strain. Now you've got the idea. Keep him coming right over the net. Don't reel up any more — just walk backwards along the bank and he'll swim along like a barge following a tug. I've got him! I simply lifted the net when he came over the top and raised the net ring clear of the water. Now I'll just hold the net ring clear to send the fish down to the bottom against the mesh, reach in and grab a handful of mesh between my outspread fingers, and with the fish confined in a bag of net, carefully lift it out and onto the bank It is a mistake to wallop the net out like a scoop. It strains the net, and with a heavy fish can cause the handle to snap.

Well away from the water, I carefully open the mesh just enough to allow access to the head of the fish so I can remove the hook. Keeping the catfish smothered in the mesh prevents him from rolling and jumping around and makes handling easier. Always do this in a boat, for it will keep slime off tackle and clothes, and in the case of lively fish — such as pike or muskie — will prevent them from landing in an open tackle box and spraying lures broadside.

The catfish bumps the marker on my pocket scale to 11 pounds — a nice, fat fish that will supply us with some great fillets. No, don't put it on the stringer — it's too big. Here's a sack. Take hold under the gills and don't get stabbed by the sharp spines on the pectoral fins (they are the ones just behind the gills on each side) or the other on the front of his dorsal fin. Lower him in, tie the neck tightly with this length of cord, put the sack in the water to keep him alive and tie the other end of the cord to that stump.

A stout sack and a length of strong cord are just two of the odd items I carry on a fishing trip. After a while you will find yourself with a tendency to collect many useful things, including a corkscrew/bottle-opener, a sharp knife, a washcloth and a small piece of soap, plastic bags for fish, and one of those lightweight foam coolers for taking the catch home in hot weather. Then of course there will be cans of insect repellent, suntan lotion, a small first-aid kit, a container of waterproof matches, and so on, not forgetting such important accessories as vacuum flasks for hot drinks. I carry a six-cup flask for coffee and in chill weather or for night fishing, two smaller, wide-topped flasks which I fill with hot home-made soup.

On this note, let's break for lunch. We will put out minnow baits while we eat, and afterwards I want you to change tactics and enjoy a little spinning with a pike bait in that shallow area along the edge of the marsh. There are usually a few pike roaming around, and I know you must be anxious to try out your precious lures.

Lunch by the waterside never lasts long and I see you are ready to go again, so let's change tackle right here. I am going to show you how to do it and then leave you on your own, so first I'll take out my tackle, put the minnow back in the bucket and, after setting the hook in the wire loop above the butt, I'll leave the rod propped up against the bridge.

Now, take off your leger, saving the hook and weight but snipping the nylon off above the split shot. Don't throw away the nylon — it tangles the legs of water birds and can even sever them. Roll it up in a little coil and stick it in the middle of the empty sandwich paper. We'll dump it in a litter can, with the rest of our debris, on the way home.

Using the clinch knot, tie a 6-inch-long light leader to the end of your line. A 10-pound-test leader is fine, and I see you are beginning to make a fast neat job of the knot. All you need now is a lure, so take a look through the box and see what you think best for fishing that shallow, weedy area. That's great, I'm glad you remembered what we discussed in Chapter Five. That wide, 3-inch-long, red and white spoon will work perfectly and its weight will balance nicely with your 8-pound line. I've got the gaff, so let's see what you can do.

Working a spoon for pike is harder than just stillfishing with live bait in a known hole. You must throw to the right spot and be able to work the lure to get all the action it can give. Since pike have a greenish body with a mass of lozenge-shaped camouflage spots, it should be obvious that they prowl either the reeds or the edge of the weed. They lie in wait by the weeds, and when a chosen prey happens along, they coil and launch a spearlike attack at lightning speed, turning to one side at the last moment to make a superb deflection shot which is aimed at the greater length of the prey, rather than at the smaller target offered from astern. This spearlike attack is suggested by the name *pike*, an old word for spear, derived from the Middle English *pik* for sharp-pointed, meaning in this case, the head of the fish.

If you see a pike approaching your bait, don't stop reeling. Give the lure a little more action, making it dart and swerve by turning the rod to one side and then the other. That will sometimes make them attack.

Use the overhead cast, but this time reel in till the swivel of the leader is just short of the rod tip. This, with your 6-inch leader, gives a nice compact length. It is much easier to throw than leger gear with the double weight of the sinker and the bait. Make the cast as before, and try to get it right on the edge of that line of reeds. Then you can reel it back past a whole line of places suitable for pike habitat.

A good cast — too far out from the reeds, but better than landing right in them. Put the rod point to the right side and half turn in that direction, away from the water. Keep the rod at an angle to the run of the spoon, so that if there is a strike it will come on the limber tip and at a position where it will be easy to rear back and set the hook. Reel a little more slowly. Your spoon is too high and a slower rate is best, as long as it keeps the spoon off the bottom. Finish the cast and don't haul out when the spoon is 10 feet off. In fact, run it back and forth at least a couple of times on the end of the rod. You will often bring on a fish that way.

Cast again and try to get a little closer. Good. Now it's travelling right down the length of the weeds. No fish, so keep going. The spoon might be making a hungry but wary pike a little excited and several casts in the same place will often bring a fish. Right where you are spinning, three of us took 11 pike in less than two hours. The bay holds quite a number at this time and while very big pike tend to be solitary, it is quite common to find a place of this type holding a couple of dozen fish weighing as much as 10 pounds or more. So it is up to you to cover the water carefully and thoroughly.

See that? As you pulled the lure out, a good pike slid underneath the place that it had been. He was following to take and you pulled it out from under his nose. It would have been a different story if you had fished the cast right out and run it back and forth a couple of times along the edge. No, don't make a short cast to try and get that one — throw out to the line of weeds again and fish the full length of the cast. Pike are tremendously fast fish and he will find it if he wants it. Whoops! You had a grab at the lure and didn't try to set the hook, so the fish let go. You must react quickly and rear back to set the hook. He probably grabbed it above the hook and your strike would have slid the thin metal spoon through the mouth and driven the hook into the outside of his jaw. *That's* it. He came again and you did it right this time. Up he goes in a full jump, almost clearing the water. You lowered your rod point at the same time, which must have been instinct, but make sure you do that on every jumping fish. If they come out and land on a tight line they snap it like cotton.

It isn't a big fish and he won't put up a fight anything like the one you enjoyed with the channel cat, but keep that rod up or old speedy there will snap the line. I'm going to use the gaff, so, with its point up, I put it under the water, just as I did with the landing net, and you bring him to me using side-strain. Be careful. The pike came out shaking his head. You're pulling too hard, and when that happens they come out and often throw the lure. It waggles as they shake and the weight of the spoon often jars the hook loose. You brought him in, but not close enough. I'm not going to slash out with the gaff — he has to be right over the top. That's better . . . got him. See how I slid the gaff point up

Using a home-made gaff costing less than 50¢ and consisting of a loose gaff hook bound to the end of an old broom stick, the author holds up a pike that has virtually engulfed the plug and is hooked in two places. Note that the gaff point has been slipped in from underneath, cutting only through thin skin; thus there is no damage to the fish. With the pike held firmly and safely, the author removes the

through the thin skin of the lower jaw and in one smooth lift pulled up the fish dangling on the bend of the gaff. Now you can take out the hook with the forceps without touching the fish. Some people shudder at the use of gaffs and then do worse damage by man-handling the fish and wiping off the natural slime that protects it. There are no vital organs under the jaw and often I have landed a pike in this way, returned it to the water and had it take the lure on the next throw.

Transferring the pike from the gaff to the balance-scale is simple and shows that he weighs 4½ pounds; I suggest you put him back to grow bigger, since pike of this size are boney. You will? Fine. Take the scale by the ring, and without touching the fish, lower it gently back into the water. Jiggle the scale and the fish will come loose.

Carry on casting. You should cover the whole of this shallow bay with crisscrossing casts. Fish the lure as slowly as possible and don't

plug with a pair of long-nosed hook removers. Holding and handling the fish in this fashion, it is easy to unhook it and put it back without touching it or removing its natural slime. When fishing from a canoe, as here, the method is not only more convenient but safer, for a large, active pike dumped into the bottom of a canoe can be quite a hazard.

hesitate to cover every weed- and reed-edging several times in succession. It is poor technique to rush a piece of good water. Call me if you get into trouble, I'm going back to catch a few more white bass.

Hello, where's your tackle? What's that? It caught in a snag and you can't get it loose? Hang on a second — I have a white bass nipping the tail of my minnow. There. He took it and I've hooked him and out he comes. Just put him on the stringer and I'll come along and see what I can do. It was a good idea to lay down the rod and fetch me. A lot of people get into a huff, put on too much pull and lose the lure — or worse, damage the rod — by doing it all wrong.

Pick up the rod, I'll tell you what to do. First, apply a slow, even strain, in case it's buried in weed and only needs to be pulled loose. That's enough. Now, with a good bend in the rod, try tapping the end of the butt with the other hand. That sometimes jolts a hook out. No? Well, let out line and first come to this side to try again and, if that doesn't work, to the other side. Hmm, we'll need to try something else. Right . . . let some slack line out of the rod, and put it down while you hold on to the line. Get a fair bit of slack, pull steadily until the line is perfectly taut and then let go. That did it — your lure is free, so reel it up quickly to get it off the bottom.

Snagging is one of the things anglers must learn to live with. Since most fish are taken on or close to the bottom, it is essential to send lure and bait down to where the fish are feeding, and this means that we will get caught from time to time.

When this happens, the unskilled angler usually pulls the line tight and starts tugging with his rod, straining the tackle and doing little more than driving the hook firmly home into the snag. This is simply not the way to do it. As I have suggested, give a slow, straight pull, in case it is tied into a small sunken stick which will be pulled out of the mud by this action. The tapping on the butt also will help jog a snag from the mud or, in the case of the hook being caught in a weed, will either dislodge the weed's root or help the hook to tear the weed, freeing the hold. Try the same thing from several places to get a range of angles of pull, as the object in which the hook is fast may be jammed behind a rigid obstruction and a pull from the side might bring it clear.

If this fails, strip the line out of the tip to give a long length of spare, put the rod down, slowly pull the line taut and then suddenly release it. This takes advantage of the stretch in the nylon so that, when the line is released, a shock wave is sent back which can jump the lure free if it is caught lightly between two small rocks, or a similar obstruction. This shock wave technique is repeated several times from the front and each side, and if this doesn't work, there is need for the last and drastic method. This either kills or cures, so it pays to give the previous systems a chance to work.

But when all other methods fail, put down the rod, take hold of the line and start a long, steady pull. The monofilament will stretch, so it will be necessary to reach out and take another hand hold. In the end, something will give. Usually either the hook comes free, or the obstruction is eased out of the bottom and comes through the water to the bank. If this floating snag is heavy don't use the reel, but continue to pull in the line by hand.

About 3 per cent of the time you will lose hook or lure by the line parting at the knot; but don't stand around for an hour or more playing with the snag. Angling time is much too precious and it is a mistake to fritter that time away jigging at the line. Run through the outlined procedures right away, and you will save a lot of time.

Lures and hooks brought up from snags must be checked to make sure that all is in working condition and it is usually a good idea to cut off the knots and retie. The end length of the line is run through the fingers and inspected for fraying and any part showing wear must be cut out and the tackle reassembled.

Snags are a natural hazard and the angler who never catches bottom is simply not fishing in the proper manner.

Well, you have run the line through your fingers and found an uneven section of about 9 inches long, 12 feet up from the leader. No, don't cut it out and knot the line; throw out the whole length and retie the leader above the spot.

Hey, come on now. You've forgotten what I told you. Pick up that waste piece of nylon, coil it and put it in your pocket. No, you shouldn't throw it in the water, it's liable to float and catch in water birds' legs, or get sucked into the prop system of an outboard motor and cut the seal. It only takes a second to wind up a bit of nylon to throw away at home, or in a proper litter bin. Make a point of doing this. I hope you will never see what I have seen - a gull with both legs amputated by a tangle of nylon, or a robin starving to death because it became bound in a loose coil of waste nylon that it picked up while pecking at worms dumped out on the bank. The angler has a special responsibility to leave the wild lands clean, and to protect and conserve every part of nature.

On this note it is time to end our first day's angling together. We have caught a few fish, tried out a few different techniques, learned an important knot and found out how to use the gaff and landing net.

There is a lot to be learned still, for now we are going to turn to the specialized side of the game. We will pick up more knots and lots of techniques in the chapters to come, and we will discover that there is a lot of tackle yet to be tried out. It is going to be a lot of fun.

7 🐟 Catching Carp

~~~~~~

Our lawyer friend pulled up, looked at us with suspicion and said, "You can't go fishing, There's no season open."

Busily loading down my wife with spare coats, tackle and vacuum bottles from the trunk of our car, I smiled sweetly and told him that we were going fishing for carp, a species that has no closed season in our area. "Carp," he snorted. "You must be crazy to waste time on a garbage fish."

My wife struggled out from underneath my big parka. "What do you mean, wasting time?" she asked hotly. "We are going *fishing*. What are you going to do? Watch TV?" But, used to this attitude from people weaned on game fish, I just invited him to come down later and watch the fun, then picked up the heavy gear and led the way down the winding path to our favorite carp-fishing spot on the local river. Both of us thought that this was the end of the incident; but no, a couple of hours later, our friend approached us as we sat on our folding chairs, screened from the water by a tall row of growing reeds. He sat on my tackle box, took a big deep breath of fresh air and said, "It's not such a bad idea. It's rather nice here, after a day in the city." And at that point, the loose line dangling from the tip of my wife's rod became taut and sped off 20 feet from the open spool, before she picked up the rod and set the hook hard.

Her rod whipped sharply down, and as the sound of her reel drag rose to a scream, I reeled in my tackle to prevent a tangle with her running fish. Leaping to her feet, Joy kicked her folding seat out of the way and screamed with delight as her fish boiled to the surface 40 yards out, before shooting off on a new run downstream.

Pushing past us, she ran along the bank holding her rod high and reeling furiously to keep a taut line into the fish. As we followed, John asked in disbelieving tones, "What has she hooked — a big muskie?"

"No," Joy yelled back. "It's just one of your old garbage fish."

Forty minutes later, when the carp bounced the spring scale down at 37 pounds, John was still in a daze. "All my life I've lived just a few hundred yards from this spot," he said, "and I didn't know carp could fight like that."

So with a wink at my wife, I offered him a spare set of gear and the first step in making a new carp angler was taken.

When Joy and I wrapped up our evening's fishing at 11 p.m., John was in a dreadful state. He had missed four certain runs in pop-eyed astonishment, hooked one fish and had the hold give way, and had fought two beautiful carp for a while, only to lose them in a big snag 100 yards downstream from our fishing spot. Wearing only a thin jacket, he was shivering in the chill wind blowing up the river from the lake, but wouldn't give up. So we left him with my spare outfit, all the bait, some hooks and another line spool, and went home to bed.

He was at our door around 9 a.m. the following morning to return the tackle and to show us his one fish of the night. It was a 9-pound common carp — quite a small fish really, but in his eyes something special.

Over coffee in the kitchen, he told us of hour after hour of missed bites, mishaps and troubles. Finally, at 3.30 a.m. he had hooked the 9-pounder and had gone waist deep to net it, then carried it home in dazed delight.

At last, he shook his head in self-pity. "I've lived here all my life," he said, "and didn't know what I was missing. Good God, I fly up into wilderness lakes every year and I've been ignoring fantastic sport less than a mile from my own house."

This is a typical incident in a decade of planned carp-fishing propaganda that I have conducted and shows how carp is by far the most neglected game fish in our waters. When I started, I met ridicule from game-fish oriented anglers who thought the pursuit of a big minnow (for that's what it is), to be beneath their dignity.

Anglers who think nothing of driving a couple of hundred miles for the chance to tackle a 2-pound bass, often have a strange reaction to the idea of fishing close to home for a tough, hard-fighting fish that can reach 50 pounds. "Can you eat them?" they ask. "I thought they fed on garbage."

The carp is an excellent food fish and this was why it was planted here in the first place. In Europe, extensive fish culture raises millions of pounds of carp for the market each year and in some parts of Germany it is given live as a gift for Christmas, to be eaten as a festive dish. I eat carp and have a box full of recipes, some of them dating to the 15th century.

But this is surely not the point. Classifying a game species by its edible qualities is foolish. Bonefish, sailfish and big bluefin tuna are all inedible, but are correctly admired as magnificent sporting species. I don't pursue carp because I want food, but because they are smart, tough, big, and available close to home, where I can get out and enjoy a couple of hours of first-class sport and relaxation after a hard day at work. Many people who know my delight in this fish, try to tell me that they are sluggish and poor fighters. This may well be true of small fish hooked in very warm waters, but proves that the speaker has never hooked one weighing over 9 pounds.

CARP (Cyprinus Carpio)

This is a minnow of the family *CYPRINDAE* with the name *Cyprinus carpio* (Linnaeus). The family is found in Europe, Asia, Africa and America. Outside of carp, which was introduced from Europe, North American minnows are small. The indigenous species include creek chub, redbellied dace, pearl dace and a number of others that are valuable as forage for predators, and in some cases, as live bait for angling.

The domesticated goldfish *Carassius auratus* is a close relative of the common carp and is found wild in many waters where unwanted stocks have been dumped. On reverting to the wild state, goldfish lose their bright colors and appear as rather plain fish that can weigh as much as 2 pounds. I have also seen Crucian carp in limited distribution. Named *Carassius vulgaris*, this rather attractive European carp reaches 4 pounds and has a compressed, heavy build.

The common carp comes in a variety of body shapes and scale patterns. Some have long, slim bodies, and most take on depth with size. The common scale form is an even covering of large, well-shaped scales. The mirror carp has one or two rows of wider scales running the length of the lateral line, and an oddity known as the leather carp has no scales. None of these variations mark different species. Carp have been cultivated over so many centuries that any of the above might be encountered. We have such a variety of races and scale patterns that almost any type can be caught. Being all mixed together, there is wonderful confusion.

The use of descriptive names such as *leather* carp and *mirror* carp is misleading and unnecessary, so let us drop them. The devoted carp angler can expect to catch a wide variety during the year, and in some waters just might get a wild goldfish, or even a crucian.

The carp is a robust, heavily built fish compressed from side to side into a dish shape. The fish with highly pronounced dish configuration appear to be slower fighters than the slim fish which average about 9 pounds. These smaller and more round-bodied carp still have a massive tail, and being quite streamlined, are fast swimmers. I have had these slim carp run so quickly that they have made the line sound like a razor slicing through silk. It is quite a dazzling effect.

The difference between the slim fish and the massive old lunkers can be deceptive. If you have experienced a fast fight and then tie into a healthy old slab-sider, it usually appears that the big fish is not an effective fighter. Then, before you realize it, the lunker has calmly bulldozed his way to a snag and you are beaten before the fight has started.

Carp are olive-green on the back, shading to yellow on the flank and belly. Depending on water conditions, some are golden, others coppery or even greyish-green. There are two pairs of barbels around the mouth, the larger pair trailing.

One native fish that can be confused with the carp is the northern redhorse sucker. At first glance this large sucker seems quite similar. But it lacks the barbels, and has an inferior sucker-mouth.

Carp grow very large indeed, weighing over 80 pounds under ideal conditions. I have seen carp in North American waters that I estimate to be over 50 pounds, and indeed I played one about that heavy for better than an hour before losing it in the tangle of a sunken tree. An authenticated report tells of a 56-pound carp caught by commercial means in Lake Erie, and I have no doubt at all that there are fish well above this weight in places suited to fast growth. The average size caught by anglers is around 4 to 5 pounds, but fish of 10 pounds are common, and anglers with skill will find it fairly simple to hook into 20-pounders in most waters. You will see monsters basking on the surface that are easily double that weight.

Feeding Habits

The carp is omnivorous, that is to say, it eats just about everything, including insect larvae, weed, plankton, and — at certain times of the year — small fry. It is almost hair-raising to see a school of carp feeding in a clear lake. They root along the bottom, wrenching out weeds and spreading a massive stain of mud outwards from the shoal as they move slowly over the bottom. This habit alone makes it an undesirable species in any game-fish water, as the reduction of weeds and the clouding of a lake with mud creates less than favourable conditions for predatory fish.

Carp spawn in spring or summer, according to local water temperatures. They gather in vast shoals in the weedy shallows where the small eggs are carelessly broadcast. This act is accompanied by great splashing, with some of the smaller fish jumping clear of the water. I once came across a boat load of anglers on the edge of one of these agitated shoals, and found the men getting more and more furious when the fish wouldn't take their baits. They enjoyed the joke however when I pointed out that the fish were spawning and that food could be expected to be of less importance.

These are the basic facts about carp, and it is apparent that they can form a worthwhile angling quarry for many anglers, as they range across the continent. They can usually be found close to cities and towns and are often the only big fish readily available.

Carp lack the style of the trout, but are generally smarter and harder to catch; they are not noble jumpers like the Atlantic salmon, but seem to keep cool in a fight, and after the first rush, work to tie up the line in weed or any convenient snag. The truly big specimens are rarely hooked by accident. There must be a planned campaign, in which the angler makes no mistakes. The dedicated carp hunter soon comes to realize that this fish, the often maligned river-pig, has its own kind of appeal.

Peter Brewster, a keen carp catcher, poses with five moderate-sized carp of slim build, big tails and powerhouse dispositions. He holds his basic carp rod, a nine-foot spinning stick of hollow glass, with a full-length cork handle that gives better grip in a prolonged fight. His standard spinning reel is loaded with 12-pound test nylon; his landing net is salmon-sized and big enough to handle a 40-pound fish. These carp were caught in Lake Ontario during a couple of hours fishing in the evening after work. The location was less than 15 miles from the heart of the city.

Just about all basic angling outfits can be used on carp, but for the best effect, a long, powerful spinning rod has a number of advantages. I use a slender, powerful, 9-foot hollow-glass, steelhead rod with a standard spinning reel on which is spooled 12-pound-test line. For the very large fish I often exchange the 12-pound test for a spare spool of 15-pound test. But a standard 8-pound line will handle big fish, and indeed my largest catch, a 38½-pound beauty, was landed with standard tackle.

Just for fun, I sometimes fish for carp with very light spinning gear, using 4-pound or even 2-pound test line. In some waters this can be effective, but where there are weed-beds or snags, the tackle is inadequate, as it is not strong enough to give the extra bit of pressure needed to wean a running carp away from a haven of safety.

Do not use leaders in carp tackle. This is a wise fish and every part of the terminal gear must be simple. The fish has a soft mouth, and its teeth, which are in its throat, do not come in contact with the line, so it is never necessary to have more than a plain hook tied to the end of the nylon line.

Similarly, sinkers must be kept to a minimum. When fishing for carp in a current, it may be necessary to add weight to keep the tackle in place. Sometimes one large split shot 2 feet up from the hook is sufficient; sometimes two shots will be needed. But if more weight is required, the best thing to do is to arrange a sliding-shot leger, or to try and find a feed place situated in a slow eddy or a piece of slack water by a bend. Carp are primarily stillwater fish, so when you select slack water, you are putting yourself at an advantage.

The choice of hook is dictated by the type of bait to be used. For doughballs, I find the standard shank gives a better hold and allows a larger piece of bait to be put out. On the other hand, worms are better when fished on a short shank, but no more than 1-X Short. Long-shank hooks are useless for carp fishing, since they are clumsy and can thus be felt quickly by a fish mouthing the bait. Also, they are much more easily shed by a hooked fish. For reasons I have never been able to fathom, carp seem quite good at getting a hook out of their mouth and the angler should be prepared for this to happen quite often. The fish takes the bait, you set the hook, a good fight develops and then for no accountable reason the tackle goes slack and you reel in to find the hook in good shape, but the fish gone. By now I am so used to this that I shrug it off as an unsolvable mystery.

Since carp have big mouths, and the larger fish have a preference for a bait as big as a hen's egg, the hook size can be fairly large. For a doughball as big as an egg (that's a graded *small* egg by the way), a size 8 or a size 6 is about right, and this must be buried completely in the bait. The bigger the hook, the better the hold it will take in the fish, but carp are such wily fellows that they will pick up a bait to mouth it. If they feel the hook, they'll spit it out faster than a rattlesnake's strike, and there will be many false bites and few fish hooked. Used with a worm bait, a short-shank hook should be no bigger than 8 and indeed 10 is even better. So the range for carp is between 10 and 6 and if there are a number of false bites, it would be a good idea to change the hook to the next smaller size.

Since carp should always be killed, and never put back, a gaff can be used to get them out of the water. I have used gaffs, and still do at times, but believe that there is nothing better than a really big landing net, and my faithful old salmon net with its deep mesh pocket is a fine piece of equipment for this.

The completion of the carp tackle requires containers for bait and a pair of rod supports to hold the rod at a proper angle for allowing the first run, and to put the butt in a convenient place, so that the angler can quickly grab it to set the hook. These rod rests can be either a pair of forked sticks cut from a tree, or home-made metal rests with welded forks. I have a beautiful pair made by a fishing friend who is also a good machinist and my rests slide together into lengths short enough to fit into my tackle box.

Baits

Being omnivorous, carp eat a wide range of foods, many of which cannot be used on a hook. Strange as it may seem, the carp's natural foods are seldom used in carp fishing. My favorite is a cooked bait — a doughball of cornmeal that is not found in the wilds, yet seems to be tremendously effective. Another useful bait is the small, peeled canned potatoes, that come in just the right size. I have used a hunk of moulded cheese, small red worms, bread and bread crust, garden slugs, freshwater mussels, and even fly maggots. Doughballs, however, appear to be acceptable to all carp.

Every dedicated carp angler has some special bait recipe of his own, and, I am no exception. I have enjoyed the greatest success with cornmeal balls and since I hold to the unexplained superstition that carp have a sweet tooth, I add a slug of corn syrup. This is probably nonsense, but I rest my case on a quote from Izaak Walton in *The Compleat Angler*:

' . . . but doubtless sweet pastes are best; I mean, pastes made with honey or with sugar . . . '

The author with his biggest carp to date, a 38½-pound fish that took a cornmeal dough-ball and fought a rugged 40-minute battle. The fish is of a beautiful size and proportion, being fat but not too deep. Note the huge tail, as well as the massive mouth which is capable of taking in a bait as big as a golf ball.

Tiny's Best Carp Bait

Put a large measure of cornmeal and exactly the same quantity of water into an old saucepan. I use a tall water-glass as a measure, and this makes a substantial amount of bait.

Add a couple of large slugs of corn syrup, place the pot over fairly high heat and stir throughout the cooling process.

At first, the mix in the pot is fluid and appears to be too diluted to ever form bait. But as the cornmeal cooks, it absorbs all this water.

Turn the mix thoroughly from the bottom with a big spoon, keeping it moving to avoid burning. It will stick, so it becomes necessary to use a strong stirring action.

After a very short cooking period the bait will form into a solid mass. But it is not yet properly cooked. We must wait for the cornmeal to lose its gritty feel and become a smooth dough. This can take as long as ten minutes more, during which time it is essential to keep stirring up from the bottom.

When the bait is smooth and heavy, take the pot off the heat, cover it and leave it at the back of the stove for half-an-hour. Then turn it out onto a surface that has been dusted with plain white flour, and taking care not to get burned, knead thoroughly after carefully washing your hands. Add dustings of flour until the bait is moist and soft (yet not sticky), and is solid enough to stay on the hook for hours.

Carefully wrap this ball of bait in clean cloth or aluminum foil, to prevent the air from turning the outside hard and crumbly. It can be stored in any cool place for fishing the next day, but for use later in the week it should be placed in the refrigerator.

Essence of vanilla added to the mix imparts a fetching odor to the bait, as does oil of aniseed. I don't know that this attracts more fish, but by masking man-scent it performs a useful function. Go easy on the aniseed, by the way — three drops will perfume the whole neighborhood.

The finished cornmeal bait is kept in the wrapper in one large piece, and the cloth is opened just long enough for the angler to reach in and pinch off a hook bait. The best size is that of a small egg. This is pressed flat, the hook is put in, bend first, and the ball is brought up to form a cover around the whole of the hook, including the eye.

The bait fishes better if it is rolled between the palms of the hands, to form a streamlined bomb on the hook. A round ball doesn't cast as well, and having less hold on the hook and greater water resistance, washes off when the line is reeled in. Smokers should always wash their hands before handling the bait.

It is important to have confidence in the ability of the bait to stay on the hook throughout the playing and fiddling that often goes on before the carp takes properly. This is never a problem if the bait has been cooked long enough, and anglers must learn to leave the bait in the water and not scare off fish by constantly reeling it in to see if it is still on.

Ground-baiting or chumming the waters is seldom practiced in freshwater angling, but it is important in the art of catching big carp. None of the dough baits used are natural food, and the scattering of chum in the form of mixed cereal, aids in conditioning the fish towards accepting hook baits not found in the wild.

I know from experience that good water, properly chummed either in advance or during angling, can give double the number of bites, and even produce fish that otherwise might not be caught.

I get spoiled loaves from my local bakery, and during carp season we save all crusts of bread and toast, until we have a couple of buckets of stale, but sweet bread. Town- and city-dwelling anglers can buy stale bread or, if necessary, buy half a dozen fresh loaves and let them go stale.

To make chum for carp, soak the bread for an hour in a sink filled with clean water. Then allow the water to run off, squeeze out as much of it as possible, and dump the bread into a clean plastic bucket. Mix it thoroughly by hand, adding small quantities of plain bran meal now and again, until the chum forms a heavy, dry pudding that can be rolled into firm balls as big as oranges.

If you have a good spot where nobody else goes, it is a good idea to put a bucketful of chum into the water two nights in a row before fishing. Just mark the spot and cast out balls of chum in a fan shape from where you plan to fish. If the water is heavily fished this would be a waste, and the chum should be used only when you are angling.

In the latter case, throw in about one-third of the chum on reaching the water, and then add a ball every fifteen minutes during the angling session.

With cornmeal doughball bait, use the simple chum suggested

above, but when using a worm or a potato on the hook, the chum must contain some of the intended hook bait.

In the case of potatoes get a medium-sized can of the size used as bait and chop the whole can into the bread-and-bran mix. Never allow whole potatoes to get into the chum, but only smaller bits. Your whole, small potatoes will be that much more acceptable as bait.

Dew worms should be broken into small pieces and mixed in, and the same applies to other baits.

When ground-baiting, it is important to angle at the point where the bait goes in. If the chosen spot has some degree of current, the chum must be put in high enough upstream to have time to sink and to be carried down to where you intend to fish. When fishing, make sure that the balls of chum are tossed far enough upstream, and if in doubt as to where they will land on the bottom, throw them in shotgun style to be sure to cover the area where the hook bait sits. If the stream is fairly fast, the chum can be sunk with greater precision, by sticking a few stones in the heart of each ball.

Chum made up according to my formula will hold together long enough to hit the bottom and maybe roll a little. But in a short time, it becomes water-logged and tends to flow as a sort of gruel. This quickly coats quite a considerable area of the bottom and every time a carp swims over that ground, the chum will lift and form a swirling mass of exciting food odors, with very little substance to ease the hunger pangs. So the fish become excited and quest around, until, hopefully, they come upon your hook bait forming a large hunk of food.

This technique, with variations, can be used with great effect upon a number of other game species. I have used it for channel catfish, using fish oil, steer's blood, and even chopped chicken's guts. But each time, the basic material is stale bread with plain bran used as a stiffener.

CARP TACTICS

Carp, while normally bottom feeders, often swim or bask on the surface, and at times will accept baits at all levels, including the surface and the margins of a lake. They have a good sense of smell, excellent vision and a sharp sense of what might constitute danger. Don't confuse them with the attacking predators that will sometimes attack a bait in the face of obvious danger. Carp often sink out of sight and go off feed when disturbed.

Because of this, and of the other survival factors they possess, these fish must be approached with extreme caution. This has also produced some strange differences between those in quiet waterways and those in busy ones. In Britain, where the finest carp angling is found on private estates, the carp are not used to numbers of people walking the bank. Just one person wandering along the edge of the moat or the lake can scare the fish at once.

It is different in most carp waters here, for the shores of the lakes and the banks of the rivers are often heavily used, and there are usually outboard motors humming across the surface, so the fish have a general acclimatization to noise, people and disturbance. They tend to be less sensitive and, since I have fished in both lands, I would not hesitate to say that they are also far easier to catch.

This, however, applies more to the smaller fish — the really big carp are never easy to catch. Many carp fishermen don't know this, and they sit on the bank in full view of the water, happily taking a quota of fish that weigh up to 12 pounds but never getting hold of one of the monsters that can be seen. For this reason a lot of people believe that big carp won't take a bait, but this is not true.

It is all in the approach. If it is a crowded water, select an angling time when nobody is around: maybe late in the evening, in the early morning, or even during the middle of the night. I fish mostly in the evenings, arriving at my spot when people are leaving for home. Let me tell you of one trip.

When I arrived, I threw out several balls of chum, then sat down on a log behind a screen of tall weeds to make up my tackle. This river is just 12 miles from a major city, and high overhead an eight-lane highway crosses the river valley. The bridge is so high that the noise of the traffic comes down as a faint rumble, and best of all, at nightfall the sodium lights on the bridge shed a soft, moonlight effect down to my fishing spot, with just enough illumination to see.

With my tackle put up, I was throwing more chum when I was hailed by two young couples heading out of the valley. They had recognized me from the picture at the top of my newspaper column, and they sat down on the log for a chat. "Are you just starting?" asked one of the girls. "We came down here to fish because you wrote it up as a good carp spot, but we've been here most of the day and haven't even seen one."

I explained how difficult it was to catch carp with the gross disturbance of people wading in the river and playing on the bank. Then I baited my hook, and threw out, scattered a series of balls of chum well across our front, and invited them to fish with me for a while. I explained that we should all stay down behind the weeds, sit quietly, and only move our tackle when there was a good run. They were delighted with the idea, and on my instruction, put up spinning rods, tied standard size 8 hooks directly to the end of their lines, squeezed on a ball of my cornmeal bait and threw out.

We could see the water through the screen of weeds, but were less visible ourselves, being covered in front by the weeds and behind by a row of trees which prevented our being shown against the skyline, and after a few minutes I was able to point to a series of bubbles over our baits, where carp were nuzzling at the chum.

Just as I finished explaining that this was a sign of feeding carp, my line came up quietly and started to peel swiftly from my open-spinning-reel spool. With a fast grab I threw in the flier, set the hook and told them in urgent tones to get their lines out of the way. This is an essential precaution that prevents a running fish from getting tangled. I landed a nice fish of 15 pounds, put out some more chum, and we all rebaited and cast again.

The sun slid down, the lights popped on above us and the river came to life. A hail of bait fish showered out over by the bridge butt-ress, and these were followed by the zigzagging back fins of a school of hungry white bass. A great boil, followed by a slurp, marked the spot where a carp had taken an item of food off the surface, and a few early bats zoomed and hawked at a rising hatch of insects. Then the peace was broken by a clatter as the rod of one of the girls slid madly towards the river.

She had forgotten to release the line on her reel spool to allow it free run, and a carp on a fast take was making off with it. She grabbed it up, and wonder of wonders, hooked the fish. The rest of the lines were swiftly hustled out, and passing the landing net to her husband, I settled at her shoulder to advise on the fight.

Her fish was smaller than mine, around 6 pounds, but it was the biggest fish she had ever caught and the long fight left her almost shaking with excitement. We baited up and threw out again and this time I sternly warned them to leave their line fliers open and their lines lax and ready to flow on a bite.

They told me that they had used fixed sinkers all day and one of the fellows confessed that they had been worried by little jigs and taps at regular intervals. "Your no-sinker rig is great," he said, "I've never seen fish hit like the two we have."

More and more fish moved out on the now dark waters of the rivers, the carp boiling and giving out with peculiar kissing sounds as they swirled up to take the food that was floating down. But not just carp were on the move. Small fish leaped and went flying across the surface, and the ever-active white bass broke surface in pursuit. "It's a different river now," one of the girls said in quiet awe.

Two hours went by in which the bites came fast and furious. Most of these were slow run-offs with the bait, but for something like twenty minutes one of my young companions was bothered by small lifts of the line and little pulls. "That's what happened earlier," he said, "but every time we tried to set the hook in the fish, there was nothing there."

This is a common occurrence in carp fishing. It is caused by the carp nudging the bait, or washing against the light line with its powerful tail. People attempting to set the hook into this form of line movement spend frustrating hours without success. It is possible to hook a carp if he is pulling and you hit at the moment the line comes up. But most of the time on this form of half bite, he has dropped the bait before you pull on the line. The only thing to do under these circumstances is to stay alert, but to leave the tackle alone until there is an actual take.

When my wife and I have an evening carp-fishing session with a group of people, she is usually the first to catch a fish. I'm often prowling back and forth, advising, baiting, suggesting where to cast, and so forth, without a bait in the water. Joy knows from of old that it is a waste of time to mess about with a jiggling fish, so she sits back with her hand poised over the butt, and ignores everything but the firm takes. The rest of the crowd find it diffucult to believe that they can't set the hook, so they keep trying and missing. Then Joy's fish finally whizzes off with her bait, and she hooks it.

I told the young fellow of this, and he waited (a very difficult thing to do), and was rewarded by a sizzling run from what turned out to be the biggest fish of the evening. The hook was set, and our lines were pulled out, when the carp stubbornly started to edge downstream fighting the pull of the rod, and getting in a few licks by hitting the light line with jolting thumps of its tail. I realized then that it was a big, smart fish, and warned the angler that it was working down to a heavy weed bed.

I may be giving carp credit for more intelligence than they have but I feel strongly that they are aware of snags and havens of safety, and that after their first scared rush at the sting of the hook, they settle down to catch the line in these snags.

I guided the angler to a vantage point below our position and suggested the use of side-strain on the fish to swing it away from its intended path. He turned the rod over so that it was parallel to the water and away from the weed-bed, and giving line under strain, he slowly turned the head of the carp before it could reach safety. Balked, the carp shot off fast to the middle of the river, sulked a little and then made a power dive back for the weeds. The side-strain turned the fish short of the mark again, so it turned and rammed hard into the bank. Luckily it is a clean, hard bank and nothing caught — another reason for the minimum use of terminal accessories. Then, moving out into the stream again, it slanted once more towards the weeds, and he had to turn it again.

At the end of a long, hard fight, the net came up under his fish, which weighed 27 pounds and was in perfect shape. By then it was time to go and we walked out of the valley to our cars, dazed with joy by the sport we'd had in just a few quiet evening hours.

Carp can be caught just as easily in daylight in those quiet places where a solitary carp angler can guard against disturbing the fish. When carp fishing, I wear a pair of khaki pants and khaki shirt to better blend into the background; stay well concealed from the fish; and keep all movements to a minimum. It is most important to keep off the skyline as the carp's vision is keen enough to take warning from a figure outlined against the sky.

Here I have dealt with what I regard as *the* basic bait — my cornmeal doughballs — and one of the many techniques of angling for carp. There are, of course, many other effective baits, and variations on my method of bottom fishing.

A warm, sticky loaf of fresh bread makes a good bait as well. Open the crust, pinch out a hunk and flatten it in the middle to form a hard centre. Stick the bend of the hook into this centre and then, drawing up the loose outside edges, squeeze it tightly around the line above the the hook shank. This bait, called *flake*, holds well where it has been squeezed and sinks well. When it reaches bottom, the loose, unsqueezed bread melts off and forms a chum that attracts carp.

Where carp are cruising and feeding on the surface a hunk of fresh bread crust can be hooked on, cast out and allowed to float where the carp will slurp it down with gusto.

Fishing for small school carp with fly tackle and a small wet fly is a fairly new innovation, and this can provide exciting sport.

But the big fish offer the challenge, down on the bottom where they grub away and happen upon your big ball of bait. This is the peak of carp fishing: the waiting in anticipation and the sudden shock of action when some massive, gold-flanked fish speeds off like a train on the end of your flimsy tackle.

Any angler who becomes skilled enough to regularly catch carp of more than 20 pounds, need never fear the other species. They are nowhere near as smart or as tough.

Best of all, the finest sport is to be enjoyed in the quiet times, removed from the crowds and the noise and the bustle of daily life. In the sweet of the evening, by lake or by river, we may commune with nature as we fish for carp.

8 🐟 The Catfish

In folklore, catfish conjure up a picture of barefoot boys, cane poles, and an idyllic southern scene. This truly exists, but the catfish family is large, and includes big fish that can test the toughest tackle and the artful wiles of the skilled angler. Catfish are common in salt- and freshwater. In Europe, the giant wels runs to 400 pounds; India has a brute of a fish, known as the goonch; South America is rich in catfish species, and on the North American continent there are enough to keep biologists and anglers in a happy frame of mind.

Catfish of all sizes and species form an important sports fishery, accounting for millions of happy man-fishing hours per year. Every single species is good to eat, and the larger fish such as the channel and blue catfish are lusty roughnecks that never give in, until brought ashore by net or gaff.

NORTH AMERICAN CATFISH (Ameiuridae)

The North American catfishes make up around fifty species found from Canada to Guatemala, from the Atlantic to the Pacific. Many sporting species have been stocked outside their natural range and thus are spread throughout the land. These are indeed hardy and aggressive fish that plant well, and in a suitable habitat, thrive to the extent that

All catfish are identified by their eight rubbery whiskers or barbels: four below the mouth, one at each corner of the mouth (the long whiskers), and a small one on each side of the nostrils. It is obvious from the size of this fish's mouth that a big bait is normal fare for large channel catfish.

various official organizations maintain special catfishing lakes where the fish are scientifically produced to provide healthy and hardy stocks to benefit commercial and angling needs.

All catfish lack scales, possessing instead a tough and rubbery skin that can be the very devil to remove if the angler lacks the necessary skills. Of more concern to the beginner, however, are the sharp and dangerous spines found in front of the dorsal and pectoral fins. Careless handling can result in a painful wound that usually stings for quite a while and will turn septic if not treated. Some of the smaller cats actually have poison glands located at the base of the pectorals and a jab from one of these is less than pleasant.

The obvious identifying marks of all catfish are the long, rubbery whiskers or barbels that give the fish their common name. There are eight, all told: four under the chin, one at each corner of the mouth, and one on each side of the nostrils. These barbels are sensory organs that help the fish locate their food.

Catfish have an adipose fin, a small fleshy little tag set on the back just in front of the tail. This fin, also found on salmon and trout, used to be regarded in Britain as the mark of the true game fish. Told this once by a crusty old British game fisherman, I almost sent him into apoplexy when I innocently mentioned that all catfish are so endowed.

A number of North American catfish species are too small to be regarded as sporting fish, and in this group we meet the madtoms, which reach around 6 inches in length and own those previously mentioned poison glands. But even when we take away the tiddlers of the family, we are still left with a rich array of sporting fish, so let us look at the important species.

Channel Catfish (Ictalurus punctatus)

This is my favorite catfish and a species I pursue with love and devotion because of its fighting power and superb edible qualities. Usually, the eating status of the fish is the least of the points I ponder, but not with the channel cat. I regard these fish as a sweet and toothsome quarry and there is always space in my deep-freeze unit for as many as I can catch.

While not the biggest catfish, the channel has a very large range, being found from north of the Great Lakes and the waters of the Saskatchewan River, south into Mexico, with many planned plants well east and west of this range.

This is our only spotted catfish with a deeply forked tail. These spots are prominent in the smaller fish of up to 4 pounds and less apparent in specimens over this size, so a better form of identification for the beginner is in the count of the anal-fin rays — a typical method of separating similar species of one family.

The anal fin, sometimes called the ventral fin, is the one running back along the belly, from the vent of the fish to the tail. The rays are the spiny portions of the fin, with a count of 24 to 30 for the channel catfish, 30 to 36 for the blue catfish and 19 to 23 for the white catfish.

Channel cats range in color from blueish-silver on the back, and silver-white on the belly, in the smaller fish, to a dark steely blue-grey above, and almost pure white below, in the bigger fish. Color is a poor identification system though, as I have caught cat almost black on the back; so, where there is doubt, the anal-fin ray-count should be the guide to species.

This is a catfish that enjoys fast water, and at times it is taken in extremely rapid currents such as may be found below a dam or a weir. They seem to enjoy working around cuts between lakes, where moving waters are often found, but at times can also be caught in almost stillwater locations, where the rocky bottom and depth suit their ideas of a home away from home. These are active fish, and in spring they will ascend fast rivers, usually those with clean sand, gravel or rock bottoms. It is rare to find them in weedy or shallow places, for their obvious preference is for deeper holes and cleaner waters.

The average-sized channel cat caught by anglers weighs between 1 to 2 pounds and these little fish can provide good sport and good eating. Specialist tackle, techniques and timing are needed to take the larger fish, as I have proven on one of my favorite waters. In this spot, fishing on the bottom during the day with a live dew worm, it is nothing to catch a score of small channel cats in a day. However, at that same spot at night, using a large, dead bait such as a 7- or 8-inch minnow or smelt, the size of the fish taken jumps to a minimum of about 5 pounds, and the bag often includes some lunkers better than 20 pounds in weight.

I should perhaps mention here that all catfish tend to be more active in feeding during the hours of darkness, and it seems that in the case of the channel cats, night fishing usually brings home the lunkers.

The top weight for the channel catfish is suggested at around 60 pounds, but there is no reason why larger fish than this could not be found in particularly suitable habitation. The upper-weight estimate has been made from a wealth of data, for unlike many other game fish species, channel cats are the object of important commercial fisheries throughout North America and the tremendous catches made every year provide us with reliable information.

This is an omnivorous species that will eat every form of aquatic life, with special emphasis on other fish. I once found a 2-pound rainbow trout in the belly of a 15-pound channel catfish. This shows that we are dealing with a tough creature with a fair amount of speed and a healthy appetite.

Blue Catfish (Ictalurus furcatus)

Most of what has been said on the angling qualities of the channel catfish applies equally to the blue catfish with the added fact that this species is one of the largest North American cat species.

Known to reach 180 pounds, the average size caught is 2 to 3 pounds bigger than the average of the channel cat, but the largest of this species have not yet been taken by fair angling means, and this in itself offers a challenge.

More limited in range than the channels, blues are found in the larger rivers, from Ohio and Minnesota south to Mexico, and they have been planted in suitable habitats east and west of this natural zone.

With a decided preference for fast waters and clean bottoms of sand, rock or gravel, this superbly streamlined catfish is obviously suited to feed in its favorite holes close to white water at the base of dams and chutes. It has a well-shaped tail with a deep fork, and while it generally feeds on all available aquatic life, it is primarily a predator.

Pale blue above and milky white below, the blue cat has a distinctive feature in that its eyes are set in the lower part of its head. The anal-fin ray-count is 30 to 36.

In common with the majority of their family, these catfish build a nest at spawning time and both parents stay to guard the eggs and rear the young to a size where they can take care of themselves. In this parent-brood relationship they are fiercely protective and will swiftly slash at any object approaching their nest. Some anglers take advantage of this by searching out nests and then dropping a baited hook, with a good chance of it being taken by one of the parent fish.

Possibly I am exhibiting an over-protective attitude when I suggest that this is an unfair practice, but that is the way I feel. I wouldn't fish for black bass when they are on nest guard, and they, too, are easy to hook under these circumstances. Yet on the other hand, I do not hesitate to throw plugs at another nest-guard fish, the bowfin, or grindle. I have decided that the catfish and black bass are game, sporting fish, and the bowfin is not.

White Catfish (Ictalurus catus)

Unlike his cousins, the channel and the blue catfish, the white cat is a smallish fish, running to 18 inches and seldom exceeding 3 pounds. It is a good sporting fish with a blue-white color effect that often looks blotched. It has a forked tail and only 19 to 23 rays in the anal fin.

The original range of the white catfish was from around the Chesapeake Bay to Texas, but it has been planted in the West and also the Northeast.

Preferring sluggish water conditions, the white's choice lies somewhere between the white-water habitat of the channel and blue, and the muddy conditions favored by the bullhead. It is omnivorous, gobbling up almost every kind of aquatic life that passes by.

Since it is regarded as a superb food fish and is also an eager biter, the white catfish has proven an excellent stocking fish for a range of pay-for-your-catch establishments where the angler can fish stocked water and be charged according to the size of his catch.

Flathead Catfish (Pilodictis olivaris)

With the flathead cat we start to move away from the fast, clear-water, speedy cats, and get into the more general field of fish that live in warmish waters and have an affinity for mud and a life of leisure. The flathead is a big fish, running to at least 100 pounds. The average size of 3 to 4 pounds too, is larger than the average of the other catfishes.

This is that big, old Mississippi catfish of tale and fable, sitting fat and happy in those glorious rivers of the Mississippi Valley as far down as Mexico. I went to see a movie called *The Southerner* five times, some years back, because the focal point of the movie was a situation involving a monster flathead. The lead role, played by the late Zachary Scott, was that of a sharecropper who was in competition with a well-off landowner to catch a monster cat known locally as 'old lead pencils,' because of its massive whiskers. The whole movie was enjoyable, but I got a special kick out of the scene in which the two arch enemies got together waist deep in the great river, to haul on the trot line that had been set by the sharecropper and had at last fooled the big cat. It was a monster fish; at least 70 pounds by my estimate.

This catfish gets its name from its flattened head, and it has a brown-colored body overlaid with darker brown blotches. The anal fin is short and the ray count is 14 to 17.

The flathead prefers slow-moving, deeper pools in very big rivers where it is often taken on trot lines baited with a live fish. All kinds of fish make up its diet, plus most types of organic matter.

Bullheads

This is a recognized division of the North American catfish family and it includes most of the common small varieties that give angling pleasure on light tackle.

These are eager-biting, husky little fish seldom exceeding 4 pounds, and actually averaging closer to half-a-pound on rod and line. The three main species — the black, brown and yellow bullheads — provide tremendous sport to anglers of all ages, and are considered among the finest of all freshwater fish for eating.

The three bullheads we shall cover are quite similar to each other and few anglers ever bother to identify which species is being caught. For most people the fact that it *is* a bullhead is enough, but it is worth-while knowing our fish, so we'll deal with the more important points of their make-up.

Black Bullhead (Ictalurus melas)

This typical species is distinguished by darker-colored chin barbels and a shorter, more robust body, and it can be separated by the fact that its pectoral spines lack serrations on the back edge. The top color of the fish is less certain as a means of identification, as it can range from black, through dark-green, to yellow-green; underparts can be bright yellow through milky white. It is closer in looks to the yellow bullhead but can be separated by those serrated pectoral spines.

The range is from the southern edge of the Great Lakes across to North Dakota, and south to Texas. It has been widely stocked. This is the so-called *horned pout* of central North America and dwells in slow-moving waters with scant vegetation; sometimes it enjoys a spell in clear water over gravel or sand.

Brown Bullhead (Ictalurus nebulosus)

This popular little catfish has an almost square tail, dark chin barbels and an anal-fin ray-count of 22 to 23. The back edge of the pectoral spines is serrated and the top weight is about 3 to 4 pounds, with the average running 10 to 12 inches long, between 3/4 pound and 1 pound. Color patterns for the brown bullhead run through yellowish brown to almost a dark chocolate, with mottled patches on the upper part of the body. The belly can be white, but is usually more on the yellow side, even to a bright yellow.

The natural range is from the Great Lakes east to Maine, and south to Florida and Mexico, but of course it has been planted all over in suitable habitation. Where the water temperatures allow, the brown bullhead will thrive in the weedy parts of deep bends in rivers and in lakes; yet I often catch them over a clean, rock bottom in the same place inhabited by channel cats. So it would be fair to suggest that it is not too rigid in its choice of living space.

The brown, and indeed the other bullheads, will dine happily on whatever comes along in the form of food. A worm is the bait supreme, but they take cheese, live bait-minnows, bread, grubs and even stink baits concocted from richly odorous materials.

This also is a good table fish, and being a freely biting species, is valuable in terms of angling and of the economy. It is one of the truly common catfishes and is taken in some commercial quantities, for market use, in the lower Great Lakes and other areas.

Yellow Bullhead (Ictalurus natalis)

The yellow bullhead is often confused with the brown, but it is fairly simple to separate the two, although this doesn't matter from the angling point of view. This fish has white chin whiskers and a very long anal fin with a count of 24 to 28 rays. It reaches 15 to 16 inches and a possible weight of 3 pounds.

This is a most common catfish, ranging from North Dakota east to the Great Lakes and the St. Lawrence River, south to Texas and south from New York State down the coastal plains to Florida and points west. I have taken these fish in salt chuck in South Carolina, while bait fishing for river-run stripers and channel bass.

The yellow bullhead will feed happily in streaming currents as well as in clear waters and quiet, weedy parts of lakes and ponds. In common with the rest of the family, it will bite eagerly on everything from a live shrimp to a stink-bait sponge.

Madtoms (Notorus)

The madtoms are small, thin-skinned catfish of almost no value in angling, because of their size. However, since some of the tribe are armed with needle-sharp pectoral fins connected to poison sacs, it is useful to be able to recognize them on sight.

They appear to be all head, and have an almost square tail with a blob of an adipose fin that is tied down to the back and merges into the upper margin of the inferior tail.

The group includes: the brindled, eastern, freckled, mountain and tadpole madtoms, few of which exceed 6 inches. Some make an excellent live bait for smallmouth black bass, but must be handled carefully by the angler.

CATFISHING GEAR

The range of size of the catfish calls for a division of tackle. For the bullheads, any basic outfit will do and indeed a simple cane-pole rig is excellent. However, for the really big cats in fast water, there is a need for tougher and more specialized gear. So, ignoring the species as such, let us lump the channel catfish and blues together and deal with them; and later, we will do the same for the bullheads.

Big Catfish Gear

I own two 9-foot, hollow glass rods each with a spinning reel to match, for use against the bigger cats. The lighter model is a steelhead rod with standard spinning reel loaded with 12- or 15-pound-test line; the second is identical, except for being staged more powerfully in the stick with fittings to match. With the second stick, which is a light surf-caster, I use an oversize spinning reel capable of carrying 350 yards of 15- or 20-pound-test line.

Standard spinning sticks are too light for the biggest cats, but can handle fish up to 10 pounds, if the angler is willing to conduct a careful fight for quite a long time. This can be dangerous in very powerful water and stouter gear is definitely recommended.

Big catfish are not only heavy, but are powerful swimmers with deep reserves of stamina. Add to these qualities the fact that they are usually found in fast waters, and it becomes obvious that we are meeting rugged customers. Our tackle, then, must be balanced accordingly.

The heavier spinning gear I use is rather expensive and for readers who don't wish to pay out the money involved, there are some excellent substitutes in the form of sturdy boat rods of solid glass, used with plain but effective level-wind, star drag reels. An effective outfit of this type can be bought for less than a quarter of the price of the spinning gear and in boat-fishing situations could be considered the better, and certainly stronger, set of tackle.

One of the best rods for this work is a standard boat rod in hollow or solid glass, around 7 feet long, with the double-length popping-rod butt. With this can be matched a star drag reel taking 25 to 30-pound-test line. An outfit of this type is useful in that it makes a good heavy-fishing set that can be used for stillfishing for catfish and also as a trolling rig for pike, muskies and a range of other fish.

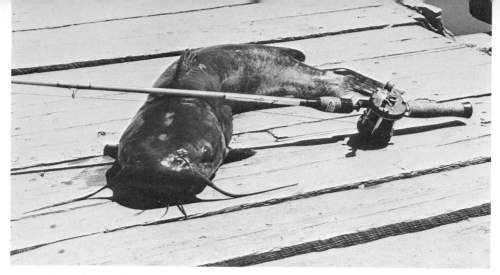

A star drag reel and a powerful baitcasting stick make an excellent rig for tough fish such as this 15-pound channel cat. With very large baits a star drag reel is best used on a bigger, stronger rod with a double handle for superior purchase during a prolonged fight.

Popping Rods

In hollow or solid glass, these are quite inexpensive when fitted with a good long wooden butt, fixed-reel setting, and plain but solid line-guide rings. A long butt is preferable so as to give good holding purchase for fighting heavy fish and standard or medium-fast tip action best handles the heavier baits.

Star Drag Reels

These moderately priced units are made to cover hundreds of tasks from heavy-duty freshwater angling to medium saltwater uses. For this style, the reel is fished on top of the rod, with the reel handles to the right side. A slim metal lever mounted on the side-plates is pushed back and forth to throw the spool in and out of gear for easier casting. Below the reel handles sits a star-shaped unit like a capstan which, when screwed in or out, applies or takes off drag. On retrieve the line is spread evenly across the spool by a level-wind apparatus geared to the inner works. Reels of this type can be obtained to take line from 10-pound test, all the way to 100-pound for big-game angling, and the smaller end of the range provides a useful scale from which to select a suitable model for this heavier style of freshwater angling.

Most catfishing for the larger species is from boats, but in certain waters bank fishing is the rule and for this it becomes necessary to know how to cast this gear, which is less simple than spinning tackle. In boat fishing, the angler can simply put the tackle over the side, click forward the free-spool lever and, with a thumb on the spool to check overrun, allow the weighted terminal tackle to slide down to the bottom. At this point, when the sinker is felt to be holding, the free-spool lever is clicked back, the slack line carefully wound in and the tackle allowed to fish.

To cast with a free-spool, star drag reel takes quite a bit of practice and even the highly skilled continue to suffer overruns and "bird nests" or tangles in the reel spool. So here is how it is done — with an educated thumb and a prayer.

Using a double-handed rod, the caster grasps the butt at the reel seat with his right hand, thumb clamped firmly on the line spool to prevent it from running when the reel is put out of gear. He slides the free-spool lever forward with his left hand and then takes firm hold on the end of the butt to form the power leverage of the cast. With both arms raised level with his shoulders, the caster faces down the bank, left elbow pointing to the spot intended to be fished, with the rod also lined up, but behind his right shoulder. A sharp thrust of his left hand powers the rod in an arc overhead in direct line with the chosen fishing spot; as the tip hits 10 o'clock out front, the caster lifts his thumb from the spool and allows the line to peel off the sharply powered, revolving reel spool. He swings his body around in a follow-through until the rod tip points to the target. From the moment of releasing the line, the caster must control the speed of the reel so that it doesn't overrun, and speeding faster than the line flying through the guides, start a double-back action and bring the cast to a wrenching halt. This is accomplished by applying pressure with his thumb to keep down the spool speed to that of the line, and to prevent it from bunching out in a big loop before flying up the first line guide. As the tackle curves over to the target, he touches his thumb directly to the spool and slows the cast, so that the reel's forward movement is brought to a firm but gradual stop as the tackle lands.

This is not an easy casting system, but a very effective one, and an important part of angling technique for those wishing to avoid the higher cost of heavier spinning outfits.

Terminal Gear

All big cats are bottom feeders and being usually in flowing waters, the sliding leger is by far the best bottom rig. However, since we will be using heavy tackle and need more weight to hold to the bottom, we must use a stronger system than the two split shot which form the standard sinker-stop. Our heavier leger is fitted in the following manner.

The chosen sinker is slid onto the line and a small swivel is tied to the end of the line to serve as the sinker-stop. This must be big enough to prevent the sinker from sliding down to the hook. To the end of a 2-foot length of lighter nylon we knot our chosen hook, using the improved clinch knot (see page 118). The other end of the hook length is tied to the swivel, also with the improved clinch, and we have a

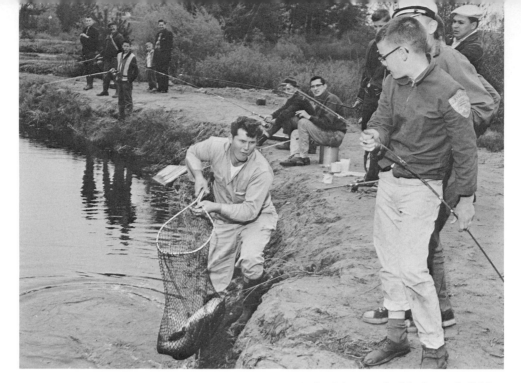

A fine catfish caught in a public fishing pond. Catfish are valuable for such fishing because they can adapt to waters that would not support more delicate species. They offer the thrill of landing large specimens in regions where big fish may otherwise be scarce.

sliding leger that will break in the hook length when snagged and save the loss of the sinker and swivel.

Sinker Technique

      The sinker weight needed to anchor the bait will depend on the speed of the current and the weight of the line. A light line has less water resistance than the heavier, thicker line so we must carry an effective range for different jobs. When fishing downstream from a boat, however, the sinker can be lighter, since all we need do to anchor it is to simply keep letting out line as it lifts in the current, until it reaches a point downstream where it holds. This helps to bring bites, since the bait covers more water. The simple principle is like that of using a small anchor for a boat and then letting out enough anchor cable to hold the boat in the tide. When walking back the gear in this way, it is necessary to stay in touch by holding the line, so as to be able to respond to a swift bite.

Chumming For Cats

      Although chum is not generally used when fishing for cats, it can produce a tremendous increase in bites and in fish caught. I have used this system for everything from channel cats to bullheads, and the only difference is in the amount of chum used and, to a degree, in the ingredients.

Obviously, in fast waters it is possible to put in up to six or seven buckets of chum, without overfeeding the fish, where a small pool holding a big head of bullheads would be properly baited with much less chum.

All the fish in this family have a keen sense of smell and can sense the odor of food in the water from a fair distance away. The use of chum has two major advantages. We can bring fish to our bait from some distance off, and then keep them concentrated in our hole by the judicial application of tantalizing, fragrant foodstuffs.

To make catfish chum, start off with the basic bread-and-bran bulk material that was used for carp (see page 144). For cats, which delight in all kinds of different foodstuffs, suitable additives are needed. These can consist of any form of fish or fish product that the reader can easily obtain. People living close to places where smelts or herrings make spring runs can collect and freeze these fish when they are available. Fresh- and saltwater clams, shrimp, chicken guts and other such delights are all valuable. I keep an old meat chopper for whatever I have to add to the basic bread-bran mix. I pour in a bottle of coarse, cheap cod-liver oil, and stir it all up with an iron mixing spoon.

There seems to be a general idea that baits for cats must be decayed, and yet I have found that fresh chum is better than a batch that has gone rotten. With the mass of smelly materials in the chum plus the strong odor of the oil, I feel it is best to use chum that has no sour smell — and it is certainly nicer to have around the house during preparation.

To put the chum out I use my big iron spoon to simply drop it over the side of the boat, or throw it upstream so that it hits bottom where my bait is set. When fishing from the bank, the chum can be tossed out, using the spoon as a bait hurler, again making sure that it goes where it will do the most good.

Hook Baits

I have yet to find anything better for the big cats than a fresh dead fish between 8 and 10 inches in length. Oily fish, such as smelt, gizzard shad and freshwater herrings are best, but if I can't get these, I'll use hunks of saltwater herrings bought from a store, or suckers soaked in cod-liver oil.

However, catfish are not particular about what they take, and perch and even small sunfish can be used. A large dead frog is a great bait, and while this often works better in slower waters, I have enjoyed a great deal of success with it in fast channels. Live minnows work well, too, but are not as effective as the more easily used dead baits.

In many areas there is a strong local practice of using stink baits, that is to say, baits made from a mess of fish allowed to go rotten in the sun and to turn into an oily mess in a container. To use stink bait, a sponge is fastened to the hook, dipped in the guck and then put out to lure the catfish. I have never used this system, mainly because of the unpleasant work involved, and because I have always enjoyed a high degree of success with the standard baits mentioned here.

However, the reader should remember that it is wise to take notice of and try local baits and preferences. Nobody knows all there is to know about angling and it is a truth that very often local technique is based on good sense. Fish in different locations have preferences which are hard to explain, and this should teach us to always listen carefully when a successful local angler tells how he takes his good catches.

The lists of baits used for big catfish are long and varied. Don't neglect one because it is new, but give it a try and see for yourself if it has value.

Hooks

The important factor in using hooks for cats is matching the sizes to suit the baits.

With a slim smelt dead bait between 7 and 10 inches long, I use a size 1/0 standard length shank. With a single or double dew worm, a size 6 is fine. For a dead frog, it may be necessary to use from size 1 to 2/0, depending on how big the frog is.

Cats have big mouths and are not particularly shy, but the bait should contain the hook — with point and barb free — so the fish is not put off by a mass of hardware. When you get bites, but the fish won't take, rebait, using a smaller-sized hook; it often makes all the difference.

BIG CAT TECHNIQUES

The bigger catfish are seldom shy and the major problem is first to locate a good spot. Local knowledge is helpful in this, but knowing that the channel and blue cats are fast-water, deep-hole species, we can sort out likely places ourselves. Any white-water chute below a dam is potentially a starting point, as is a gut between lakes where the water flow has dug deep holes. I found one place by a boat dock on a big river when I dropped a sinker down and discovered a lovely, deep hole with a sturdy current pushing through. The flathead, which has a narrower range, is located by searching out deeper spots on the big rivers through the Mississippi Valley, where they live.

Above all, don't be afraid to ask, for many people who will protect a favorite trout spot will be only too willing to tell where catfish are to be found. It is the snobbery attitude at work again.

The best catfishing is at night and I have found that I catch ten big fish during the night for every one hooked during daylight. I prefer the very hot, sticky nights when it is painful to toss and turn without sleep in a humid bedroom, and a night on the water becomes a joy indeed. I arrive early, load the boat and moor into place in good time to get well-organized before nightfall. A gasoline lantern set in a box with one side removed protects my night sight, and yet gives plenty of light to see around the boat; and of course I load up with heavy clothes, as any night can be chilly out on the water, even though a heat wave has the city folks gasping for breath.

Let us look at a typical night out — a trip, I might add, that was enjoyed while this book was in preparation. I took with me a young friend, Peter Brewster, who had never been out after channel cats before, although he is a highly skilled angler in all other departments.

We picked up our boat — a big, roomy old punt, with a 5 hp. kicker on the stern — checked all our gear during daylight and made sure that the anchor had a long enough rope to hold us securely in the fast channel where we planned to fish. The motor thumped away at the first pull on the cord, and I guided it out of the dock, pointing it to our chosen spot not more than 200 yards away.

With Peter in the bow to handle the anchor I edged the big boat slowly up against the current, running it straight upstream directly over the fishing mark. This was important, because when the anchor went over the bow I wanted the current to push us back down towards the deep hole. Judging that we were in the right position, I gave the word and Peter *placed* the anchor into the water and allowed it to sink swiftly to the bottom, without splash or thump. Why scare off fish with noise, when just a little care will prevent it?

Sure enough, with all our anchor cable out, our boat came to a stop and held in the current, arrow-straight at just the right spot. At this point, I grabbed my old iron spoon and flipped in load after load of chum directly upstream of our position, starting off with almost half a bucketful.

Using heavy spinning rigs, we slipped on sliding-leger ends with 2-ounce sinkers and size 1 hooks for the frozen smelt baits. In such a fast-water situation, I thread my bait so that it streams back from the tackle, with the head facing the current. To do this, I push the hook right through the mouth and out the gills, then push it cleanly through the back in front of the dorsal fin and, pushing it through the body in front of the tail, pull gently on the line until the hook rests neatly by the tail with the point and barb exposed.

Peter did the same and I walked mine back down over the stern while he walked his downstream to its resting place over the offshore side of the boat. Both baits were now sitting amidst the chum, but separated from each other by a safe distance.

We propped both our rods firmly in the boat so that the rod points sat at a shallow angle to the lines, with the line taut to the sinker to let the slightest nibble register on the rod tip. Now that we were set, we tidied up the boat, set out food and drink, opened the big gaff and parked the salmon-sized landing net over the bow, out of the way. I then flipped in another bucket of chum.

There were a few small taps during the lingering moments of daylight, but nothing came of them, and as it became dark, I lit the gasoline lantern and set it up to shine on the rods and give us baiting light, shading it so that it would not shine directly in our eyes. More ground-bait went in, and just as I poured the first of my many cups of coffee, there was a heavy slam at my rod.

This is the moment of truth in this particular channel catfish hole for I have found that the fish will quite often leave the bait if there is too much resistance. I picked up the rod, and pointing it to the fish, provided a short length of slack line. I held the rod forward at the full stretch of my arm, the slack was taken and I set home the hook.

I swiftly pulled up the rod, point in the air, and the angry cat slashed it into a strumming bend, shooting across the channel as the spinning drag purred delightfully. "Good heavens," said Peter (who is a very polite angler). "What have you got, a monster?"

It wasn't one of the big fish of the channel (only about 5 pounds), but it put up the usual dogged scrap, and when the powerful tackle brought it boiling to the side, it went into the net on the first try, and was grunting away as I took out the hook with my long-nosed pliers seconds later.

More chum went over the side and then the cats came on feed with a fury, getting bigger and bigger as the night wore on.

By midnight I had seven channel cats in the sack and Pete sat there without any, taking a little time to get used to the system of pushing the rod out fast on the first thumping bite. But at last he clicked. There was the usual wallop, he jabbed out his rod and, as the line immediately went iron hard, reared back into his first good-sized channel catfish, a nice specimen weighing about 11 pounds.

By 2 a.m. we had lost two very big fish that became tangled in the anchor lines, and had a couple of sacks filled with smooth-skinned channels from 4 pounds to 24 pounds in weight. And I had sold another keen angler on the joys and delights of night fishing for these superb sporting fish.

We slept a little, until dawn, then tidied up the boat, changed tackle and went out into the weedy bay for a little dawn fishing for largemouths before settling down to skinning and filleting our catch. And this itself is worthy of description and instruction.

Filleting Big Catfish

My fishing buddy, Peter, is not only a keen angler, but like me, enjoys cooking and appreciates good food, so he was all ready to learn the filleting method when, after a couple of hours of casting for bass, we returned and anchored in the channel and I settled down to prepare the catfish for taking home. During hot weather this is always best done on the spot, for with big cats there is considerable material to be thrown away and dumping it all in the garbage as I once did, will draw every racoon for a considerable distance.

Preparing these fish is simple to do, but difficult to describe, so bear with me. I want to make this quite plain, because it is a shame to waste such delicious fish. The smaller bullheads are prepared in a different way and it will be described later.

Catfish have tough, rubbery skin that defies all but the very sharpest of knives, and the matter is further complicated by a head structure that is different from most other fish. To fillet a big cat properly, a blade that can be honed to a razor edge is required, and if you don't possess a really sharp knife, the best bet is to make the initial cuts with a good razor blade. I use a very old Green River skinning knife of the type that was carried on commercial buffalo hunts, and between cuts I hone it carefully with a steel and an Arkansas stone.

Here's the method. First, all the skin is removed from the body and the fillets are then sliced off close to the bone. So make the first cut from the root of one pectoral fin, over the back, behind the head, to the base of the other pectoral fin. Make all these cuts just through the skin, stopping short of the flesh.

With the skin severed through right over the back, behind the head, start the second cut from the first, moving down the length of the back to the tail. Make two more cuts running down along the belly and flank towards the tail, one each side, to divide the fish's skin into two patches covering the whole of each side of the body.

Now rip off these patches by catching hold of the top edge with a pair of tight-fitting pliers, winding a couple of turns around for better purchase and then following through with a strong pull back and down towards the tail.

When both sides are done you should have a fish completely skinned from the back of the head down to the tail, with a patch of skin left covering the belly.

Set the blade of a sharp filleting knife against the tail, and keeping the edge down along the backbone, separate all the meat from the bones on each flank. When you meet the curved bones of the belly, curve the knife to follow them and ease all the flesh away without cutting into the abdominal cavity.

Once you have learned how to do this, you will finish with two massive fillets, which can then be sliced lengthwise for ease in cooking, and you will have head, backbone and guts contained in one large piece which can be dropped over the side to provide feed for crawdads, shrimps and, of course, other catfish. The clean fillets should be wrapped and put in a cooler for the journey home, where they can be eaten right away or deep-frozen for later use.

With catfish from cool, clean waters, this is a feast fit for the gods, or as old Isaak Walton put it so well, "fit for anglers and other very honest men."

And now for the simplest pleasure that any angler can enjoy in peace and comfort during a nice day in spring, summer or early fall: a session of fishing for bullheads, be they horned pout, chuckleheads, yellow, black, or brown; or even half-pint editions of the larger cat-fishes.

BULLHEAD TACKLE TECHNIQUES

Since these fishes are small, they can best be caught with standard gear, a good cane-pole rig being about the best obtainable. The angler can use spinning, baitcasting or even fly-fishing gear, with a simple bobber or sliding-leger terminal tackle, and enjoy a day's fishing that is completely lacking in sophistication, yet rich in sport.

The best bait is a small worm, or a short stub of a large worm, but these fish will take just about anything that is offered. I have caught them on stale shrimps left over from a fish fry, on scraps of cut-up oysters or clams, on cheese, grubs, macaroni, liver and the unwanted innards of chickens. Use whatever is at hand and be sure to make a bucket of chum that includes a basic bread-bran base to which is added some of the material to be used on the hook.

The best sport is achieved with bobber tackle close to a weed-bed off a deeper hole and channel. Set the bobber to allow the bait to sit an inch or so off the mud, bait the hook, cast out and sprinkle a little chum around the bobber. When the bobber starts to jiggle, pause, then set the hook and haul in your catch.

The best hook for these smaller cats is a size 8 hook with a 2-X Long shank which will help when you want to unhook the fish, but since the bullheads are gobblers, don't forget your forceps or slim-nosed pliers, to aid in this task.

There is much fun and deep satisfaction in spending a few hours on the banks of a good water landing husky catfish such as this one from the famed Santee-Cooper system of South Carolina. Though small compared to some of the monsters caught, it is still a nice size both for catching and eating.

About the only problem in this type of angling is in getting these little fish ready for the table, and since they all have viciously sharp spines, handle them with care at all times.

Skinning Bullheads

Since I am very fond of eating these delicious little fish, I often make up a family bullhead-fishing party with all the kids that want to come along. The children and adults alike are fitted with cane poles or similar tackle, and I prowl around, chumming, baiting hooks, taking off the fish and skinning them on the spot. We take along a couple of big coolers in which there is ice in waterproof packs so that the fish can be kept fresh without going soggy through contact with water.

The tools needed are simple: just a sharp knife with a steel and a honing stone to whet the edge, plus a plain length of clean plank on which to make the initial cut.

For protection from the sharp spines, I wear an old glove on my left hand, with steel pot-cleaners stitched to the palm to provide a better hold on a slimy, wriggling fish.

I put the freshly caught fish belly-down on the board and kill it with a straight cut down through the backbone, from in front of the dorsal fin, almost to the bottom of the gills. Once through the backbone, I take it easy, and taking the fish in both hands, snap the smaller bones down to bring the head of the fish flat to the underpart.

With the fish held firmly in this position, I edge the fingers of my right hand in under the ledge beneath the back that offers good purchase. With a firm grip established in both hands, I then pull the head of the fish down in a steady pull to the tail, freeing all the edible meat from skin, head and guts. Everything in the left hand is thrown back out to feed other catfish and everything in the right hand is popped into the cooler. On reaching home, and sometimes on the spot, I clean out the blood trail against the backbone, clean up the fish and start work on that most delightful of all meals, a catfish fry.

This process is easy to learn and will enable the user to quickly prepare these fish for eating. I might add that in the time it took to commit this to paper I could have peeled out a score or more.

CATFISH SUMMARY

Some people of a snobbish attitude scorn catfish, suggesting that they are of less value than other freshwater fish. But when we look at the true picture, both the large species and the small form a tremendously important part of the angling scene. Quite often, waters that could not support cold-water game fish can be made into outstanding catfish waters that will provide thousands of happy fishing hours each year, where otherwise there would be no fishing.

The big catfish species often provide strong sport in places where there are no other game fish or species that can put a good bend into a rod.

The smaller fish are excellent for introducing a youngster to the grand sport of angling, and I must say that I think less of any man who turns to me and sneers at catfishing as an unworthy sport. Catfish are fun, and that's what angling is all about.

9 🐟 The Walleye

~~~~~~

Walleye are sluggish-fighting, easily hooked fish that are extremely popular species with many anglers. It would be easy to suppose that this popularity is based on their superb edible qualities, but it is not as simple as that.

I rarely take a trip just for the purpose of fishing for walleye, but when I do catch them, it is with a genuine feeling of delight. There is something rather grand about the sight of a big walleye rolling beside the boat. I have never attempted to analyze this reaction; I just accept it.

Of their edible qualities there is no doubt at all, and on most of my northern trips, a big part of the joy is in fishing for walleye around lunch time, in an all-out meat-hunting sense. On one three weeks' trip into Northern Saskatchewan, my Indian guide, my companion, and I ate walleye every day for shore lunch; catching all we needed in the time it took for the guide to build the fire and unload the grub box.

Small- and medium-sized walleye are indifferent fighters at best, even on light tackle, but fish of 8 pounds and up are capable of good action, as long as the tackle used is on the light side. Once on a trip to Lake Temagami in Ontario, I tied into a good-sized fish that gave a good account of itself. I was drifting down a large bay, eating lunch with my Indian guide, and to see what was around, I put out a 4-inch live fish on an ultralight spinning outfit, using a slender bobber and 4-pound line.

This particular bay holds pike as heavy as 30 pounds and as we washed down sandwiches with cold beer, my guide, Archie Lalonde, a keen angler in his own right, wished aloud that I would tie into one of the bruiser pike. "I've never seen a good fish played with really light tackle," he said. "It looks as if it could be fun."

The words were hardly spoken when my bobber quivered and then slid away in a series of shuddering jerks. I set the hook and the fish hit back, slashing the rod over into an arc. Archie put a paddle over the side to keep the boat faced towards the fish and to check our drift, and while the reel drag kept up a whine as the fish ran off, I began to think that I just might have hooked a big pike.

The fish slowed down and began to slug solidly around a small area, thumping away at the line with its tail, and then rose and boiled on the surface. I didn't see it, being busy, but Archie's keen eyes recorded the fish. "It's a fairly big walleye," he commented. "He'll give you a decent fight on that light gear."

Twice the walleye attempted to run under the boat, but was foiled by deft work with the paddle. It was a good ten to fifteen minutes before I got him over the net, and Archie brought it up with a beautiful fish weighing a shade over 9 pounds.

Since that day I have been just a little more respectful of the fighting power of walleye — at least on light tackle.

WALLEYE SPECIES

Walleye are members of the perch family *Percidae*, found in North American, European and Asian freshwaters. In North America the family includes the perch, the walleye, and a group of smaller fishes of small angling interest, known as darters.

Often confused with the pikes, the walleye have been given a number of inexact names. Older North American publications call them Walleyed-Pike, and in many parts of Canada today the yellow and blue walleye are known as pickerel, even in areas where true pickerel are present. In Quebec they are known as *doré*, but being a French word this is regarded as permissible. A similar species found in Europe, known now as Zander, was named pike-perch; until recently.

There are three walleye species of interest to us, the yellow walleye, commonly called simply "walleye," the blue walleye, and the sauger. It is worth our while to take a look at each individually, and then deal with them as one type from the angling standpoint, for apart from matters such as distribution and size, the three are similar in habits that affect angling techniques.

Yellow Walleye (Stizostedion vitreum vitreum)

This is the largest of the three, reaching a possible 30 pounds, with fish of about 10 pounds regarded as very worth-while specimens. It has a robust, elongate body, a large head, and formidable, sharp teeth. Its eyes have a glassy centre — hence the name walleye.

The natural range of the yellow walleye includes the whole of Canada, from the Hudson Bay drainage system west to British Columbia and the Northwest Territories, and in the United States, south to the Alabama and Tennessee rivers' drainage. In the past fifty years man has extended it outside this natural zone to lakes and waterways considered suitable.

This is a cold-water, deep-dwelling fish that seldom does well in small waters, and the suggested minimum-size water is about 100 acres. If prefers cleaner waters and a water temperature of less than 85° Fahrenheit is held to be necessary.

The yellow walleye is usually a bronze-olive-green on the back and sides, with six or seven dark, narrow bands crossing over the back in perch fashion. The quickest way to separate it from its nearest look alike, the sauger, is by the silver or milky-white tip prominent on the lower lobe of the tail. This is easily seen and is often the first distinctive mark visible on a fish fighting deep down in clear waters. The sauger lack this feature.

Yellow walleye spawn in spring, moving up rivers until a dam or barrier blocks further progress. Then, in water running over gravel, sand or small rock, the fish drop eggs and milt in what seems to be a careless

This string of yellow walleye from ice-cold water will make a superb meal to give added pleasure to the joy of the catch.

fashion. Where there are no suitable spawning tributaries, the fish spawn in shallow waters with suitable bottoms. The apparently careless spawning act is modified by the large amount of eggs, with a large female carrying up to 700,000.

In many places these spawning runs form a tourist attraction, as the fish lose any caution they may possess, and cram into clear, shallow streams where their massed numbers often force smaller fish above the surface. In a number of places the fish will still be massed in white waters below barriers when angling seasons open and, for as long as the fish are around, tremendous catches are enjoyed.

In their natural habitat walleye are a school fish, tending to shoal with other fish of similar size, living and feeding close to the bottom where they prey on all kinds of marine life, other fish forming a major part of their diet. They also feed during winter, and in many northern regions are a popular quarry for ice fishermen.

Blue Walleye (Stizostedion vitreum glaucum)

In all features save color and size, the blue walleye closely resembles the yellow walleye. The species are separated by the slate-blue body and white pelvic fins possessed by the blue walleye.

This rather small fish was for years thought to be young yellow walleye in an early stage of color development, and in this there is the rare incident of naturalists being wrong and commercial fishermen being right. In the Lake Erie fishery around the turn of the century the blue walleye were marketed as a different fish, even though a number of scientific authorities insisted they were immature yellow walleye.

The average size is stated to be around 1 pound, but although I have caught quite a number, I have yet to land one better than ½ pound.

Strictly limited in range, this smaller version of the popular yellow walleye was once common in Lake Erie where there was an important commercial fishery for them. Pollution and other factors have done untold damage to their numbers there and today they are found in patches in many areas connected with the Great Lakes.

Offering little to the angler that is not better given by the yellow walleye, this species has not been spread around by man and today it is little more than a subject of mild interest when caught.

Sauger (Stizostedion canadense)

This cousin to the yellow walleye is physically similar and is separated by the previously mentioned lack of the silver or white tip on the lower lobe of the tail. Also it has three or four dark saddle-marks across the back, in contrast to the perch-like bars found on the yellow walleye.

The sauger has quite a strong preference for larger bodies of water, being native to all the Great Lakes, the St. Lawrence River basin, and all the larger lakes of the northern States and Canada. The creation of major lakes through great dams on the Tennessee and Missouri watersheds has also produced notable angling for sauger in these regions, and there is little doubt that the best sport obtainable is in these waters. For, like the yellow walleye, the sauger runs rivers until halted by barriers, and the large concentrations of big saugers makes for hot fishing.

The average size of sauger in their northern habitat is around ¾ pound to 1 pound, and they seldom attain 2 pounds. But it is a different story on the Tennessee and Missouri rivers, where they grow to much greater size and have created important sports-fishing facilities for delighted anglers. On the Missouri, fish are found up to 8 pounds and the anglers who work the tail races below dams catch quite a few fish between 4 to 6 pounds. Under similar conditions on the Tennessee waters, an upper weight of 3 to 5 pounds may be expected.

But enough of introductions. We have seen the differences and should be able to recognize each of the species. Let us now get down to the basics of walleye angling. The blue has little angling value, and what will work for the yellow walleye will also cover most of what we need to know about the sauger. None of these fish are hard to catch, and the toughest part of the game is locating a school.

FINDING THE FISH

Every week I get letters and calls from people asking where they can go fishing. Most of these are requests for particular and usually simple information about accommodation, desired services and areas where certain species may be found. But every now and then, there is a hidden message contained in the request. The caller or writer wants me to tell him an exact spot that he can go to and catch lots of big fish without any problems.

Because I am a professional outdoorsman, engaged in full-time angling writing, many people believe that I have knowledge of a whole list of secret spots where success is assured.

This childlike faith in the infallability of some secret spot is also shown when a fisherman showing off a big fish is asked, "Where did you get it?" This is a good enough question as far as it goes, but the *how* and the *why* must be asked.

Finding fish is an important part of angling for all species of game fish, but in the case of the walleye it becomes tougher because most of the best angling is on large waters and many factors come into play to affect the search.

I know that there are some secret waters that do hold much bigger fish than those generally caught. Brook trout, for example, are often discovered to be present in small numbers but great size in some little-fished wilderness lake, and the man who finds one of these places would be a fool to broadcast the information. But this is a highly specialized matter, with little bearing on the problem of approaching a lake and saying to oneself, "They say there are big walleye here. . . Now, where do I start to fish?"

The skilled angler who is consistently successful is the one who can take a look at a piece of water, and noting conditions and a hundred other important factors, will push off to a *type* of spot that he believes will be harboring fish. If his first choice is not confirmed by bites he will then go to another place that is deeper or shallower, and continue this until he finds what he is seeking.

It is tough for the beginner to stand on the shore of a massive lake and pick where he will go and what he will do to get into fish. It takes experience and the realization that location according to conditions is 90 per cent of the game.

The only time walleye are easy to find is in spring when they pack up against tail races. Everybody knows they are there and the crowd fishes shoulder to shoulder.

All good fun indeed, but when the fish leave and head back down to spread through the whole of the lake, you must then find them in order to catch them, and in the case of walleye this is not at all a difficult task.

These fish prefer cool water, and because of the peculiar structure of their eyes, they avoid bright light conditions. Obviously then, on a warm bright day they will be in deep and thus cool and dark water. Since they are also predators it can be taken for granted that they will pick a spot where there is a head of bait minnows on which they can feed. It is only logical then to suggest that on a cool, overcast day they may be in shallower waters, and that at dusk and dawn, and during the hours of darkness they may be inshore in very shallow water, pursuing prey around the edges.

So, taking into consideration the light value and the air temperature, we should do well if we learn to select the correct area that is also rich with food.

In all the northern lakes on which I have fished for walleye, one type of place has always been a good bet, and that is at the base of rapids, or anywhere that white water tumbles down into deeper places. The water below rapids is always cooler and rich in oxygen. It becomes a gathering place for fish because of these factors and because the food washed over provides rich feed for small, prey-sized fishes. In the majority of cases, a live minnow dropped into the deep part will bring fast action, and because the walleye is a schooling fish, once you have one, you have many.

Another sure situation is the point at which a river flows in or out of a lake. This forms a gathering spot for fish of all kinds, and if there is a drop-off of the right depth, walleye will be present. A place of this type should be remembered for evening or night fishing, for as the light goes down the walleye will move out of deep water and prowl for food through the channel.

Rivers and rapids are fairly obvious places to fish, and it is in the lakes with neither of these features that the harder test comes. But here again, a simple understanding will lead to success.

On a plain lake my favorite walleye fishing stations are the points of islands, land sticking out into the waters, sharp reefs with obvious depth, and the channels between bays. All these places are subject to winds that set up currents which scour the bottom, removing mud and exposing sand, gravel and bare rocks. The current may be so slight as to be completely unseen by our eyes, but it creates excellent habitat for millions of aquatic creatures on the bottom, first attracting slightly larger creatures to feed, and in the natural chain of life, minnows and then the bigger predators.

On a windy day I always go to the upwind areas of an island and test for depth. If the bottom is clean and the water shelves off into greater depth, I carefully fish the bottom at different places until the fish are located. On many trips after trolling for lake trout, I have made a number of zigzagging trolls over the end of an island, off a point of land, or through a channel, and picked up all the walleye needed to supply lunch for three men.

The Light Factor

I cannot emphasize too strongly the important role played by light conditions in the movement and feeding habits of the walleye. Let me tell of an incident that really made me see how strongly it affects these fish.

I was out fishing for lake trout in a giant bay of an immense Canadian lake, probing deep with 450 feet of metal trolling line out, when a massive electric storm came raging in from the west.

It is basic safety to get off open waters when lightning is around and since I was also attached to a 450-foot lightning rod, I wasted no time in reeling out, so that we could run for cover.

My Indian guide, Joey Twain, gunned the big motor, and we shot off to take shelter in the mouth of a narrow channel where a river drained water from the big lake. With the anchor down, we donned rain-gear and there was just time enough before the storm arrived for me to put a big live minnow on my old faithful bobber tackle and drop it over the side to work along the bottom, 12 feet down.

The sun was blotted out and savage lightning slashed and made us wince. Far out on the big bay we spotted a solid curtain of rain advancing towards our boat. By now it was almost as dark as night, and just before the rain engulfed us a bolt of lightning hit a tall pine on the height of land, sounding a curious sizzle that hung in the air. Then, just before the hissing, icy rain hid all from view but a small area around the boat, we saw the tree lurch and topple slowly forward, like a frail old man starting a courtly bow.

The rain was a hissing hammer on our bowed heads as we stood in the boat and let it run in sheets down our slickers. So torrential was this sharp summer storm that it quickly filled the lower hull and rose over the floorboards to chill our feet in their soft boat-moccasins.

I looked over the side in abject misery and was surprised to see my bobber make a swift lunge under, with that unmistakable slap that denotes a good fish. Later it would bump the scales down to the 7-pound mark, but right then I was in the middle of a bonanza and too busy to care, as I hauled in five more fine, fat walleye. Before the storm abated, the sky lightened and the sun at last came out, hot and bright, to raise tendrils of vapor from our drenched gear. We fished on while getting the boat back into shape, but not one more walleye hit, although I did hook and land a 12-pound pike.

The important part of the tale is that the spot happens to be a famous walleye fishing hole for late evening and night sessions. It was midday when those fish came on feed, obviously responding to what was, in effect, night fishing conditions. Far from being an isolated incident, it is only one of any number of times that I have enjoyed a sudden upsurge of walleye strikes to match a darkening sky from a swift-moving summer storm.

TACKLE

Since walleye are pure and simple predators, angling for them follows a pretty straightforward system of live-baiting, plug-casting, spinning, or trolling. They are not good fighters and standard spinning, spincasting or baitcasting gear is normally used.

The type of tackle chosen depends then upon what system is being used and what technique is adopted. For most of my walleye angling I use standard spinning tackle with 8-pound-test nylon line, and I find that this works well for just about every circumstance.

Since these fish are often found in the same waters as the sharp-toothed pike or muskies, a short, steel wire leader is sometimes used next to the lure. This has double value in that it prevents damage to the

One of a school of walleyes, feeding beside a deep rocky ledge, attacks a deep-diving plug bumbling slowly by. Walleyes, closely related to the perch, have a special magic all their own and are keenly sought after by many anglers.

Lunch is coming ashore: On a smooth rock of Canada's pre-Cambrian Shield country, the author reaches out to grasp the line and to slide a plump walleye out of the water. In this fertile fishing region far to the north, every cast brings a hit, until the guide calls out that there is enough for lunch.

Two anglers have moored their boat in a fine hole, where the walleye gather in the area between the fast water and the still deep water close inshore. A sure way to catch a fish is to stillfish beside a steep slide of rock, with a live minnow worked down near the bottom, or plugs and spinners run deep.

leader and allows for the easy changing of bait. However, I never use metal next to my bait hook when using live fish as bait and I have never found that walleye's teeth are much danger to nylon line.

Hook sizes should match the baits used and since walleye have big mouths and hearty appetites, minnows as big as 6 or 8 inches long will be found effective in places where larger fish are expected. With a fish of this length a fairly large hook is needed, but a 1/0 size is sufficient.

All standard plugs and spinning lures are used for walleye, but again the type used depends a great deal on the technique. In most cases the fish are found deep, and because of this I prefer to use deep-diving plugs that will zoom down and scratch bottom by nature of their design, rather than those requiring the aid of added lead.

Jigs and other lead-head bottom bumpers can be counted as top walleye lures and some of the biggest are caught each year with a Doll fly or a lure of a similar pattern.

Spinning lures such as the Mepps are deadly under certain circumstances, but have a basic disadvantage in not working well on the bottom. However, there is nothing better than a good vibrating spinner for fishing the cutoff or drops beside a steep-shelving rock, and the Mepps No. 3 has long been my standard for walleye fishing under these conditions.

About the toughest proposition in catching these fish is getting them into the boat. They are long for their weight, and since they are armed with sharp spines on their backs and gill covers, it is unwise to attempt to lift them out by hand. Since they also have very sharp teeth you can't grab them by the mouth as you can a bass. Since the meat is too good to spoil by using a gaff, the best bet is a landing net; and for the larger fish it is best to use a wide-mouthed unit like the one I suggested earlier for use on carp.

Incidentals of tackle include long-nosed pliers to keep fingers clear while hooks or lures are being removed, and a stringer on which the fish can be kept alive in the water till the time comes to prepare them for the table.

Walleye tackle then, is fairly standard. It is the system of fishing for walleye that plays the important part in making the angler.

WALLEYE TACTICS

There are three major styles used in catching walleye. These are stillfishing with bait, casting a lure, and trolling some suitable rig behind a moving boat. They are all effective methods for walleye, and the well-rounded angler will master each of them. I find it difficult to understand why an angler will sneer at stillfishing and then go out and troll all day. I can understand on the other hand, a man preferring to cast, for this is a delight in itself. But I strongly advise the learning and use of all methods, for this, in the end, makes a better angler.

Angling techniques used for walleye are those used to take predatory fish, so while fishing for this species we can expect to take other predators, from pike and bass to such low-life creatures as bowfin and gar. For example, late one night, while trolling the medium shallows with a diving plug, I walloped into three nice lake trout in a row, which gave the evening rather a zestful touch.

But we have covered how to find the fish. Let us now look at the different systems and where they can best be applied.

Stillfishing

Stillfishing usually means a form of live-bait angling in one spot. Anywhere that walleye are known to be located, a properly set bobber rig, sliding leger, or similar system, can be an effective way of making a good catch. This works especially well at the bottom of rapids when searching for the fish, and of course, when walleye are gathered against a dam in spring, their concentration makes stillfishing highly practical.

There is, however, a mobile form of stillfishing that covers the water and is especially valuable when in an unknown area. It is simply a matter of drifting down an area with stillfishing gear out and a live minnow bumping along the bottom.

If the water is fairly shallow (which is rare), a bobber rig can be used; if deep, a slider-bobber, or better still a plain hook and clinch sinker. This last is easily prepared. All that is needed is a hook tied to the end of the line, with a sinker clamped on 2 feet or more up from the hook.

The hook is baited through both lips of a live minnow and dropped over the side on the upwind edge of a likely spot. The boat drifts down, covering the water, and all the angler needs to do is to make sure that the minnow is swimming along close to the bottom. Of course, to drift like this requires some breeze, or a strong enough current to keep the boat moving. In a strong wind it is often necessary to use a heavier sinker, and sometimes, to let out more line. The bite is usually signalled directly to the tip of the rod and then it is best to give a little slack and set the hook when the fish moves off.

In one place where I fish, the walleyes come inshore along a featureless beach which provides no way of knowing where they will school. Since the waters are of pretty uniform depth, this drift/still-fishing is by far the best technique to use, certainly superior to the method generally used there, which is to go out, drop anchor and sit, hoping that the fish will happen along.

Drifting with live bait is an accepted saltwater fishing method, and will take just about every type of freshwater fish that feeds on the type of bait used. Not too long ago, on a winter fishing trip to South Carolina's famed Santee-Cooper waters, I drifted down a 20-foot-deep channel picking off big white crappies with ultralight spinning gear and small live minnows, when what I thought was a thunderbolt hit the bait. It proved to be a glorious largemouth black bass of 6 pounds. So make sure that this technique is an active part of your angling repertory.

Casting

The use of plugs, spoons, spinners and all kinds of artificial, or natural-and-artificial baits is a well-known part of walleye fishing, but what is less well-known is that it is most important to run the baits at the slowest possible pace.

Jim Kennedy, one of the best baitcasting anglers I know, taught me a lesson I have never forgotton. I was out casting for walleye with him on the end of an island one time, and while I tossed out live minnows to swim around the end of the island, Jim rigged up a red-head/white-body pikie-minnow sinker-plug and added a slug of lead just in front of the lure. He then threw out, allowed the lure to sink to the bottom, let it rest a while, and then began to nudge it back an inch at a time over the bottom. He moved it so slowly that there could have been only minimum action from the lure, but he was outstandingly successful in catching the walleye on that shoal. He not only caught more fish than I did, but every one of his was bigger.

Jim knew that walleye won't bother with a fast-moving bait and this is an important point. The best plugs and baits are those that can be fished slowly along the bottom without too many snags occurring. One of my personal favorites for this is the egg-shaped Arbo-Gaster, a plug with an extended diving vane that drives the lure down deep and acts as a guard against snags. I own one about nine years old that has rumbled along so many rocky shoals that the front edge of the diving vane has burred, and I couldn't begin to count how many walleye it has taken.

To fish this lure for walleye, when using the casting method, I toss it well past my chosen spot, reel swiftly to make it dive to the bottom, and then bring it along on a slow retrieve, just fast enough to bring out the killing vibrations. At that, I still work my lure faster than Jim, but it is a system and pace that better suits my angling temperament. And it certainly works well.

Weedless, weighted lures such as the jigs, and those eel or worm combinations favored in fishing for southern largemouth bass are just fine for this bottom-hugging, creeping style of fishing, and should be in more general use. They closely resemble northern leeches and small non-parasitic lampreys that most fish enjoy.

But the lure itself is less important than what it can be made to do. Revolving spinners are handy, but the larger bottom-baits take the bigger fish every time.

Trolling

In some northern walleye waters, trolling has become almost the sole method for many anglers. In one way this is good, but in another it is subject to criticism. The top-notch angler who understands the game can catch many walleye by trolling, for he knows the waters, runs his lure consistently through all the best places, and so spends more time with his lure in front of fish than does the caster or stillfisher. In this case, trolling can be one of the most deadly of all the systems in use.

But then there is the other angler, the one who I feel is wrong. This fellow accepts trolling as a good angling method and gets out on the water and burns up a lot of gas. It is an unfortunate fact that all too often he trolls in places where there is little chance of catching fish, but without ever knowing it, because every now and then he runs over productive water and catches a fish. Although he seldom realizes the truth, this angler — and there are many like him — has rejected the essential fact of skill, in favor of the overworked angling god, Luck.

Yet, for the troller who cares to take the trouble to work in the proper places, the rewards can be great, and this is probably one of the reasons why so many beginning anglers who go out with a good guide bring in a first-class catch. The *cheechako* (Siwash word for tenderfoot) doesn't know what's going on, but almost without thinking, the experienced guide will run the *cheechako's* lure in all the best places at exactly the right pace. Once again, it boils down to knowing *where* and *how*, according to prevailing conditions.

Earlier in this chapter, we dealt at length with the importance of selecting where to fish, and it should be obvious that when we get down to trolling, there are definite places to start and a number of things to work out.

Once, while fishing a turbulent water, I found the base of a rapids crammed to the brim with hungry pike. I stood on the edge and cast every poor lure I had been given over the previous months, without finding one that they would not hit. I knew there had to be walleye in the lake, and since we urgently needed some for dinner, I tried all kinds of swiftly sinking lures in an attempt to get under the pike to the walleye. But when I lost my third 4-pound pike to another pike, I realized that even if I did hook what I wanted, it would be stolen by those lean and frantically hungry pike. So I took the car-top boat off the rack and pushed off to look for a walleye hole.

On the other side of the lake, about half a mile away, I saw a lovely, sleek rock running along for about 300 yards. So I rowed across, and found to my delight a beautiful drop-off falling down to a twenty-foot depth with gravel and broken rock on the bottom. I rowed up to the top end, threw over the stern a diving, wobbling plug, and then started back, rowing the boat parallel to the reef of rock and about 10 feet off. My spinning rod stuck up over the stern and I had one of my size 14 boat-moccasins placed firmly on top of the butt.

That proved to be a smart trick, for about a quarter of the way along, the rod bent with a no-nonsense wallop, and when I dropped the oars and grabbed the butt, I found that I had *hooked* an eating-sized walleye.

Tossing the fish into the stern with the thought that I had got *my* dinner, I rowed back again to the start and repeating the manoeuvre, came down again seeking fish for the other two men in the party.

Sure enough, at the same spot, there came a similar belt on the rod, and into the boat came another eating-sized fish, the twin of my first at about 1½ pounds. At this point I thought it might be sensible to try a little casting, but it didn't work, so back I went again and rowed the lure through the obvious hotspot.

This time I hit the fish about 40 yards further down the reef. It was obviously from the same school, for when I tossed it back in the

On the rocky side of a Manitoba lake a group of anglers takes it easy while the scent of frying walleye wafts from the fire. Few moments are more satisfying.

stern with the other two, it looked as if I had captured triplets. So this time, instead of going all the way back to the start, I rowed back about 40 yards, threw out and came down once more, and hooked the fourth fish, exactly the same size, a further 20 yards down the reef.

Knowing that my companions liked walleye as much as I do, I kept this up, until I had taken three fish for each of us, on the basis that what we wouldn't eat for dinner we could have for breakfast with bacon and hush puppies. Although I didn't catch two fish in exactly the same spot, I did catch them all at the same distance out from the reef. The school, all fish of the same size, were running and feeding in a regular pattern up and down the rocky shelf.

So when trolling for walleye, remember that they are a school fish that stay with their own size class. They may move from one place to another, but their route follows a path suited to their cool-depth requirements in which the light factor is acceptable. If you keep this in mind when you choose a trolling run, all that is then needed to ensure success, is the choice of a lure that will wriggle close to the bottom, with a minimum of snagging, a maximum of action, and the ability to work at the slowest possible trolling speed.

Walleyes are not hard to catch if you know where to look for them, and it is my sincere hope that now you do.

10 🐟 Pike

The North American members of the pike family *Esocidae* are game fish ranging in size from the 10- to 12-inch little pickerels up to the 20 to 40 pounds of the northern pike, and the potential 100-pound weight and 7-foot length of the mighty muskellunge.

Of the five species, two — the redfin and the grass pickerel — are small fish that provide small sport. A third, the chain pickerel, is a larger fish and is the object of widespread angling. Finally, the giant pike and muskellunge provide two of the most challenging hunts in our fresh waters.

There is a great deal of emotion involved in fishing for the big members of the family, for these are the predators supreme. Both pike and muskies are extremely fast swimmers and powerful fighters, and are among the few fish in the world that can give back a full-face stare from unwinking eyes set in a flattened face. Little wonder that one of the oldest names for the pike is *Luce*, or waterwolf.

It is completely unscientific to attribute human emotions to a fish, but it is difficult to be scientific when discussing the big pikes. They can send a shiver down a human's spine when they press home an attack on a lure or a fish. They are not fierce killers in our sense of the term, but it is quite easy to fit some with this description.

I once met with one of these on a large northern lake. Some friends and I were fishing at the foot of a rapids and the lean and

A superb 54-pound muskie from Eagle Lake in Ontario. Note that a big muskie like this is not unduly deep, thus retaining its speed and fighting ability far better than the large specimens of some other species. This is less than half the weight of the largest muskie recorded.

savagely hungry pike hit every lure we threw no matter how big, although the average weight of the fish was only 6 to 7 pounds. They were speedy and hard-fighting, but we wanted to try for larger fish, so we left for the deeper waters of the big bay.

The first casts there produced fish around the same size, so I suggested to one of my friends that he drop his red and white spoon right at the top of a big log, a likely resting place for a big fish. He did this, and there was a swift hit by a pike weighing around 10 pounds. It boiled to the surface, then dived and Harvey's rod slammed down, as a bigger pike grabbed the 10-pounder and took off with it at a frightening speed. Suddenly the monster let go, and as the hooked fish swam up weakly to the surface, it came after it and grabbed it again. Harvey kept up a steady pressure and jiggled the rod so that the big fish would keep biting down to kill the smaller pike while he brought it to within range of the gaff. Just short of the gaff, the pike let go once more and the strain on the line shot the mangled small pike right to the boat, where I got hold of it swiftly with the gaff, wrenched it off the hook and threw Harvey's lure out, yelling for him to work it back and forth to see if the big fish would hit it.

I sat breathlessly, holding the dead pike out over the water, clear of the boat to keep the blood and slime off my clothes, and waited for the take on Harvey's spoon. The giant pike took all right, but not what I expected. There was a tremendous boil by the boat and the pike came head out of the water, grabbed the fish I was holding, and cruised off with it set across its massive jaws. The big fish weighed possibly 30 pounds, and I sat in the boat quivering like a jelly and counting my fingers.

I received quite a bit of gentle ribbing about my "maneater" pike, but I heard that two weeks later at the same place an angler who had filletted a few pike, was sluicing his knife to wash off blood and slime, when a pike attacked and clamped down on his hand and the knife handle. The man jerked his hand back and flipped a 7-pound wriggling pike several feet up the bank.

THE PIKE SPECIES

The pikes are freshwater species found in the northern parts of North America, of Asia and of Europe. They prefer cold water, feed well on all but the coldest days and, in the case of the northern pike and the chain pickerel, are popular game for ice fishermen.

There are five species of pike in North America, all so alike that they are classified as members of the single genus *Esox*. The angler can learn how to tell them apart by such characteristics as color, size and scale pattern, but it would take a keen eye and more than a smattering of science to correctly separate a collection of immature specimens of the five North American species.

All the pikes are pure predators, built to hunt, catch and eat other fish, as well as a range of aquatic life from frogs and baby muskrats to full-grown ducks. From the pike's earliest moment of life it is a case of kill or be killed, which makes these fish difficult to raise in hatcheries, as even the baby fish eat their weaker, slower or less determined brothers and sisters. It is an incredible fact that a five-inch-long pike will swallow another pike of the same size.

The development for a life of fast hunting can be seen in every part of these fish, especially in the soft, rayed fins that give superior swimming power, as compared to the more rigid, bristling fins of the bass and perch.

The dorsal fin is set so near the tail that it acts with the tail and the anal fin to provide the sudden snap of power that is the final part of the pike's attack. You could say that the position of the dorsal fin increases the *propeller* surface area, and the sudden bend-and-flick action used by an attacking pike provides the extra speed that spells doom for the victim. In this final stage of the attack, a pike can slash in so quickly that it seems to the human eye to be little more than a blur.

If the attacking motion of the pike is like a hurled spear, then the tooth-filled mouth represents a grim portcullis from which few victims escape. The mouth is shaped like that of a duck, and the teeth are of different shapes and types. The long canines at each side grab and puncture, and row upon row of small hook-like teeth set in the roof of the mouth, facing back down the throat, lessen the chance of a prey fish escaping.

As a rule, the color and pattern of these fish provides them with camouflage, and it often varies with the habitat. Pike in the weedy, shallow bays are quite green with lighter ovals on their backs and sides, so that the fish blends into the background. Muskies in similar places are usually heavily striped in an excellent system of camouflage, differing from muskies in large, open bodies of water, where they are usually far more plain.

The bigger fish in this predatory family are solitary in nature, a useful — in fact, necessary — trait in species that attack and eat their own kind. About the only time these fish pair off or school is when spawning, and the large female northern pike often follow this act by grabbing and eating one of the smaller males in attendance.

The smaller members of the tribes, however, seem to be able to live fairly close together at times. After spawning is over, it is quite common to hit pike after pike in a limited area, and chain pickerel appear to live fairly close to each other. I have often waded around a lagoon, casting slim silver spoons for chain pickerel, and caught a dozen or so in a small area of water. This does not mean that I ran into a *school* of chain pickerel, but into individuals feeding quite close to each other.

Pickerels

The three smaller members of the North American pikes are called pickerel, a word used centuries ago in England to describe a small northern pike. They are the redfin pickerel, the grass pickerel and the chain pickerel. The first two are very small fish with limited angling appeal. They are known as the *little pickerels* and are often mistaken for immature fish when caught. It is impossible for the layman to tell the two apart, as the physical points of distinction only show in dissection.

Some scientists argue that the two fish are one and the same, and are nothing more than western and eastern varieties of the same species. Others insist that there are two well-defined species involved, and they support this argument with data on differences found in autopsy. The debate matters little to the angler, as the fish involved offer little in the way of sport, having a full growth of only 14 to 15 inches in length.

Redfin Pickerel

The redfin ranges from the Atlantic drainage system of Quebec and the upper St. Lawrence River, down through the coastal plains of Maryland and Georgia to Florida. It extends west from Florida to the Gulf States. It has a preference for the remote backwaters where, through its scrappy nature, it gives some sport on light cane-pole gear. Owing to its small size, it has not been widely planted.

Grass Pickerel

The grass pickerel is considered by some to be a western form of the redfin, being found westward from the St. Lawrence River to the tributaries of Lake Ontario and Lake Erie, out to the Appalachian drainage, into eastern Kentucky, Tennessee and Alabama. It is found in Ohio, Michigan, Indiana and Illinois and where its range touches that of the redfin, the two are believed to intergrade. This fish too has not been planted because of its small size. If taken within the area occupied by northern pike it is usually dismissed as being an immature member of that species.

Chain Pickerel

This fish is not one of the lesser breeds but a fully qualified sports species that is eagerly pursued in most of the places where it is found. Exactly pike-like in shape, it is popularly identified by black chain-like markings covering its green-bronze body, and by the fact that it grows to a possible weight of 9 pounds. One of the best aids to identification for the layman is the fact that it is usually found in regions where the larger pikes are rare, or limited in distribution. This range extends from Maine to Texas and north to some parts of the Great Lakes. It is most common in roughly the centre of the area mentioned and on one trip to South Carolina's Santee-Cooper system, I found these fish biting well during cold weather that had sent most game species off feed.

The chain pickerel provides great sport on light tackle, and for angling purposes, the only difference between this and the larger pikes is size. They hit slim silver lures, plugs and fly-rod poppers, and go hurtling up into the air when the hook strikes home. They take live bait on most types of rigs, and being active right through the winter months, are an important species for ice fishermen.

Chain pickerel fishing is actually a miniature form of northern pike angling, with all the methods used for the larger species forming excellent catch techniques for the smaller. For this reason, I advise the reader to follow the techniques that I later suggest for pike. The only change needed is scaling down tackle and baits to a size suited to these smaller fish.

Pickerel Identification

The chain pickerel stands out vividly because of the chain-like pattern covering the body, but while this works well in identifying mature fish, it is less valuable in separating immature pickerel from the young of the northern pike and muskie. For this difficult job we must take a look at the scale pattern on the cheeks and gill covers.

All three pickerel species have fully scaled cheeks and gill covers, whereas the larger pike do not. The chain markings also separate the chain pickerel from the "little pickerels."

Northern Pike (Esox Lucius)

The northern pike is the senior member of the tribe and one of the most glorious species for which we can angle. I get a feeling with this pike that just doesn't happen with any other freshwater fish. It grows big and tough and is the fastest of our freshwater species. When it gets really big, it can become as difficult to hook and land as the smartest carp that ever swam away with your tackle.

It is unfortunate that this fish has never been given full marks in the angling literature of this continent, and has been so neglected that few people are aware of the sport awaiting them.

There's a place about 35 miles from my home where people go every spring to fish for the pike in the shallow waters of a vast bay. Most of the anglers are content to catch pike of any size and to take home a catch of fish averaging 6 or 7 pounds. Yet in that bay I know there are monsters, fish that will weigh up to and over 35 pounds, and not one person in a thousand sets out seriously to get one of those big fish.

I have mentioned this any number of times while waiting for my boat and bait and have been met with blank stares. The anglers are after pike, and they row offshore a few hundred yards, drop an anchor and then put over a live bait to accept in docile fashion any foolish little fish that chances on it. True pike angling has never been a part of the North American scene, the fish has never been held in high regard, and it is difficult to explain that there is more to the game.

The most expert pike fishermen in this world are found in the British Isles, where pike fishing for many years has been about the only way most anglers could enjoy pursuing a *big* fish. All the salmon waters are costly. There are only limited species, and far too many anglers for the available waters. So an intensive type of pike-fishing technique has grown, and many anglers spend all their fall and winter angling-time pursuing the very big fish. This accounts for the secret of their success — they specialize.

In most of the places here where pike are caught there is often local contempt for these fish, often because the angling is done in small lakes, where an excess of numbers has produced a reduction in the size of the fish. These places are regarded as suitable for beginners or for people who have never caught pike, and are often given some name like "Hammerhandle Lake." I took two small boys into one such lake a few years back and set them up with ultralight spinning tackle to fish for the pike which I knew averaged around 4 pounds. The boys nearly went out of their minds with delight as they hooked fish after fish on 2-ounce rods and 4-pound-test line, and enjoyed dazzling acrobatics and sizzling runs. I don't know how many they caught, because we put them all back, but it was well over 50 each, and they were tired and delirious with joy when they finished.

A day like that can be tremendous fun and teaches kids a great deal about casting, working a lure, and playing a fish, and when I suggested the next day that we fish elsewhere for pike, the kids were ready and willing to spend quite a bit of time in this quest. So even the stunted pike in the smaller places can provide sport of a rather special nature. The very big specimens are another story. The size reached by northern pike is one of their most exciting qualities from the standpoint of angling, yet most fishermen settle for fish of a small average size, when lunkers that reach 50 pounds are waiting to be caught.

The largest known pike, which I believe weighed 73 pounds, was caught sometime during the 1700's in Loch Ken, in Kenmure, Scotland, a game-fish area where the pike is not even called a fish. I cannot vouch for this weight, but there is no doubt that the Loch Ken pike was a monster, as the skull and body were examined in 1910 by an eminent British authority, Tate Regan. He took measurements and reported that the fish was 8 inches across the back. The stuffed specimen was subsequently lost. Then in 1952 a curious angler rummaged around the Castle Kenmure seeking the remains of the pike and duly found the head in a chicken run. The width of the jaws was so great that there is little doubt that this was a monster pike.

In 1920 an angler fishing in Ireland landed another monster, a pike of 53 pounds that was recorded and weighed most carefully before being mounted for posterity. Any number of fish above 40 pounds have been taken recently, in Europe and in North America.

It would be fair to say that the average pike caught weighs around 3½ pounds. A first-class fish is anything over 20 pounds, and there are lone fish swimming around that will make that 53-pound fish look small.

Distribution and Habitat

Northern pike are distributed through all northern parts of the northern hemisphere, where they can enjoy their preference for the cooler waters. Found across all northern Europe and Asia, pike are concentrated in North America through most of Canada to Alaska, and from New York to Nebraska. This species is not native to the south and has only been planted in places within, or close to, the natural range. It is rather interesting to relate that Ontario, which must be considered prime northern pike range, has a number of places (usually highland country), where the species is absent, and these form pockets surrounded by superior pike-fishing waters.

The preferred habitat of the northern pike is shallow, weedy places such as bays and lakes fringed with reeds and water weeds. This preference is so marked that in the north, on open, rocky lakes with an edge of reeds or a shallow bay with weedy edgings, it is almost certain that a lure flashed through close to the edge will produce a strike from a lurking pike. The experienced angler becomes so aware of this that it becomes almost automatic to pitch out a big spoon on sighting this natural habitat.

This, however, is not all that is involved. In many very large northern lakes weed growth can be sparse, and the pike in these lakes tend to lurk beside rock ledges, by the side of shoals, or indeed any place that provides a suitable shelter from which to launch an attack. Water and air temperatures also play important roles in the choice of location.

When the spawning urge comes in spring, pike move towards the edges of the lakes, the marshes and the feeder creeks, sometimes moving under the ice towards the chosen place. They spawn and leave the fertilized eggs in the reeds, and weedy shallows and even flooded marsh lands. It is most exciting to observe huge pike working their way up some tiny little creek during this period, and quite a few very big fish fall victim to a poacher's spear or gaff each year.

After the spawning act, the pike break up and seek the slightly deeper waters where there is suitable cover, and at this time they will often go on a wild feeding spree. As the waters warm, the bigger pike tend to drop out to deep waters and even the smaller ones move to water of a more desirable temperature. In the full heat of summer very big pike are known to go down into water as deep as 60 feet and more, where they prey on big whitefish and suckers.

This deep-dwelling habit of the big fish helps to explain the fact that relatively few very large northern pike are caught each year. It will vary according to the locality of course, but there is little doubt that the giant northern pike of the southern edge of the range are seldom around *fishable* spots at a time when most anglers are out and active. Pike and muskies are somewhat similar in their behavior patterns and a later open season for muskies in some Great Lakes waters has enabled the fish to be caught in greater size and numbers in the months of October and November, during which time they were in available waters. The biggest pike, then, should be sought at every available moment outside late spring and summer when they stay in deep water, for in the fall, as the waters cool, the big fish move in again and seek a comfortable hole, from 12 to 30 feet down.

These holes become winter quarters for most of the big fish, but as ice covers the lakes and the water clears, many northern pike once more move into the shallows where they hunt perch and other school fish amidst the weeds. In many northern regions this provides an ice-fishing sport of almost numbing intensity, with artificial decoys flashed in water that may be no more than 5 feet deep, to lure a lurking pike to charge in and grab a struggling live bait. Since the water for this must be perfectly clear, the angler in his dark hut can peer down into a magical green world of nature and see every movement of the ensuing drama.

At this point, detailed data on how to catch pike might be expected, but the northern pike and the muskellunge are so similar that it will be a space-saver to first take a look at the muskie and then do a tackle and technique roundup for both these big pikes.

Muskellunge (Esox Masquinongy)

The northern pike is exciting quarry, but his mighty cousin, the muskellunge, is magnificent. This is the biggest of the great pikes, a fish of incredible power and speed that, in my opinion, fights twice as hard, pound for pound, as the pike. Add to this the fact that the muskie grows to weights in excess of 100 pounds, and it is easy to see how this fish got its gilt-edged membership in the game-fish lists. There's a dash and vigor to the fight of a muskie not found even in the Atlantic salmon. Even the largest muskie are incredibly fast and the medium sizes, as I found out many years ago, are startling.

I had accepted an invitation from a government agency to catch muskies for their camera chief, as they had received a request for film footage of muskies jumping. It would be a brave fisherman indeed who would promise to catch muskie on assignment in open waters, and I only accepted because I knew of a suitable location, a rearing area where muskies were grown for planting in other waters. The fish would be plentiful and the right size for some first-rate aerial acrobatics. On the day arranged I set off from the dock in a canoe, closely followed by the camera crew, who were comfortably set up on a flat-bottom scow fitted with a small outboard motor.

My first choice of location was on the bend of the river where a deep hole nestled close to the weed beds, but my first cast with a deep-running plug produced a largemouth bass. Moving from this place, I spotted a super-muskie setup, a shallow bay on the river receding away into deep water. So I moved in, waited for the cameraman to give the OK, and spun a cast into the deep part.

As my plug worked out of the deep water and started its run across the shallow, a muskie of about 9 pounds sliced up, hit and then flew straight up in the air in a curving clean jump that made all our hearts leap with appreciation when we saw it on film (by sheer luck the cameraman had switched on to record the cast and was right on top of the fish when it came out).

The fish barreled into the deep water, bored, sulked for just a second and then came flying out once more, hit the water, and putting on speed, rushed straight at my canoe. It went under the canoe, came up the other side and jumped clean over the boat, flinging away the lure, and landing safely and free on the other side.

And there I sat, soaking wet from the spray, with the tail treble of my plug caught over the side of my sunglasses. If I hadn't been wearing them, there was a good chance that I would have been hit right in the eye by one of the hooks. A fantastic episode, and one that leaves no doubt of the fighting fury of these fish.

Muskellunge then are prime quarry, and being bigger than the pike, are fish that must be treated with respect. Most of all, since they are not as common as most other North American species of game fish, the most rigid rules of conservation should be practiced by all anglers. I have never killed a muskie, although I have landed better than one hundred at the time of writing. I am told that they are good to eat, but I don't intend to find out if that is true. As far as I am concerned, this is one of the great angling game fishes of the world, and I take them off the hook with extreme care and put them safely back into the water. It may be that one day I shall land one so big that I will not be able to resist killing it for a trophy to hang on the wall, but I hope that I will have the sense of duty and the courage to resist the temptation.

I should add here that these remarks do not apply to a world's record, for under those circumstances the scientific and sporting value of the specimen would be too valuable to lose.

Distribution and Habitat

The muskellunge is native only to the waters of northeastern North America, including the Great Lakes region, the Ohio drainage, west to Lake of the Woods, Minnesota, Wisconsin, Michigan and down through Pennsylvania to Tennessee and Georgia in the TVA system. It is strictly confined to North America, where there are a small number of subspecies, and one fish — the tiger muskie — that is strongly suspected of being a hybrid between the muskie and the northern pike.

There are three subspecies of muskellunge, the Great Lakes, the Ohio or Chautauqua, and the tiger or northern which may be simply a pike-muskie crossbreed.

From the practical angling viewpoint these classifications mean

Lancing through a clump of water lilies, a muskie opens its savage mouth to engulf a fleeing bait fish. Found in strictly limited areas around the Great Lakes, the muskellunge is the highest prize of all freshwater angling. It is a swiftly moving predator that will attack and eat its own kind. A tackle buster, known to grow to over 100 pounds, the muskie provides fishing filled with a special excitement that few other sports can match.

It pays to take care when unhooking a muskie, even as small a one as that shown here, which was caught by the author in a thickly weeded bay. To remove the hooks without damaging the small fish, the author has wedged its mouth open with a gag, a spring-loaded device that allows hooks to be removed without hands coming in contact with those wicked teeth.

Big pike and muskies can be tough to handle by the side of the boat. They often come in quietly, and when they see the boat they begin a boiling, raging fight and frequently escape. This wary angler was prepared for this sudden tearing battle; note how his rod is angled to minimize the strain on his gear.

nothing, and might even form a basis for confusion if people attempt to draw conclusions from available data. It might seem that the Great Lakes muskellunge grows bigger than the others, because all the largest fish recorded are of this type. The more sensible viewpoint however would suggest that the Great Lakes subspecies grows bigger because it lives in larger waters. The old rule of thumb, "big water — big fish," really *is* true.

Muskies are found in rivers as well as lakes, and in suitable streams they can survive very well and provide great sport. These river fish, however, never reach the size of the bigger specimens from the lakes, and the angler seeking to catch a record muskie would be wise to look for it in such well-known giant-muskie habitat as the Georgian Bay portion of Lake Huron, or the St. Lawrence River at its wide, deep points, where the muskies are known to be present.

One of the reasons why big muskies are great prizes is that they are not easy to find in open waters. Their range is small, compared to that of the northern pike, and even in those places where they are found, it is seldom in anything like the occasional concentrations of pike.

Quite a few muskellunge are caught each year by people fishing for other species and this always makes for a red-letter day. But anyone seeking to land a good specimen has to work hard. It is a question of first locating good waters, then selecting an area to fish, and lastly, going at it in a fury of concentration. There is no assurance of success and the man who intends to fish seriously for this magnificent species had better be a dedicated, serious-minded angler with an intense love of his craft.

Like the pike, muskies move into flooded marsh lands and weedy shallows to spawn in spring, usually around two weeks later than the pike. If the two species inhabit the same waters they tend to use the same spawning beds, with disastrous results to the baby muskies, for the earlier spawn of the pike means an earlier hatching and by the time the baby muskies turn out of the egg, the little pike are husky enough to eat them.

At spring spawning-time, muskies pair off and work their way inshore and up creeks and small streams where, like the pike, they sometimes run into two-legged predators armed with pitchforks or gaffs. After spawning, the fish drift off, hunting for a while in shallows and heading into deeper places as the water warms. In summer, some very large fish move away from the shoreline into very deep waters, and as the water cools again in fall, come inshore to feed on the suckers and whitefish gathering on the shoal grounds. The medium-sized fish are often found at this time in far shallower waters than those used by the pike at the same time, but the big muskies too have been known to roam and feed in shallow, weedy regions.

Identification of Pike and Muskellunge

Anglers who are used to catching both pike and muskies usually have little trouble in separating the two, and can often tell the species while the fish is still in the water. This comes with experience and is based on recognition of the color-key of background and pattern. For the inexperienced, however, the color pattern is a poor system unless the angler is lucky enough to have one of each species and can make a comparison. Location is an important factor, for in many places either one or the other is present. It doesn't pay to take chances on this indentification, for in many places muskies are protected by a closed season at a time when the pike is fair game.

Color

Both fish have classic color and pattern formations that are usually enough to set them apart, but this can vary from fish to fish and from one water to another, and where both species are in one spot they often tend to become more alike in looks.

The basic color and pattern of the northern pike is a green to dark green back and flanks, with lighter-colored bean-shaped spots scattered all over the body. In dark peat water this coloration is often most noticeable, whereas fish in open-shoal areas tend to be less vivid.

The coloration of the muskellunge usually consists of a light-colored body, with either bars of a darker shade or dark dots producing a faint speckling against the lighter background. Muskies, however, run through a considerable range of color and pattern styles according to location. It can be readily seen that when the extreme patterns of the two species are encountered, it can be a tough job to tell them apart in that excited moment of capture. Luckily, there are two sure-fire methods, based on scaling of the checks and gill covers, and the number of sensory pits on the under-part of the lower jaw.

Scaling

When dealing with the chain pickerel, it was noted that these smaller members of the pike family are fully scaled on the cheeks and the gill covers. The northern pike has a fully scaled cheek and only the upper part of the gill cover has scales. The muskellunge has only the upper half of the cheeks covered with scales.

All Pickerel: Cheeks and gill covers fully scaled.
Northern Pike: Cheeks fully scaled, upper part of gill covers scaled.
Muskellunge: Upper part of cheeks scaled.

Sensory Pits

These provide far more accurate identification than the scaling, because it is so easy to forget which has the scaled cheeks and which has not. The sensory pits are located underneath the lower jaw where these holes show up in vivid contrast to the sheer white of the jaw. The pike has ten and the muskellunge has from twelve to eighteen. I remember which is which by the following simple formula:

Pike, the *smaller* species, have the *smaller* number of pits, with *ten*. Muskies, the *larger* species, have the *larger* number of pits, with *twelve* to *eighteen*.

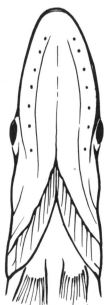

Pike

Muskie

Oddities

Pike and muskies come in such an array of color patterns that it is easy to take a well-marked fish and believe it to be some rare subspecies. In waters in which both pike and muskies are found there *is* the chance of coming up with a hybrid and since these fish are important to science it is a good plan to see that such a fish is handed in for full examination.

There is one type of pike, however, that leaves no room for doubt, and this is the silver pike, a mutant found in a number of lakes in the northeast. These fish breed with others of their kind rather than with plain northern pike and the results are very attractive fish indeed, having plain, dark-silver bodies with a fleck of gold on every scale. Most of the waters in which these fish are found have been classified, but there is always the chance of new waters being discovered, so it is important that any silver pike caught be reported, together with a pinpoint account of where the fish was caught. This fish is seldom heavier than about 10 pounds.

PIKE TACKLE

I grew up in good pike-fishing country and so I learned at an early age to enjoy these fish. I knew I needed special tackle to fish for pike, for about the only system I had for catching them was to suspend a live-bait fish from a substantial bobber the size of a small orange. The bait *and* the tackle *and* the hooks were all big, so I used stronger line, a bigger reel and a much stiffer fishing rod than in my general angling. These rods were usually plain hardwoods such as greenheart, hickory, or combinations of the canes, cut to about 8 feet long. They were stiff and heavy, but they did the job, and were powerful enough to throw the heavy baits we used in those days.

Today I still believe one of the best systems for taking pike and muskies is with a fairly large live-bait fish, and indeed I now extend this to include dead baits too. Whenever an angler intends to use big natural baits, he should go to bigger tackle to handle the load, and to have the power to set those big hooks that are needed to cover the bait.

The serious and dedicated pike fisherman *must* get into the specialized tackle field. He must use more powerful rods, reels and lines, and when the biggest fish are hunted, his tackle kit must be expanded to take in treble-hook rigs, large bobbers, and a fair amount of accessory gear. Since this will sound like an entirely new idea to most readers, let me explain my feelings about this aspect of taking on pike and muskie.

Small- and medium-sized pike of up to 10 pounds are among the easiest of all freshwater fish to catch. They are often little more than all mouth and swimming appetite and they will hit almost any lure or bait that the angler cares to send their way. I include the chain pickerel in this generalization, which may shock some people, but I have never found them at all hard to catch once they have been located. It is my opinion that this easy-catch status of the smaller pikes has put a kind of damper on thinking of pike fishing as one of the higher skills in angling. People tend to sneer, suggesting that any fool can get a pike.

The muskies are held in a different light, not because they are harder to catch than pike, but because they are so thinly spread around. Locating muskies becomes quite a chore, with the result that these fish are placed in a higher bracket than the pike. But make no mistake about this: where muskies are present in numbers, the small- and medium-sized ones are every bit as easy to catch as the small- and medium-sized pike. Few North American anglers recognize the truth which is that both the big pike *and* the big muskies fall into a different class, since both are difficult to locate, hard to make strike, and more than tough to handle, even on powerful gear.

So, pike tackle, whether for northern pike or muskies can be divided into two classes: the basic gear for those that just want to catch any pike, and the specialized tackle for people seeking the biggest fish. I am not suggesting that big pike cannot be landed on ordinary tackle, it is often done on ultralight tackle. What I am suggesting is that there is a much better chance of getting the big fish if much larger baits are used, *and this calls for a complete range of special gear.*

Basic Pike Gear

The angler who wants to catch a pike now and then, or who finds himself in a northern region where such fish are in good supply, can fish for these species using any basic tackle he possesses. I have caught pike on ultralight spinning tackle, my medium spinning gear, fly rods, cane poles, bobber-fishing rigs, even hand lines, and while there have been exciting moments, the pike so hooked have all been handled without any trouble.

The basic spinning or spincasting outfit that was picked earlier in the book is fine for pike and about the only change I would suggest in the tackle make-up, is the addition to the end of the line of a 6-inch steel leader when using lures, or the use of a hook-to-steel wire, when using live bait. This aids in guarding the line against those needle-sharp canine teeth in the side of the jaw and should be accepted as standard procedure for all pike fishing.

For the reader who might laugh at my using specialist tackle for connecting with the monsters of the pike family, I suggest the use of the basic tackle outfit with the baits scaled down in size. I use three weights of tackle for these fish, choosing a basic medium-action spinning rig for those waters where the fish have over-bred, a heavier steelhead-weight spinning rig for spinning with the bigger lures for larger fish, and then a special, lunker pike and muskie outfit designed to handle all big trolling jobs, plus the throwing of the largest possible live or dead baits available. So the specialist pike angling advice that follows may be adapted to suit the tackle you prefer to use.

Specialist Tackle

The important factor in selecting tackle for use on the biggest pikes is the weight of the baits to be thrown or handled by the gear. For the secret of specialist angling for big pikes is in the use of quite large live or dead baits, such as a 3 to 4-pound sucker. And no matter how well-versed one may be in the joys and sportsmanship of using light tackle, there is simply no way at all that these heavy baits can be worked, except with balanced tackle strong enough to handle the extra strain imposed.

Rods

The heavy surf-casting sticks made for saltwater spinning are valuable for use in this specialized game, if the angler has the quite expensive big reel to match the outfit. I have a big surf stick of hollow glass and substantial weight that I use with 20-pound-test nylon line on a surf-sized spinning reel. This combination is tough to beat, for it makes it possible to throw heavy baits quite a distance without any strain on the angler's skills. The easier casting that is possible with spinning tackle also allows for a more delicate entry of the bait into the water, with less of the solid slap that tends to quickly reduce the liveliness of a bait.

This tackle, however, is not cheap. The rod and reel together cost about $100, although it is possible to buy a specialist set of gear for about half that cost.

One of my favorite heavier live-baiting outfits consists of a surf rod of hollow glass, 9 feet in length, with a standard long hardwood handle on which is fixed a screw-reel fitting with double-ring tightener. These are pretty common rods, selling at about $15 and up, according to the quality of fittings and furniture used. I have two that I use. One, which gets 90 per cent of the work, is fairly light to use, yet will handle line up to 30-pound test and live and dead baits to 1½ pounds. The second rod is a monster that I'm keeping around for the time when I get the chance to pop out baits of 4 to 5 pounds for the world's biggest pike or muskie. It, too, is hollow glass and is big enough to handle 50-pound-test line.

For this heavier range of tackle the fisherman is faced with a rather unusual choice. The upper-sized spinning reels of good quality are pretty expensive, starting at around $50 and climbing up and up. I have a couple that I use and find them really worth their cost, if only for the way they permit gentle casting and the soft entry of a live bait into the water. These reels, of course, are for use with my heavier surf-casting spinning sticks.

Now, the unusual choice results from the fact that, pushing aside the expensive spinning reels, and looking at the star drag, free-spool, level-wind casting reels, you will find a big list of reels available at quite a moderate price. I'm not talking now of standard-sized bait-casting reels for use in bass fishing, jewelled delights which in recent years have climbed in price. What I mean is the slightly oversized reels used for light sea fishing, which have no refinements, except for their simple but effective free-spool, star drag, level-wind abilities. Built to accept around 300 yards of 20-pound-test line, these excellent reels can be bought new from about $16 to $30 or so. I have about a half a dozen of these and although at least three have been heavily used for ten or more years, they all still possess that bright, new look.

With this type of reel the angler must learn to cast well, for it is quite easy to get an overrun and a tangle if the spool is not properly thumbed. The low cost of these reels is made possible by the lack of automatic aids for casting and I, for one, highly approve. Used with a wooden-butt moderate-weight surf stick, one of these excellent models can do everything the high-cost gear can do, and all that is needed is for the angler to learn how and when to thumb the spool at the end of the cast.

Line

For all basic pike angling with standard tackle, nylon mono-filament, in a test to match rod and reel, is the obvious choice. For the heavier work, and most especially when using live bait, I prefer braided dacron of either 20- or 27-pound test. This may appear to some readers to be excessively strong, but it won't feel that way at all when the time comes to swing out a large live fish, or to troll a 14-inch-long plug behind the boat. Monofilament can be used of course, but I prefer the braided line when I am after big fish in shallow water and may wish to add dressing to my line to keep it afloat. For a middle range of baits, using my lighter surf-casting rod with star drag reel, I prefer 15-pound-test dacron which handles better with the lighter baits than does the heavier line. It is also more sporting and sensible — *in all but the weed-choked waters.*

Hooks

Because of the large size of the biggest pikes and their method of taking big baits, gang hooks (or treble hooks, as they are sometimes called) are quite often more suitable than single hooks. These gang hooks come in a full range of sizes and consist of high-quality single hooks joined in a triangular form, with one eye for attachment to the line and a solid braize joining the three hooks to make one tough unit.

Single hooks are perfectly suitable for small-and medium-sized baits and the size chosen should match the fish used. A minnow of 4 to 5 inches, for example, would call for the use of a size No. 1 or No. 2 hook. A 9-inch minnow is too big for the effective use of a single hook, and in this case the angler might use one gang hook nicked lightly through the back of the fish, just in front of the dorsal fin. For fish bigger than this, and for dead-bait work, it is sometimes necessary to use as many as four separate gang hooks. The reason is plain if one examines the way the big pikes take a bait. Unlike sharks, which slice off a hunk or bolt a fish whole in one gulp, the pikes turn in at the last minute, and grabbing the fish across the middle, shake it and bite it until assured that it is dead. They may remain still for a while just biting down on the bait, and this can seem like ages to the person on the other end of the tackle. Then the fish usually moves off, and the strike must be timed according to the hook arrangement used.

To ensure that at least one hook is in the mouth of the predator, as many as three gang hooks are used with the bigger dead baits. These are set up on a length of steel leader. The end hook is fixed in the cheek of the bait, the centre hook in the middle area, and the third up by the tail. Using this spread of hooks across the centre of the bait's target area, it is almost certain that at least one will be in a hooking position, and an immediate strike is given when the bait is taken.

If that big bait just discussed was *alive,* then a two-gang-hook rig would be used, with the tail or end hook fastened in the root of the pectoral fin, just behind the gill cover, and the second gang hook fixed lightly through the back, just in front of the dorsal fin. A lot of anglers strike on first contact with this arrangement (called snap-tackle), but it is better to wait until the fish has turned the bait before the hooks are set.

Leaders

Leader wire between the end of the line and a lure is always needed in this style of angling, and indeed the serious fisherman will find it necessary to arrange his own hook rigs for attachment to the wire. There are two reasons for making them up yourself. First, the use of different-sized baits calls for many variations in length and the number of hooks used, and secondly, there are no commercial rigs on the market (as far as I know) that will do the job.

The grim tooth-filled mouths of pike and muskies make a wire leader standard gear. For safety, anglers should keep their hands clear of the duck-shaped mouths. The proper technique for releasing a pike is shown here.

The best and simplest kit for making steel leaders and hook-to-wire rigs, consists of a pair of crimping pliers, a series of coils of different-test wire, and boxes of soft metal sleeves which are squashed flat for making the connections.

It only takes seconds to make up a plain single-hook-to-wire rig and for the sake of convenience, a plain wire loop is fashioned on the end opposite to the hook, to allow for simple attachment to the line snap. Here's how this plain hook-to-steel-wire leader is made:

A length of wire 14 inches long is cut off the main spool and a sleeve matching the gauge of the wire is slipped up a few inches. The end of the wire is then turned back on itself to make a loop and is then pushed into the metal sleeve. The loop is drawn small, the end hidden in the sleeve and the metal sleeve is crimped hard with the pliers at two opposing points. The procedure is repeated on the other end of the wire, but this time, before the loop is made, the wire is first pushed through the eye of the hook. Using different lengths of wire and the right-sized sleeves it is possible to make all kinds of different hook systems that will be as neat and as tough as anything obtainable in a store.

Accessories

Apart from the leader-making kit, spare wire, sleeves and a set of good wire cutters, there are a few modest items that can enhance our specialist big-fish tackle collection.

A pair of long-nosed pliers is standard for removing hooks, but for the long-jawed pike and muskie it pays to buy a special rig which operates clamp jaws by a sort of pistol-grip arrangement. With this I would advise the use of the wire gag, an ingenious gadget from England that springs the fish's mouth open so that hooks may be removed without danger to the angler.

Finally, I would suggest the use of a short blunt weapon to quickly and neatly finish off any fish the angler wishes to retain. It is better to carry a special tool for this purpose than to improvise. All that is needed is a short length of metal piping, with one end filled with lead and then covered with plastic or rubber hose. This accessory is known as a priest, because it ministers the last rites. A short, sharp chop with the weighted end to the top of the head and behind the eyes will kill any big fish.

Catching the Lunkers

There is little doubt that there are giant pike and muskie swimming around North American waters that will never be caught, because most anglers don't realize that there is a special art to catching very big fish.

Small- and medium-sized pike and muskie are easy to catch and they will strike at most lures and any live bait small enough to swallow. I have on occasion caught pike that were actually a shade shorter than the plug they hit, which should tell us part of the story.

The size of the bait plays an important role in deciding the size of the fish that will be caught. Really big pike and muskies simply do not accept small baits, because they are out of their prey-size-preference range. The heart of the matter is that you must use big baits to stand the best chance of getting the big fish.

The reason is this. Most predators, animals as well as fish, have a certain limitation of size in the prey they will pursue. Lions do not, as a rule, hunt small animals, but pick on substantial creatures, such as the zebra, which make fairly good meals for the pride of lions involved in the hunt. The energy gained from a killed zebra exceeds the energy expended in the hunt, and the lions make an "energy-profit." Wolves prefer fairly large animals, for they are pack predators with several mouths to feed, so the prey-preference is for deer, caribou and moose. Beaver are about the smallest prey-animals regularly killed by wolves, and even these are fairly big animals. Wolves have been seen hunting mice at times when the mice have been numerous, but this is comparable to a man snacking on peanuts.

Pike and muskies will attack and gobble small fish, but this is in the same category as the mice/peanut situation. A 60-pound fish couldn't make an "energy-profit" by hunting and feeding on small fish. A fish of this size needs something in the nature of a 12-pound fish, or several in the range of 4 to 5 pounds. Convincing proof of this was given when a new style of pike angling was started in England during the 1950's. It was a simple system of rigging a dead fish with a series of gang hooks and throwing it out to rest on the bottom of a hole where pike were known to roam. The anglers who started it reported that very big pike could be caught this way, as they seemed more than eager to pick a motionless fish off the bottom.

As more and more anglers turned to this leger system, it seemed that the innovators were correct and that this was a system for the taking of lunker pike. But when all the facts were gathered in, it was realized that it was not the method that was bringing home bigger fish, but the larger baits being used.

In England the cheapest and easiest way to get dead fish for bait is from the local fish store. And the cheapest fish available all year round is the saltwater herring, a fish that is about 1 foot long and weighs ½ to ¾ pound. Anglers were using herrings nearly double the size of the freshwater roach commonly used there as pike bait.

However, the important thing to remember is that during every week of the English pike-fishing season, monster fish are taken on massive dead baits fished in simple yet effective systems. I know there are fish in North America that can challenge the English pike in size, and of course there is the muskellunge known to reach weights in excess of 100 pounds. Since I have proven that these English dead-bait methods will take fish here, I suggest that the angler who turns to the big dead baits is in for some great sport.

Baits

One can get through a tremendous amount of dead baits in a season, so it is necessary to start collecting as early as possible in the fishing year. One of the reasons for having a very large deep-freeze unit in my home is that I need a way of keeping baits in good condition from the time they are caught until I'm ready to use them.

The best fish for pike and muskies is without doubt the sucker, the white and the northern sucker being about the best of the family. These fish are tough, brightly colored, properly shaped for drifting and casting, and have a range of size that is perfect for our purposes.

In my home area there is a big run of white suckers into the stream in spring, at which time they are taken in dip-nets, and by leger fishing a worm on the bottom of the river. I get as many as two to three dozen big ones in a day and never have any trouble trading the biggest ones for a number of the 10-inch fish caught by the dip-netters. I come out ahead on the deal, although I am sure that some of the dip-netters think I'm nuts to exchange big fish for those too small to eat.

During rainbow-fishing time I also get a supply of slim northern suckers, when these fish are foul-hooked by trout anglers spinning for the big migratory trout. I simply take a big plastic bag along to the stream and every time a cursing trout angler snags into a sucker, I just ask for it to be dropped into my sack.

When suckers are not available, look for any cheap and easily obtained fish — smelts, alewife, shad, lake herrings, whitefish (if you can spare such delicious fish), perch, or anything that shoals and can be caught in quantity. Of course you can *buy* whole fish, such as saltwater herrings or mackerel, but this is less satisfying than building up a stack of *free* fish caught or put aside from times of plenty.

With live bait it is necessary to buy or collect a supply of fish on the actual day of fishing. If there is a reliable bait dealer on hand, order and pay for a range of fish bigger than those ordinarily stocked, and in my experience, once the dealer recognizes that you really do want such big baits, there is little trouble in getting served. However, in the chill times of the year when the best fishing is enjoyed, live bait can be difficult, and since dead baits work just as well and at times much better I'd suggest the collection of dead baits as a more than useful standby for the times when live bait fish are unavailable.

Finally, a word of warning about live bait and conservation. Live fish should never be transported from one watershed to another, because of the danger of unwanted species being introduced into places where they might create harm. In many regions it is an offense to move fish around, and in view of the damage done in the past, it is wise to get live baits in the area where fishing is planned.

At times it is even possible to cause harm by moving fish as short a distance as 300 yards, if that distance is all that separates one water from another. I was once fishing a lake which was set on an island in a second, larger lake. I was catching lake trout with an ultralight spinning outfit, using freshly killed minnows from the big lake. The little lake, an excellent one, is quite separate from the main water, and for this reason my Indian guide was carefully killing each minnow before putting it on the hook. When we finished for the day, he carried the remainder of the bait back down and poured them out into the big lake, running them through his fingers as he did so.

"Look at that," he exclaimed, holding out a handful of tiny fish, "that's all it would take to ruin our little lake." And he showed a dozen or so small perch wriggling on the palm of his hand. The smaller lake would soon have been overpopulated if these small fish had been left in it.

Where to Fish

The best type of place to find both pike and muskies is in a big, shallow, weedy bay where there are some nice deep holes and reeds, or rocky shelves sliding down to deep water close by a big weed-bed.

In a river, the best place is at a deep bend where the water slows and there is a line of weeds or reeds to offer shelter for lurking. Another place is the shallow marsh-land area in which there are wide creeks with deeper holes scattered here and there, supplying the fish with a temperature change when needed. Pike and muskie water is so obvious that after a while it seems to scream FISH! and the angler thinks, *Aha! That's a good-looking piece of pike water.*

I react this way when I spot a beaver lodge built on the side of a clean rocky shore of a lake in the north country. To see a lodge is to stop and fish, for in the tangle of brush put in place by the beaver, minnows swarm by the thousands and so there are always predators hanging around the lodge. It might be a small bunch of big smallmouth bass, but very often it is a lone pike, and a really big one at that.

Once the fishing area has been selected, the specific fishing spot must be chosen in accordance with the weather, the temperature, the wind and the time of day. It is fairly safe to assume that the fish will not be in the shallowest waters on the coldest day, but that they will be a little deeper, perhaps down in some snug hole. It is sensible to suggest that they will not be in extremely shallow water on a burning hot day either, but will be away seeking cooler waters. However, on a warm sunny day in the cooler times of the year, the fish will roam into the shallows, and then it pays to fish in the area where the sun is shining brightly on the waters. I don't know why, but northern pike and muskies have a preference for these sun-bright zones on warm days in spring, fall and winter.

On these warm days during the cooler times of the year, the angler can fish all day with an excellent chance of success. He can also do so on the cold days when the deeper holes are fished. But when the weather gets warmer and the fish tend to feed less, the best time is from late afternoon until dusk, when the fish move closer to the weeds and, in some cases, the very big fish are right in the thickness of the growth by a deep area.

During the very hot weather it is sensible in the southern part of the pikes' range to leave them alone and concentrate on fishing for such species as bass and catfish. In northern water, though, conditions in midsummer may be perfect and I remember a trip where I enjoyed outstanding pike fishing on chill, rainy days when it was necessary to wear heavy underwear, big wool sweaters, and a parka under a rainsuit.

Pikes really do go off feed in the hot weather, and are liable to become out of condition and to put up a dispirited fight when caught. People used to believe that this was because they lose their teeth at this time of year and won't strike because their gums are sore. This is nonsense. All the fish in this family shed teeth, as this is part of their growth, but they shed teeth all the time and grow new teeth in a dental palate under the rim of the jaw. There are a number of reasons why the fish don't strike in very hot weather, but a sore jaw is not one of them.

Now that we have a starting idea of where to find the fish, let us take a look at some of the methods used to take the big fish.

Angling Methods for Lunkers

Most North American anglers troll lures of different types for the big pikes and believe this to be the final word for the species. It is certainly true that the very big muskies are usually taken this way, mostly by specialists who use big gear and big lures and troll with unshaking determination right on top of the shoals where the lunkers are known to feed. That in itself is a specialization, and further proof — if any is needed — that the angler seeking the lunkers *must* go at the game in a hard-nosed fashion.

However, most trollers fail to realize that they are not covering the water properly, and are not sending the bait into the proper places to take the big fish. Trolling, except in the case of highly qualified specialists, is a very poor way of covering water, and while I am told that the big pikes are not put off by the roar of outboard motors, I notice that it is the manufacturers of outboard motors that keep telling me this, and I'm inclined to believe that they may be prejudiced. Much of the time people out trolling are covering unproductive water, because the type of place occupied by the fish does not often allow for a boat to be driven through.

Most people troll because it is an easy way to spend the day. There's no strain and always the chance of catching something. But this system is overplayed and very much overrated as far as the average angler fishing for pike and muskie is concerned.

The styles of angling for big fish with the large baits that we have discussed are fairly simple, and consist of drift fishing, casting, or just simply legering a bait in a known hole.

But before getting down to the styles, we must take a look at the hook rigs needed, and since these are not available commercially, it will be necessary to make them up individually as I suggested on page 201.

For the large dead baits I use two different hook rigs, and for fishing large live baits I use a third. The dedicated pike man will be inclined to vary these three simple hook systems with ideas of his own. They should be regarded as the basic patterns from which to build.

The simplest rig is the one used with a large dead bait to be legered on the bottom, and it consists of three large gang hooks fastened on an 18-inch length of steel wire. The hooks are spaced according to the size of the bait used, with the end hook fastened in the head, the centre hook in the side, halfway between the tail and the head, and the last hook just in front of the tail. The rig is mounted so that the bait hangs head down.

For drift fishing and casting a dead bait, a three- or four-hook setup is best — three large gang hooks, and one large single hook that is used to close the mouth of the bait and to form a solid hold for the thrust of the cast, and for the retrieve. This is a tricky arrangement to get right and I have found that the best way to make it up is with two lengths of wire leader, with two gang hooks on one and a single gang hook on the other. The two leaders are then clipped onto a snap, together with the large single hook. If there is any trouble with the bait not holding on well, a turn of soft copper wire across the back in front of the dorsal fin can help.

The double-gang-hook rig for live baiting is simple, and consists of two hooks mounted on a single length of steel wire leader. The end hook is fixed firmly beside the mouth, and the other is snicked through the muscle of the back in front of the dorsal fin. Held up, the bait fish hangs head down, in the right position to swim naturally beneath a bobber. When used on a drift, this hook arrangement is reversed so that the fish follows the boat head first and is not dragged backwards and drowned.

Remember that these are big baits ranging from 10 inches to 18 inches long. Using a number of hooks provides a spacing, so that no matter where the fish is grabbed a hook should be in the predator's mouth, and the strike can be instantaneous. Some people prefer to let the fish swim off with the bait and to set the hook when a jiggling on the line suggests that the bait has been turned and is being swallowed. But there are two ways of looking at this. On the one hand, while pike and muskie are not generally shy, the big fish are pretty wary. If they are pricked by a hook, they might accept this as no more than being pricked by the sharp dorsal spines of a walleye or perch, or they might drop the bait. On the other hand, if you allow the fish to really get the bait down, you have a dead fish on your hands, for you will never get a couple of gang hooks out of the belly or throat without a fair amount of damage to the fish.

I usually refrain from advising a person when to set the hook since this is only worked out by experience. I set my own when I see fit and I allow other people to do the same. However, I would like to suggest that the person using these hook rigs try setting the hook on the take.

Drift Fishing

Drift fishing is a great method to use when beginning to fish for the big pikes, as it can assist in learning where the lunkers are to be found. This method covers the water thoroughly, and since this makes it unnecessary to pinpoint a location, the angler can learn where the fish are by the strikes he gets. The only problem with this style is that it cannot be enjoyed on a still day, for there must be a wind that will move the boat down the water. Of course, it is necessary to select a spot that will allow for a proper drift according to the direction of the wind.

On those days when there seems to be no way of sorting out where the fish might be, I first drift down through deep water, and if this is non-productive, through medium depths and at last down the shallow bays. I try the dead bait at all levels and keep it on the move to create the greatest possible attraction for a lurking fish. I don't really want to make this sound difficult, for it is not. After you have chosen the place, allow the boat to drift down before the wind, and over the *upwind* side of the boat slip a big dead bait mounted so that it swims after the boat. If the water is deep you can send it down by adding a measured amount of lead to the line. Prop the rod up close at hand, the reel set to the right tension and every few minutes give the line a smooth haul so that the dead bait comes up in a wavering climb and sinks again. With this method you can effectively fish water from 3 feet deep to 60 feet deep.

Don't worry if the wind is very strong and the boat drifts quite fast, for pike and muskies are the fastest fish in our freshwater, and at times they welcome a challenge. To keep the bait fish close to the bottom, add lead to the line above the hook rig. If the bait is fresh, puncture the swim bladder to make it go deeper, and pump air into the body cavity with a hypodermic needle for shallow work.

The great thing about drift fishing is that it allows for complete coverage of a potential hotspot, without disturbing the fish. So always mark off a bay in your mind, make a drift right down, come back to the start, move over a few yards, and drift again. Keep doing this until every yard is covered. The very big pike and muskies tend to be lazy and unless they are almost starving, seldom move far to take a bait. If you drift an area properly, you should manage, on one of the runs, to present that succulent big bait right in front of the lunker's face, and this usually brings a sure hit.

Casting

This is probably one of the oldest methods for taking big pikes and yet it is seldom practiced today, possibly because we have become lazy, or have accepted the word of the pundit who says that all fish can be handled on a medium-weight spinning outfit. Casting a big dead bait is not only tough on the angler, it can be wicked punishment on even a powerful rod and I would like to see one of the everything-on-one-outfit anglers try throwing a ½-pound sucker on a 3-ounce rod.

Having said that this is hard work and calls for special tackle, I should explain that it has been included here because it is absolutely and superbly suited to taking the biggest fish. The method allows for the slow working of a big bait in all but the deeper waters and the biggest thrill is that the angler usually sees the predator move in and take. It was written up by all the old Victorian pike specialists, and even today, some people retain the method passed on by previous generations.

Dead-bait casting went into a minor decline when lures became available at prices that most people could afford. Twenty-five years ago whenever my friends and I spoke of casting for pikes we meant with a spoon, or a plug, or some similar lure, until a fellow named Joe Willock joined our crowd on a northern-pike fishing trip.

Joe had never held a fishing rod in his hand. He was a research scientist and a remarkably intelligent man, and when he found out that the most authoritative book of the time was Bickerdyke's *Book of the Pike*, bought it and not so much read it, as devoured it page by page.

When we arrived at the water, the rest of us checked our live bait and our lure kits, but Joe simply opened up a paper parcel and tipped a half-dozen herrings onto the bank. He had made up some hook rigs, and with his borrowed heavy tackle, he wandered off on his own, while the rest of us sniggered with joy, and settled down in a bunch to watch our live-bait bobbers. One of our crowd, feeling sorry for Joe, went to suggest that he come back and join the crowd, and found him happily casting a big herring and then bringing it back in a sink-and-draw wobble over the top of some weeds.

"Bickerdyke reports this as the best system for big fish," said Joe peering over the top of his frameless spectacles, "so I'll work at it. You did say he was the authority, didn't you?" The other man came back, shaking his head, and we all settled back to wait for a run — in vain, I might add.

You can guess what happened. Joe, out fishing for the very first time in his life, caught two pike, even though he couldn't cast off the reel and was forced to haul out line and then pitch out his heavy bait underhand. He caught two pike that day, while the rest of us caught none. His first fish weighed 17 pounds, and his second, 22 pounds. And for most of us present that day, dead-bait casting came back into fashion with a rush.

Mostly suited to waters of medium and shallow depths, dead-bait casting calls for a substantial outfit such as a medium surf-caster, or a heavy sea spinning-rig. I use both and employ either 15- or 20-pound-test line, plus the three-or-four-hook rig described on page 207. The bait is hooked so that it lies straight, for if it is bent, it will spin, and what is being tried for is a lovely darting wobble that resembles some hurt fish zooming up and splashing the surface, and going down again to rise and hit the surface once more.

After taking a boat down to the edge of the weeds in a bay, throw out the dead bait and slowly bring it back, imparting action by sudden lifts of the rod, or a jerk to one side when the line is taut. If there is a gentle wind, it is highly effective to allow the boat to drift down, covering all the water in slow retrieves. This can only be done in a gentle breeze as the secret of this style is the slow wild wobbling movements of the bait through the water. In a strong wind, anchor and fish each area in turn.

Since the biggest predators can be happily lurking right in the weeds it is only sensible to work the bait over the top and all around the sides of all the weed beds. If the rod point is kept high the bait will wobble back in as little as 1 foot of water over the top of the weeds, and this can be very effective.

No sinker weight is needed in this style, as it is suited for shallow-water fishing, and indeed, here again it is a good idea in very shallow places to pump a little air into the belly of the dead bait to keep it well up above the weeds.

Leger Baiting

This system of simply fishing a very large dead bait on the bottom of a deep hole probably appears to be a most implausible way of fishing for fast-swimming predators such as the pike and muskies. Yet for the angler who has a good idea of where the pikes prowl, it can be most effective. It may seem a static style, but in fact, the expert in this method knows that his bait's effectiveness will double if it is given a nudge now and then to move it a little. This movement is very often followed by a strike.

The best hooking system for leger baiting is the line of three gang hooks down one side of the fish bait, so that when the bait is picked up, the angler may, if he wishes, attempt to set the hooks right away.

Here again we deal with big baits and the need for powerful tackle to handle the weight. In the case of very big baits, it is a mistake to attempt to throw them out on the rod, as this can impose a dreadful strain on the tackle. In places where the fishing hole is fairly close the line can be pulled off the reel and layed out in a tangle-free series of loops, and then the bait pitched out by hand. An interesting technique that is more entertaining than it is effective is to put the bait on a board, allow the wind to blow the board to the right spot, then tug on the line to haul the bait off.

The legered dead bait can be made twice as effective if some small fish are cut up and thrown in a circle around the main bait. There are times when the predators go on the prowl, and finding the cut-up fish hunks quickly leads them to the main hook bait.

If I seem to have dwelt on dead bait almost to the exclusion of live bait, it is because I firmly believe dead-bait fishing to be the best way to get into contact with the really big pikes.

Also, dead baits are easier to come by and keep, and with a little luck most anglers can be assured of a regular supply. Really big live baits are difficult to keep lively, and of course, some people do have a feeling of revulsion at sticking hooks into a live fish.

However, big live baits such as suckers of 1½ to 2 pounds are superb baits for taking the big fish. Properly rigged (with a hook rig such as I described on page 207), the live fish can be left to swim around a good hole, set out under a substantial bobber, or drifted down behind the boat with a sinker on the line, to ensure that the bait works at the right depth.

A tremendous way to use a big live bait is in combination with a cast dead bait. The live bait is set out under a bobber and allowed to drift down, fairly close to the boat, while someone else throws a big dead bait into all the good spots in sink-and-draw fashion. What often happens is that a fish will follow the dead bait and not really be inclined to take it. But it spots the live bait and *wham*, it hits. The anglers should change styles so that each gets a fair crack at both casting and live baiting.

I cannot speak too strongly on the question of the size of the baits used. A 10-pound pike is nothing more than a snack to a large pike or muskie, so why use a 1-pound bait? If we are to get at some of the big fish that die of old age, we must up the scale of baits and tackle to the point where we can tempt the big fish, and then land them if we hook them.

The largest muskellunge ever taken from Georgian Bay, in Ontario, weighed better than 100 pounds; the largest pike are known to exceed 50 pounds; specimens of 30 to 35 pounds in both species should be regarded as comparatively common in the larger waters. It seems only sensible that we should use baits big enough to attract the fish to bite, for the skill is in catching the lunkers, not those easy and rather stupid small- and medium-sized fish.

11 🐟 The Bass

The smallmouth and largemouth bass are two important species of game fish that provide magnificent sport across the larger portion of the North American continent.

Known by a dozen incorrect names, including largemouth *black* bass, and smallmouth *black* bass, these are sunfishes of the family *Centrarchidae,* a small group of freshwater species common only to North America. These bass are in fact not true bass with the striper and the white bass, but belong with the bluegill, and the other sunfish.

Most authorities give a third classification to the group, the Florida largemouth bass, and in evidence that this is in fact a sub-species, it is common to trot out differences in scale counts between this very large southern fish and the more standard largemouth. However, where the Florida and the standard largemouth meet in their ranges, they tend to intergrade and when the young of the Florida largemouth have been planted elsewhere, they tend to grow only to a size similar to that of indigenous fish. So this separate classification is probably of greater value in the setting of fishing records than anything else. Certainly if the fish were regarded as one straight species, only specimens from Florida would stand any chance at all of entering the record books.

For two species so closely related, the smallmouth and the large-mouth bass are surprisingly different in almost every way. The smallmouth is generally a northern fish, the largemouth is southern. One prefers the cool waters of clear lakes and rivers, the other is happier when in shallow, brush-tangled, still waters. When the two are found in the same range it is more than noticeable that entirely separate angling techniques are needed to ensure the capture of each. This is not an exaggeration, as the story I have to tell can prove.

Years ago, a friend who owns a magnificent lodge in northern Ontario invited me to try my hand at the superb smallmouth bass he had found in a lake set in the middle of his land.

This is a crystal clear northern lake near Georgian Bay and where we launched the boat, a sheer rock face fell down into the water. At the bottom there was small rock and since it was about 20 feet deep and perfect smallmouth bass water, I was quite perplexed when none of my techniques and lures produced a strike. When I said as much, my friend, in almost an apologetic manner, told me that he had not wanted to advise an expert, but all the fish caught so far, had come from the far end of the lake. I suggested that we see what was going on at the other end. When he had rowed me into position, I got a considerable shock. The water was less than three feet deep and there were lily beds, weeds, reeds and masses of stumps and roots.

The jigs I had been using were completely out of place here, so I took off the lure, and putting on a shallow-running plug, cast to a small opening in the weed cover. And all hell broke loose. A fish actually jumped out of the water and slathered all over the plug, before bolting

The classic bass fishing style is surface casting lures into a tangled shoreline for largemouth bass. Here, an angler completes his cast and tightens his line before making his plug speak fish-talk to the bass.

with it towards the heavier weeds. In a state of near shock, I held up the rod tip, bore down and walked that fish out of its lair in brutal fashion. It jumped and rolled and bolted under the boat, and at last came to the surface, mouth open and furious. I took one look and almost exploded with delight.

"No wonder we couldn't catch the smallmouths here," I said, "This is a beautiful largemouth. Come on, let's get ashore and put up a couple of bass-bugging fly rods."

My friend had owned his place for three years and had never realized that his lake held largemouths, as the place is sited barely on the edge of the northern limit for these fish. In that area it is taken for granted that if you have bass in a lake, they are smallmouths, so my poor friend had been reading everything he could get hold of on small-mouth bass fishing, and wondering why his carefully applied techniques wouldn't work. Needless to say, from that moment on his ratio of success changed as he fished in largemouth style.

Because these fish are so different, and because there are specific techniques for each species, I intend to separate them here and deal with each in turn. Remember, however, that they do meet on common ground with reference to certain basic techniques. When a big minnow is run down a medium-speed channel where the depth is right, it is common to take both largemouth and smallmouth as a mixed bag. Late in the evening, in lakes where the two species are found together, it is not in the least unusual to catch both species on a fly, a bug, a frog, or even a surface plug. Always keep in mind that both these fish are powerful and aggressive predators. Like the pike and muskies, they will strike at anything that takes their fancy, and they won't read a book first to make sure that they are following the rules.

I'll leave any debate about the comparative fighting ability of the two species to other people. Bass drive me crazy with delight, so I fish for both species regularly, and as far as I am concerned, they are both gallant and glorious scrappers. These are also fish that I return alive to the waters – they are too good to kill as long as I can buy top-quality saltwater fish fillets in my local market.

IDENTIFYING THE LARGEMOUTH AND THE SMALLMOUTH

The two basses are not at all difficult to tell apart, and once again we have a situation where the angler who is used to catching both will be able to identify which he has caught with one careless look. There is a color pattern difference that registers to the experienced eye. In some places the color of the back and sides of the two species can be alike, in a range from light green to almost bronze, but marked on top of this is

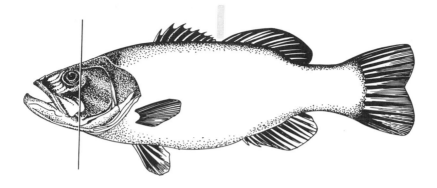

Upper Illustration: *A line drawn down from the rear of the eye on the largemouth bass will cut through the rear portion of the mouth. Note the deep notch between the dorsals.*

Lower Illustration: *The smallmouth bass has a smaller mouth, and a line drawn downwards behind the eye comes past the end of the mouth. Note that the dorsals are joined.*

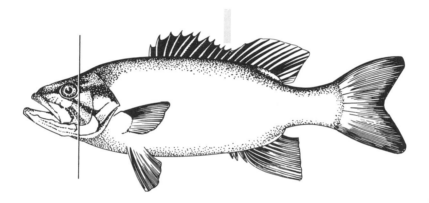

a series of vertical bars on the flanks of the smallmouth bass, and a dark irregular bar that runs along the middle of the flank of the largemouth bass. Some authorities suggest that the larger and older bass may lack this marking. Yet I have often seen pronounced bars and typical markings in very large fish of both species, so it seems that the color pattern and bar-marking varies from area to area.

However, color is the system used by the expert, and for people catching their first bass, there is a two-point check that allows for no mistakes.

The largemouth is just that — a big-mouthed fish. Its mouth, when closed, extends to a point somewhere behind the eye. On the small-mouth, the mouth only reaches back to just beneath the eye.

The other point of identification is the dorsal fins. In the case of the largemouth, there is a high spiny front dorsal then a deep notch between the first and the second dorsal, separating the two. The small-mouth has a lower, neat spiny dorsal which appears to be more broadly joined to the soft-rayed second dorsal fin. This makes for a neater and more streamlined dorsal fin arrangement, and on a quick glance, tends to give the smallmouth a kind of husky-shouldered effect.

LARGEMOUTH BASS (Micropterus salmoides)

The largemouth bass is sturdily built, a deep-bodied fish with small close-fitting scales, a spiny front dorsal fin, and a huge mouth that seems capable of opening and closing on prey of an impossibly large size. Ranging in color from almost black to light green, the dark, irregular, blotchy band down each flank is often vivid on lighter colored fish, less noticeable on the darker species and at times absent in some of the very big and oldest fish.

The largemouth is my favorite of the two, because I get an enormous thrill out of surface fishing with a plug or fly-rod bug. I find the sight of a bulge behind a plug on flat calm water in the early morning or late evening tremendously exciting, for I know that it will usually be followed by a good boil and a crashing take. Smallmouth bass are the fly rodder's babies and so you will find that the keen fly fishing angler will more often express a preference for this species. It is a matter decided by the individual and I personally enjoy fishing for both species, and once again, I wouldn't dream of getting into the argument of which fights harder.

Distribution

Originally, the largemouth was found from southern Canada around the Great Lakes, south through the Mississippi watershed down to Florida and Mexico, and then north along the Atlantic coastline up to about Maryland. But being such a great game fish, the species has been widely planted, until today it is in every part of North America where suitable habitation is found, including west of the Rockies. The largemouth has also been taken for planting in other countries, with varying degrees of success.

The largemouth is truly a fish of the south, with the best fishing for the biggest fish found in those southern regions where lush, rich, shallow marsh-lands offer the prolific feed and stumpy, snag-filled habi-tat preferred by the species. I have never been sure whether these bass

The biggest largemouth bass are found in southern waters such as this Florida setting, where a lunker rolls on the surface close to a thick bank of weed. Typical baits for lunker bass are minnows 6 or 7 inches long. This, plus the massive size of the fish, and the thick cover in which they are found, necessitates the use of stout gear, such as is used in this picture.

prefer the weedy, stumpy places because they are rich in the food enjoyed best by the fish or because of the protection offered from enemies and the burning rays of the sun. But make no mistake about the nature of the largemouth — it is a tough, aggressive fish, and when very big, can have few enemies outside man himself. Whatever the reason, largemouth thrive in the weedy, shallow, stumpy waters of marshes, lake bays, or quieter bends of rivers. They seldom move in water more than 20 feet deep and usually stay close to areas of rooted vegetation.

Habits

Both species of bass are nesting fish and the largemouth male cleans out a space on the bottom by fanning vigorously to create a nest about 20 inches in diameter, in water that is as shallow as 2 feet and fairly close to shore. This takes place when the water temperature reaches between 62° to 65° Fahrenheit in the spring. The male attracts females when the nest is ready and spawning takes place in the nest with the female dropping only a couple of hundred or so eggs at a time, and maybe moving to another male and another nest. The male fish guards the eggs until they hatch and then continues to protect the little fish for a short time before moving back into more protected waters. Naturally, nest-guarding largemouth will hit any lure thrown close to the nest, and in my opinion it is poor sportsmanship to take advantage of the instincts of protection.

Size

Anglers wishing to fish for and catch very big largemouth bass should definitely make plans to fish southern waters, such as South Carolina's Santee-Cooper system and the Georgia or Florida waters. The largemouth tends to go off feed when the water drops below a certain level, and in some of the colder northern regions this has a tremendous effect on the growth rate of the fish. Northern bass seldom reach 10 pounds and specimens of between 3 to 5 pounds are held to be first rate fish. On the other hand, conditions in the south permit feeding almost all year with an obvious effect on growth rates.

In Santee-Cooper a 5-pound largemouth is just a nice fish and a 10-pound specimen is really not so big that the locals will get excited, for fish are caught to 12 or 14 pounds. Then further south, the bass get bigger, until in Florida the fish can reach 20 pounds or more. A trip south is something to jump at if the chance comes along, but it would be wrong to feel that only the southern largemouth angling is enriching. This is a fish species with a very special attraction for the angler, and there can be as much fun with a 1-pound largemouth caught in some northern lake, as with much larger fish of the less thrilling species.

Tackle

Since the largemouth bass will take almost every form of moving life he can get into his mouth, it follows that any system of tackle that can present lures, flies, worms, minnows, frogs or bugs can be considered suitable. But this species is tough for a smallish fish, and moreover, often lives in rugged waters filled with snags and weeds. So, while it is possible to use any basic set of gear that will put a bait to the fish, it is important to use common sense and employ heavy gear under certain circumstances.

The largemouth bass is an aggressive fish, a sort of marine roughneck, a saloon brawler, always ready and eager to fight and explode into action. It is one of the few fish in freshwater that I know can be *goaded* into striking a lure, and this should form a good part of the technique of plug and bug casting for this species. When a plug is tossed into an area of open water surrounded by weeds, the largemouth will at times shoulder through the vegetation in such a determined manner that the angler can actually watch the line of route and know when to expect the fish to hit.

Even when moving forward to intercept food, the bass gives the impression of coming along to give the bum's rush to a territorial intruder. Of course, it could be that the largemouth has territorial defence tendencies in some situations outside the nesting habit, and this would help to explain the aggressive attitudes shown, but, whatever the motivation at work, largemouth bass are not particularly shy fish — not even the larger ones, which could be expected to have learned discretion. So, since the biggest fish are often found in the heart of dense weed beds, it becomes necessary to use very heavy tackle. Northern largemouth-bass fishermen can usually get away with basic spinning tackle and 8-pound-test line for a great deal of the time, but it is often sensible to move up to 12-pound test. For northern largemouth in heavy weed beds, and for all southern largemouth, a choice of 15- to 20-pound-test *braided* line should be used.

This need for comparatively heavy gear was one factor that brought about the only major American development in freshwater tackle, the baitcasting outfit. Let us examine this style and see if we should use it or the modern and less troublesome unit, the spincaster outfit.

Baitcasting

Baitcasting today is usually taken to mean the casting of a plug, lure or artificial by means of a fairly short rod, a revolving-spool reel and a short, snappy, flip-action cast. But when it was first developed, it was for the throwing of a live minnow and hence was termed "bait" casting. The introduction of the first heavy wooden plugs, usually carved out of cedar, caused a stiff, 4- to 5-foot baitcasting rod to be put on the market, and for a great many people this has become the standard to follow.

The short length of the baitcasting rod has always puzzled European anglers who are used to operating very long rods while fishing from the banks of lakes and rivers. Examining the extremely short rods in terms of their own experience, the European anglers have often offered critical suggestions for improvement. However, in most largemouth waters the short rods perform extremely well, and since the majority of angling is done from a boat, the pinpoint accuracy obtained with this type of gear outweighs any lack of casting distance, the average cast being well within 40 to 50 feet.

At first glance, baitcasting outfits appear to have changed little over the years, but in fact, a number of most valuable changes have occurred, some good, and some not so good.

Today most baitcasting rods are made in either hollow or solid glass, and in much longer lengths than previously. Many anglers prefer a baitcasting rod as long as 6 feet, 6 inches, and if they can't get one, they simply use a spincaster rod. The longer baitcasting rod makes for better casting and a greater degree of control when fighting the fish. At the maximum of 6 feet, 6 inches, it is still short and convenient for use in a boat, and even better at dabbing a lure a short distance into the exact spot the angler wants.

The revolving-spool, level-wind, multiplying reels used in this style have really been put through the design hoop, and in some cases I'm not too sure I like what has happened. Casting in this system has always been a sport that takes quite a bit of learning and a great deal of casting practice. Those of us who grew up using baitcasting learned at an early age the need for an educated thumb that would stop the spool from overrunning and yet would allow us to cast with distance and accuracy. It doesn't matter how keen one is, or how many top diagrams are studied, proper baitcasting comes down to teaching the thumb the proper way to slow the speeding spool – and there is no easy way of doing this.

Still, many reel manufacturers load all the finest reels with a designer's nightmare of special clutches, free-spool gismos, and 100 per cent foolproof brake systems – that don't work. This puts the price of the best reels out of the reach of a lot of anglers, and many people who dislike the fancy gimmicks (including myself) are made unhappy. So when I needed a good reel and was offered the choice in a bunch fitted with a free-spool mechanism, I chose the one that worked best for me, the very efficient Swedish Abu Ambassador 6000. I figured out that since I was being pushed into paying for gimmicks, I'd make quite sure that I got the gimmick that worked best. I might add that I have been more than happy with my choice.

There will be a good market in baitcasting reels for many years to come, for outside their use on traditional baitcasting rods, these jewelled, accurate reels are great for use on power rods used for heavy freshwater and light saltwater work. But I still believe the manufacturers gilded the lily with too many odd items not desired by the public and spoiled a good market by raising the price too high. Maybe I am obstinate, but I am still convinced that the best reel of this type is the pre-gismo Pflueger Supreme.

The use of the baitcasting rod and reel is a joy in itself, rather like fly casting, in that the angler can derive enjoyment out of the act of working the tackle and making a good cast. But a point that is seldom made is that baitcasting is far harder to learn than fly casting. There is no easy way to master it, and it comes down in the end to standing on the lawn, practicing with a sinker or hookless plug. Put back the rod over your right shoulder, turn the reel towards your face and power the cast with a distinct flip of the rod.

I have always believed it a little phony to try to teach baitcasting through the written word, with or without the aid of diagrams. It is not like any other casting form: the forward thrust of the rod has to be most delicately balanced with pressure from the thumb on the spool of the reel, so that a *controlled* cast is made. In the spinning cast, you simply power the stick, bring it forward and let go of the line when the stick reaches the correct spot. So I will merely pass on a couple of useful tips, with the suggestion that the best way to learn is with guidance from a skilled caster and a great deal of practice on dry land.

The first tip is on powering the rod. Reel the practice plug right to the tip of the rod and flex the stick to get the feel of the rod with the weight of the plug. When you have flexed it to almost full power, imagine that the plug is a lump of clay stuck on the rod tip, and when making the cast, power the rod as if you were flicking that lump of clay right onto the chosen target. When you lift your thumb, the line spins the spool.

My second tip is on this matter of thumbing. The only genuine control of the cast with this tackle lies in using an educated thumb to control the speed of the spinning reel-spool to avoid getting an overrun and tangle. No matter what the manufacturers might say, there is no truly efficient device that will do this automatically. The angler must learn to do it with his thumb.

Unlike the spinning and spincasting reels, which have motionless spools during a cast, the multiplying reel spool turns at a terrific speed when the cast snaps it into action. The weight of the spool plus the line is fairly heavy, and this tends to keep the speed constant so that line is pushed off the reel and up the line guides. When the lure or bait slows near the end of the cast, the line behind it slows all the way to the rod tip and down the guides, but the reel spool is still going fast and pushing off line. The educated thumb closes down almost automatically and adjusts the spool speed, with brief touches, to match the slowing down of the line.

That's how it should be done, but the beginner takes a while to learn this. At first the slowed line is fairly constant from the lure to the first line guide and meets up with the line being spun off at speed from the spool. A big curve builds up at the entrance to the first guide, angles sharply and won't enter the guide. There is a whip-back and the reel spool gathers in the slack, winding it onto the spool the wrong way, until the line comes taut. This slams the reel to a halt so quickly that it speeds into reverse, creating a tremendous tangle of line, and whips the lure back if it is light, or causes the sinker to snap off.

So my second baitcasting tip is this. Thumb as little as possible, and then only enough to avoid an overrun. This may seem a rather offhand manner of treating this form of casting, but it took me some years to learn to do it well, and after using it for 30-odd years I still get overruns and birds nests. It is practice that teaches baitcasting, not long discussions.

Spincasting

The classic baitcasting outfit has become an American tradition, and it seems almost traitorous to suggest that the same work can be done by the spincaster rig with ease and with almost no practice. But it is true, and I'm sure that if the two angling ways had been developed at the same time, the spincasters would by now have pushed the more difficult style off the market.

There are some criticisms I make of spincasters, such as their limited casting range, the limited amount of line that can be put on the reel and their inability to make a good job in a fight with a fish that makes long, fast runs. But none of these apply to largemouth bass fishing. This is a fish that fights within a small area and doesn't make long runs, so only short casts are needed to hook it and the amount of line normally used on a spincaster is perfectly suitable.

I could not suggest a better outfit to start with than a sturdy spincaster fitted with line of a minimum 15-pound test. For bigger fish and tougher waters this can be increased to 20-pound test and the rod used should be husky enough to handle a little brutal work now and then, for some fish that need to be bustled out of snag-ridden areas.

Baits

Since the largemouth bass will grab and swallow almost anything that moves, the range of baits for the species is almost unlimited. Probably the finest live bait is a big minnow, and a very large dew-worm is also excellent.

A frog is one of the most popular baits, and since these creatures are usually pretty thick in largemouth waters I have no doubt that they are a large portion of the diet of the species. But I have never liked using frogs and have never truly felt them to be all that good as bait. In fact, the thick growth in which the big largemouth hide is really unsuited to bait fishing and quite often a lure will take fish better than a live bait.

It has been my experience that, while live bait is excellent for catching largemouths, the angler who understands lures and knows how to use them will probably catch more fish of a larger average size. To put this into a sensible perspective: if I were fishing for the world-record largemouth bass I would try for him with a minnow of maybe 10 to 12 inches long. But if I was out for an exciting day's fishing for largemouth, and wanted the maximum of enjoyment from really big fish, I would use lures, such as the fine plugs made for surface work, including noisy chugger-spoons, units with weed guards and such southern specialities as the eel-and-spinner, worm-and-spinner combination baits, as well as a complete range of fly-rod bugs and poppers.

Largemouth bass have color sight and it has been proven in laboratories that these fish have a decided preference for certain colors. The order of color preference in casting-lures is red, white, silver, and black. For bugs and poppers the color preference is first plain yellow, then white with a further color such as yellow or red, and finally — rather surprisingly — brown with one other color added.

Predatory fish usually accept the same lures in every water they inhabit, but largemouth bass are an exception and often take a specific type of bait in one region and a different type in other areas. For example, there are systems of lures in the south that are fairly different from those used in the north, and it always pays to check local preferences when fishing an area for the first time. I would like to make it clear that I'm not talking in terms of Brand X lure as opposed to Brand Y lure, or even as opposed to Brand Z, Size B, but in terms of different patterned lures, such as a Hula-Popper surface plug as opposed to a weedless Black eel-spinner.

After considering local preferences and choosing the type of lure, the angler must then base his mode of attack on the fact that he is fishing for a tough predator with aggressive habits and a penchant for the worst, weedy, stump-filled water at hand. It must be remembered that bass will sink away out of sight if badly disturbed by a roaring outboard or the solid clunk of an anchor being thrown carelessly over the side, but it must also be kept in mind that these fish can be taunted into hitting. Therefore, the water should be thoroughly covered.

I find that a lot of anglers waste good water. They rush into a good bay, keeping their motor running until the last second, kill it with a corresponding disturbance and even before the wash of their boat has stopped rocking the weed beds, they have made casts into all the open holes and are ready to hit the next bay.

Fished properly, one fairly big bay will provide enough fishing for the complete afternoon-to-dusk period. The best time to approach a marshy, weedy bay is in the late afternoon when the fish are working into the shallows. The angler should cut the motor early and work in slowly and silently with a paddle or oars. The finest instrument I've seen for this work is the small silent electric motors used a lot in the south. But no matter how you get into position, it then pays to rest the water for a while and string up tackle silently without knocking the boat. Then, selecting a big channel or pothole between the weeds, the surface lure should be fired in and brought out in a hurry.

This first throw is a sort of advertising gimmick and the retrieve should be slow enough to allow a fish to strike, but fast enough to create a noisy row on the surface. Then the plug is cast back swiftly to the same spot and allowed to sit for a considerable time, with the line kept taut to the rod tip. Sometimes a bass will shatter the calm by a hit, but more often the angler must give the plug a nudge to make a noise or to spread ripples. Finally, the plug is worked very slowly back to the boat, tossed again to the original spot, and the whole pattern of action is repeated. Don't let anybody tell you that a bass won't hit a motionless lure. The secret of the plan is to have that pesky intruder right on the bass' doorstep for as long as possible, to give the fish time to find it. Then, the minute it moves, the bass will attack it.

My method is to fish a good hole in this way for a long time, keeping the lure in the same region to give the fish time to find it. I consider it a waste of good water to make one cast here, another there, and then move on to repeat this in all the holes in the bay. I firmly believe that a concentrated attack with great care in technique pays rich dividends when fishing for aggressive fish such as these.

A most effective system of angling in the stump waters of southern areas is with a jig-worm combination lure, using a vivid purple worm as long as a foot or more in length. Usually fitted with sets of hooks with weed guards, this strange-looking object is thrown into the heart of tangled weeds and slowly drawn back with slight nudges to bring it around snags and through heavy weed. Naturally for this work *heavy* tackle is needed.

This dirty work in the heart of the weeds and stumps will always take the biggest fish, but the surface fishing is so much fun that many anglers haven't the heart to turn to the slow, deep system. This is a shame, because both could be used, the weedless eel fished deep during the day and plugs or fly-rod bugs and poppers on the surface in the evening.

A bass shatters the calm by walloping a surface lure worked cleverly close to the edge of the weed bed. This angler, who has popped a bug on the surface using fly tackle, is in for a superb fight, thanks to his planned approach to working the lure.

Sleek yet sturdy, the smallmouth bass is a furious fighter, equally at home in a swift stream or a quiet bay. A bottom feeder that hunts crayfish, minnows and leeches, the smallmouth is a sports fisherman's delight that will rise to a fly, or just as readily snatch a chugging plug. It has the stamina and the will to fight to the end.

In the leafy shade of the early dawn, or at dusk, the smallmouth bass fisherman heads for quiet places to cast for feeding lunkers. There, in the peace of the dawn or evening, the calm may be broken by the furious hit of a raging smallmouth bass and the smooth waters will part as this gamest of all fish tears tranquillity into excited shreds.

Operating any popper, whether it is fished on a spinning rig, bait-casting outfit or fly rod, is simply a matter of creating a fine disturbance on the surface, as though some tiny creature had fallen in and was struggling. Fly bugs are miniature lures with open faces that issue a deep "gloop" sound when pulled down, thus harrying the bass. They are every bit as effective as other plugs and at times seem capable of out-fishing the bigger and more conventional lures.

By now it should be fairly obvious that I regard bass as *lure* fish, that is to say, a prime game species that offers the highest form of angling enjoyment when taken on a carefully presented plug or bug. It is always a heart-warming thrill to see a big, gill-rattling largemouth come flying out on the end of the line, and for me the thrill is doubled if I've fooled the fish with a lure of my own choice and presentation.

SMALLMOUTH BASS (Micropterus dolomieui)

It is no exaggeration to say that the smallmouth bass is one of the gamest freshwater fishes in the world. It provides great sport on every style of fishing tackle and is a hardy fighter that doesn't give up the fight until it is in the landing net. The outstanding scrapping ability of the smallmouth is shown further by its habit of jumping wildly into the air when hooked. All too often, the fish goes one way and the lure or hook the other.

Distribution

Confined originally to the Quebec and Ontario drainage areas of the Great Lakes, and the Ohio drainage system, the smallmouth has been carried into every part of North America where there is a suitable habitation and climate. In the early days of the railroads smallmouth bass were carried in containers in the water tenders of locomotives and planted in various creeks along the route. They were moved into isolated lakes in buckets carried by keen anglers, and state and provincial hatchery workers put them into new waters by the thousands.

Today this fish is firmly established from Nova Scotia to Saskatchewan, south to Alabama and west to eastern Kansas and Oklahoma. They are also found in California and in many foreign countries.

Smallmouths prefer clean, cool, and fairly rocky lakes and rivers, where the summer temperature warms to above 60° but does not exceed 80°. Water temperature plays an important role in growth and maturing age with northern males becoming mature at about 9 inches in their third year, while more southern fishes mature in their second year.

This species sometimes does so well that overcrowding will occur in a lake, resulting in stunted fish. I once fished a wilderness lake that was suffering from this ill and every cast resulted in a hit by a fish of about 1 pound. Summer cottages were later built along the shoreline and the lake was fairly heavily fished. I returned there about ten years after and found the fish much harder to catch, fewer in numbers, and of far better quality.

The smallmouth is more a northern fish, and the average size is bigger in the middle of the north-south range, but even in the most northern parts of the smallmouth's range big fish are encountered, and in the cooler waters, these tend to be superior fighters.

Habits

The smallmouth is a nest-building species that spawns when the water reaches between 60° to 70° This varies according to the zone, so that the more southern fish spawn in late April, and the northern fish in late June. The male fans the nest clean, using powerful strokes of its tail to create a shallow depression in small rock or gravel. Females are enticed to the nest and allowed to drop their ripened eggs. After the male has fertilized the eggs, he turns upon the female, drives her away, and seeks another. This strange multiple nesting occurs because not all of the eggs ripen at the same time, so the females have to make as many as three separate spawnings, usually in different nests. This appears to be a simple method of getting a good mixture of healthy strains.

The male smallmouth, like the largemouth, guards the eggs until they hatch, and stays with the fry for a couple of weeks, before leaving them to their own devices. While guarding his nest, the male will probably not feed, but will angrily hit any lure that comes close to the nest. Some people take advantage of this habit to catch the bass. This is not only unsporting — like shooting a tethered moose — but it is poor conservation as well, for with the male fish removed, the eggs or small fry will almost surely succumb to any number of predators.

The nest site over gravel or small rock plays an important role in the life of the smallmouth bass and even establishes the requirements for habitat. Smallmouths are found in some weedy, muddy-bottomed lakes, but they seldom do as well there as in the clean, rocky waters.

Size

Smallmouth bass cease feeding when the water temperature drops in the winter, and living at a much lower metabolic rate, go into a kind of suspended state. The slowed rate of living calls for little use of energy, but the fish doesn't grow during this period. Because of this we would expect growth rates to be affected by the amount of warm weather and by factors such as the quality of available food. However, southern fish do not get that much bigger than those in the colder climes, and smallmouths as large as 9 pounds or more are common in the northern parts of Ontario.

The average size caught is about 1 pound, fish of 3 pounds are usually considered a good catch, and anything over 5 pounds is excellent. The top size is probably around 12 pounds, although there is no knowing what might happen if the scientists ever decided to selectively breed a race of special smallmouth bass.

Tackle

As far as tackle is concerned the smallmouth is a conservative species that is taken in standard form on spinning, fly, baitcasting, or the widest range of live-baiting tackle. It is a hard and excellent fighter, but unlike the largemouth, tends to occupy open habitat where standard tackle sets should prove completely effective. Although there is little need for specialist gear, the angler must modify what he uses, so that the desired fish is properly covered.

On a camping-fishing trip through Ontario some years ago my wife and I, wanting to catch some fish for dinner, stopped by a bridge on the Eagle Lake causeway, where about a dozen anglers were fishing. With the aid of polaroid sunglasses, we could see 11 feet to the bottom of that crystal, sparkling lake water, and there, cruising from side to side with deadly intent, was a school of beautiful smallmouth bass.

The current was fairly swift, so we opted for heavy slider float rigs with big cork barrels on long quills that would take a dozen or so soft swan shot. For bait we used single dew worms hooked *once* through the collar. We slipped our baited hooks into the water, gave free line to allow the worms to dive deep quickly, and then, as the big bobbers cocked up, put our rod points slightly upstream to gently retard the progress of the worms, and make them flare up from the bottom, right in front of the noses of the school of bass. By trotting our bobbers down the stream in this fashion, we quickly caught three bass.

The other anglers were looking at us as if we had just arrived by broom and thrown magic dust on the water. "Brother," said one man, "you two are the luckiest anglers I have ever seen. I've been here all day and haven't even had a bite." And as he spoke, my wife's bobber eased slowly under, and when she set the hook, the swift bowing of her rod showed that this time she had on a dandy. The fish boiled sullenly, worked out in deep waters and then came swiftly back into the current under the bridge. I jumped down with the landing net and just before the fish came into reach, it shot out of the water, rattled its gills, and threw the hook. It was a beautiful fish, easily 7 pounds and would have broken our family smallmouth record by about 4 ounces — a record which my wife holds, by the way.

This story illustrates two important points: the fact that an ordinary roadside location turned out to be a hot smallmouth bass hole; and that a bunch of anglers fished there without hooking a smallmouth, *although they could have seen them with the aid of polaroid sunglasses.*

The concrete sidings of bridge piles appear to draw smallmouth bass, as do the steep rock reefs common to many of the northern lakes. These places form a food gathering centre where the bass can find prey, so it is always a good idea to investigate such features with care.

The other anglers were fishless in that rich location because they were not fishing properly. Not one of them was running a bait down that streamy section; no one had a bait on the bottom where the fish were swimming; and no one had taken the trouble to give the place a good look to discover the fish. Most of them simply sat with large plastic bobbers, holding a dew worm a couple of feet under the surface, in a place where the fish were in deep water. Yet every angler there had the necessary tackle to get at the fish.

Tackle for smallmouth bass is conventional and any system, especially fly fishing, may be used to take them. Fly fishing for smallmouth bass has developed into a quality sport in a number of areas, primarily in those regions where quality smallmouths are found in rivers and streams. In the larger lake waters, where the biggest fish are found, baitfishing and a range of spinning and casting lures are often best for taking the lunkers.

Baits

Generally, the best live baits for smallmouth bass are minnows, worms, leeches and crayfish, although not necessarily in that order. The larger of these carnivorous fish live mostly on other fish, including yellow perch, sunfish, and a full range of minnows and fry. Having a healthy appetite, the smallmouth will even go for a large live minnow set out for a pike, and many an angler has received a pleasant shock on finding that the quarry that has hit his 7-to 9-inch live sucker is a bruiser of a smallmouth bass.

Worms and leeches are always good baits, and in waters where leeches are present in great numbers, these two baits are often better than live minnows. I once spent a couple of hours working minnows down through a bridge channel and getting only a half-hearted response from the big smallmouths that I knew were there. Finally, in a fit of pique, I put on a great big night-crawler, a dew worm built like a diamondback rattlesnake. I slipped it over the side of the boat, bounced it along the bottom using a sliding shot leger, and immediately struck a good fish. I took four more very nice smallmouths in rapid succession, all on worm. I *know* the live minnow is the better bait, but that time I met up with a bunch that were feeding on worms, and ever since I have been less rigid in my choice of live baits.

Smallmouth can at times be very difficult to hook on a worm, because by far the finest system of hooking up the bait is by slipping the hook just once beneath the big ring near the head of the worm. Hooked this way, the worm acts up in the livliest manner and possibly resembles a leech or even one of the small non-parasitic lampreys so beloved by all game fish. But this single hook hold can make it tough to set the hook into the fish. The only way it can be done is to allow the fish to move off with the worm, giving completely slack line so that there is no hindrance, and to set the hook after a *reasonable* period.

The angler must decide for himself how long "a reasonable period" is. All I can say is that when I am watching someone else let a smallmouth swim off with the bait, it always seems a terribly long time. But I have been told that it appears the same way to someone else when I'm handling the tackle. These fish play with a worm at times and will spit it out, suck it in again and spit it out and so on for as many as five or six times. However, they will seldom let it go completely and it usually pays to wait a fairly long time between the take and the strike. In making the strike the slack line is wound very slowly onto the reel, with the rod point extended towards the fish. The moment a weight is felt, the tip is whipped back in a short but emphatic strike. This slow pickup of the line nudges the bait if the fish has let go and usually provokes a furious take.

Crayfish, often called crabs, are superb bait for smallmouth bass in many areas, and in some of the Great Lakes regions even very small crayfish will bring in big bass. These crustaceans are to be found beneath stones or loose rock along a shoreline or else can be bought from bait dealers. The live crayfish is hooked by carefully inserting the point between the last two segments of the tail. I have fished this bait from a drifting boat with a sink-and-draw action of the rod, and have taken fish *off* the bottom, but essentially it is a bottom-hugging bait.

There are any number of living baits that the smallmouth will take, but the big four are those detailed above. The hook size should be matched to the size of the bait, with perhaps a size 6 Medium shank as the best choice for all dew worms regardless of size, and a standard size 2 being a good choice for the bigger live minnows. I repeat that tackle for a smallmouth is conventional, and we simply match the size of the hook and the bait to our own satisfaction. I have used as small as a size 8 hook when very small crayfish were the only bait obtainable. But don't be fooled by the name "smallmouth," for I have had a medium-sized specimen fold both lips over a monster plug and come in to the boat with a size 5/0 treble hook firmly set in its jaw. It has a *small* mouth only in relation to that of the largemouth bass.

For many anglers, stream fishing for smallmouth with light tackle is by far the finest way of enjoying good sport. In fast streams the smallmouth put on dazzling displays, jumping and speeding through the shallows in the manner that makes many anglers swear that no other fish fights as hard.

Lures

All conventional lures in the medium range will work quite well on this species, especially those that can be worked deep. In the case of plugs, I chose those that will dive and swim close to the bottom. I have the utmost confidence in Heddon's Deep 6 and Arbo-Gaster, two deep-diving and remarkably snag-resistant plugs, they have all the qualities I require in a *deep-diving* smallmouth bait in that they are the right size and have superb vibrating action.

Other plugs for smallmouth include the range dealt with in Chapter Five. Medium-depth lures and surface plugs are useful when the smallmouth venture into the shallows in the late part of a warm summer evening, but more important are those that will zoom down to the level at which the fish usually feed.

Almost the complete range of vibrating spinner lures — long slim spoons, lead-head jigs, and spinner-worm-eel combination lures — will take smallmouth when fished down deep. In fact, the fish will strike at most baits if they are presented properly.

Smallmouth bass are fairly easy to catch once they are located, and the thing to do is to find where they are feeding and pursue them with several techniques until the right one is found for the situation. It has already been mentioned that bridge abutments, rock cliffs, deep clean holes at the bends of rivers, and streamy reaches of water where current flows over small rock, sand and gravel, are all potential hotspots. Smallmouths will feed along a medium-depth shoreline in a clean lake where there are trees fallen in at the edge to form a haven for minnows. There are usually a few big fish patrolling the front of a lakeside beaver lodge, or at the edge of a rapids where the fast water circles back to form an eddy. In big lakes such as Lake Erie, Georgian Bay and Lake Huron, very large smallmouth bass are found in the bays over the clean-bottom reaches, especially where there is good feed in the form of shoal minnows or crayfish.

I will describe a couple of places and the systems I would use to fish them. First of all, a typical streamy reach close to the gut between one lake and another. Since the water runs fairly fast in such places, I usually anchor my boat well upstream so I can fish down to the correct area.

I often fish one such place that is about 14 feet deep, and have learned that the fish hang around the tail end of the bridge, downstream in the broken-current swirl formed by the bridge abutment. If the water is not running too heavily, the smallmouths venture out into the full current, but it is always best to go for them in the eddy, so I usually start off by floating down a 3- or 4-inch live minnow on a sliding float. I adjust the float to keep the minnow close to the bottom with sinker shot pinched 18 inches above the hook to help keep the live bait deep. I guide the bobber into the eddy with the rod point and when it is in the right spot, retard it slightly so that it wanders back and forth in the feed area.

Nine times out of ten this system results in a smallmouth hit within a dozen or so "trots" down the stream. If this doesn't happen, I still continue with the float moved down a little to make sure that the bait is right on the bottom, running the float in a different path on each successive trot. Sometimes I even change the minnow for a smaller fish, or a worm. I never move off just because there is no immediate response and have often fished in this type of water without a bite for several hours, and then caught fish after fish, until my limit was reached. A decided advantage with this type of water is that other species may come along and take the bait, thus helping to enliven the day. It is common to take pike, walleye, crappies and a few other species while fishing such a spot.

When it is possible to fish this type of water from the bank, a bottom-bouncing leger with a single worm hooked once through the collar ring is a valuable technique. The worm is thrown upstream so that it sinks and tumbles along the bottom through the eddy or through the gravel or sand region, where the bass are likely to gather. This calls for an exact adjustment of the sliding leger, and the shot style described on page 93 is best.

A second typical place is an open lake where smallmouth are known to be present. First, I comb the side of the steep rocks where they slide down into deep waters, using a Mepps No. 3 or 4, tossing it right against the rock and allowing it to sink all the way to the bottom before retrieving. All fast-sinking lures work well for this, and jigs or eel-spinner combo rigs are excellent, for they can be worked down the rock face below water in little jerks and twitches which seem to send bass into an attacking rage.

Fishing these steep slides can be done very well with live minnows or dew worms, but I always try with lures first, to check the depth and the way the water is worked. Most of the time the hits come so swiftly that it is worth continuing with the lures. Quite a few people troll large waters for bass, but I prefer to drift slowly down the shoreline where possible, either swimming a bait close to the bottom, or casting into the likely spots. Lures such as the medium-diving plugs can be thrown into a shoreline tangle of trees and sunken logs and worked slowly back to the boat. In clear northern waters there is often the added thrill of seeing the fish grab at the lure. I seldom fish in the open spaces on such lakes, but in extremely large waters where monster smallmouth bass are often found on the shoals, I find that the drift method with a live bait can provide some exciting sport.

Bass, both smallmouth and largemouth are among the finest sporting fish in freshwater. They are not too hard to catch, but can be tough to locate. Believe me, they are more than worth any trouble that might be taken to find them.

12 🐟 Trout Fishing

Unfortunately, trout fishing has been set up as some form of sporting status symbol and the trout angler is given a superior rating. It is amusing (if you can keep a sense of proportion), yet mystifying that trout fishing should be classed as better than carp or pike fishing.

The gilded atmosphere surrounding this branch of the sport is not simply confined to a division between trout and all the other sporting game fish; there are sharply defined social levels according to the individual species and the techniques used to take them.

Enjoying the highest status are the brook/brown trout fishermen who angle for these two species using dry-fly fishing gear. A little beneath this elevated position are the wet-fly fishermen — still stream fishing of course — and once into the field of deep-water trolling for lake trout, the depths are plumbed and trout fishing closes up with the rest of the common herd. But even a lake-trout troller will sneer at the angler who tells about the big carp that got away last week. I suppose that on rock bottom are people like myself who have even been known to fish for eels . . . *deliberately*.

If some people prefer to fish exclusively for any one species of fish, be they brook trout or sticklebacks, I wish them joy, for there is fun in specialization. But when it comes down to snobbery, I dig in my heels. I will never believe that one species of fish is superior in all ways to all others; and to suggest that status should be applied to a species is somewhat pathetic.

The deep interest in trout that has extended through the centuries has left us a priceless heritage of literature, especially in the realm of the inner arts of fly fishing. From the very first angling work in the English language to those of our time, the world of the trout and the ways of catching it have been captured in print, enlarged and enhanced in every succeeding generation. Anyone who is serious about fly fishing should read Charles Cotton's section on this subject in the second part of Walton's *The Compleat Angler,* and follow this with the great writers of the nineteenth century: Grey, Halford, Skues, and Hewitt. Among the moderns such great craftsmen as Joe Brooks, Jr., Bergman, Charles Ritz, Lee Wulff and A.J. McClane have written outstanding books. Read all these men again and again, for they are masters of the craft.

But trout fishing for most of us today means hunching together with a noisy bunch of bleary-eyed, wader-clad men, casting spinners or sacks of roe into riffles as the spring or fall run of migratory rainbows surge up a creek from the big water downstream. There are tangled lines and arguments, and all it takes to lose your place in line is to move one step back. Trout fishing today also means probing with a metal line to send a spoon fluttering through deep holes in icy cold lakes, to search out the giant lake trout in his green and silent world; it means trolling a spoon off a river harbor hoping for a strike from a running rainbow, or a brown that has come inshore to search out the shoals of minnows; lastly, it means working a big live bait in the dark of some small stream for that old cannibal brown trout that lives in the hole by the road bridge and forages in the shallows to stalk the pallid remnants of the legal-sized, liver-fed brookies dumped only hours earlier from a state or provincial hatchery truck.

There are wild waters to the north where giant brook trout swim and are easily destroyed by the pressure of a fly-in organization. There are pretty streams and big rivers where the tangled bush droops into the white water and where a population of wild trouts will continue, until eventually that bush is cleared, or that stream or river polluted.

Realizing this is the first major step towards an understanding of the changing ways of angling in North America. It is not a pretty picture, and is not easily accepted by people still influenced by the romantic notions of those writers who are living in the past. Over much of North America, classic trout is failing before the spread of man's works, and I cannot foretell whether the new forms of game fishes being hurriedly planted in our big waters, will compensate for our past irresponsibility.

Trout are of the family *Salmonidae*, a group of northern hemi-sphere fishes that includes the Atlantic and Pacific salmons, as well as the brown trout, rainbow, brook and lake trouts. All are very much alike, have fine scales, well-developed teeth on their jaws and tongues, and similar patterns of coloration. Some of the family spend most of their life feeding in the seas, but all spawn in freshwater.

Generally speaking, the important trout for fishermen in North America are the brown and the rainbows, classed as true trout and the brook and laker, placed with the chars. The difference between the two groups is quite technical, but they can be set apart simply by a quick look into the mouth. The trout has teeth along the entire length of the vomera bone running down the centre of the mouth. The chars, on the other hand, have only a few teeth on the end of the vomer. The fish are all different in color, spotting, and minor points of shape, so the angler should have no trouble in sorting out the four species.

Breeding Habits

Although different in many ways, the fish in this family tend to follow similar patterns in general matters, including spawning. The big lakers and some of the small brook trout may be very different in size and in their choice of spawning areas, but when one takes a closer look at the family some remarkable similarities emerge.

The salmonids have very strong migratory instincts which lead most stream-dwelling species into the sea, if they have even half a chance. Because of this we hear of fishes that sound like whole new species, with names such as *sea trout, coaster,* and *steelhead.* In fact, these names apply to sea-run browns, brooks and rainbow trout, respectively.

This migratory role, adopted by fish of all species except the lake trout, has an important bearing on sport. Since all salmonids must breed in freshwater, the spawning runs create massive surges of migrant populations in streams that may otherwise be inactive, and this provides seasonal angling.

I will describe the basic pattern of spawning largely in terms of the rainbows, because every spring for many years I have observed them in my local river. While the other trout may pick different habitat, the act is basically the same, except for the lake trout, which differs markedly from the others discussed in this chapter, and which will be discussed in a separate section.

When the trouts move into a suitable spawning location, the

female at once commences to fan out a nest, or "redd," with powerful strokes of her tail. Big rainbows can shift a tremendous amount of gravel, and are helped in this by the strong current which flows over the spawning riffle. When the nest is finished, the female moves to its upstream end, with an attentive male pressed close to her side, and the fish release eggs and milt simultaneously. The female then moves a little upstream of this nest, and in fanning out a second nest causes clean gravel to roll down and cover the first batch of eggs with a protective layer. This is repeated until the female is spent, at which point she drops back downstream to feed and replace her expended energies.

The redds made by small trout of 6 to 7 inches may be only 1 foot across, but the large fish uncover a massive amount of gravel, at times spreading a series of nests over thirty feet of river bed. A big rainbow may take as much as two or three days to complete her spawning act.

The amount of time that the eggs spend in the gravel depends on water temperature but, as with all other species of fish, the eggs eventually become eyed, the embryos fill the egg case and break out. In the case of rainbow trout, the fry stay quietly beneath the sheltering gravel until their nourishing yolk sac has been absorbed, after which they work their way loose and start feeding in the stream on minute life. The casualties at this stage are immense, but some will prosper and grow, migrate and come back in turn to spawn in their place of birth.

The instinct to return to a stream has brought about a tremendous increased rainbow fishery in the Great Lakes area and in large bodies of water where rainbows have been stocked, such as New York's Finger Lakes. Although these are freshwater lakes tremendous rainbows, some weighing 20 pounds or more, fight into all the suitable creeks rivers and streams during spring spawning, and anglers await them, lining every inch of the bank and the shoreline (see picture, opposite).

The tremendous success of this inland trout fishery may be a sign of hope for rivers throughout the more northern part of the Atlantic seaboard. If some of the gross water pollution can be cured, it should be fairly easy to establish steelhead populations corresponding to the rainbow populations which are creating such incredible scenes inland. The rainbow itself, since it is a hardy, self-supporting species, might be a better fish for some of these waters than the more vulnerable Atlantic salmon.

Name The Trout

The family of Salmonids is one of the most valuable in the world in terms of sports, recreation, tourism and simple commercial fishing value. The Atlantic and Pacific fisheries for the salmon species are worth the earth — billions of dollars, when one thinks of the harvest

This scene from a Michigan river is typical of the crush that develops on rivers flowing into the Great Lakes when the rainbow trout or the coho salmon run. It is hectic, noisy, and by no means idyllic, but the rewards are great, as can be seen here.

that is taken year after year; and inland, even the dreary pieces of real estate take on a greener hue if there is a trout stream running through the property. It is strange that with this incredible value and with the way men feel about these fish, confusion continues over a number of species. I am going to attempt to clarify some of this, although within a short period of time, people may well be shaking their heads over *my* definitions.

In a scientific book on North American fish published in 1905, the authors listed 35 separate species of trouts and chars. As scientific knowledge and research moved ahead, a number of authorities reduced this number, but three decades later there were still lists insisting that at least thirty separate species existed. Many of these fish were given local names and did not differ, except in such minor details as color and possibly size/weight ratio. In works written as late as 1959, claims were laid that rainbows, steelheads, Kamloops and Mountain Kamloops were separate. They are all the same fish — the rainbow trout; and the only other name that perhaps should be used is *steelhead*, applied to those migrant members that feed in the sea and return bearing the salt color marking of steel on top of their heads.

The brown trout has escaped most of the confusion, though people still think there is a difference between *German* browns and *Loch Leven* browns, names given to different batches according to their place of origin. Much confusion surrounds the brook trout, for it seems that every time someone caught one with a color variation he claimed that it was a different species. Some old books contain pictures of as many as twenty fish that are all brook trout, but have been given local names because of some slight difference in color or shape.

In a book published in 1959 the author lists six char for North America: brook trout, lake trout, Dolly Varden trout, arctic char, *aurora trout* and *red trout*. The italics are mine, for today we would class the last two fish either as brook trout, or as subspecies too closely related to be worth separating.

So this leaves my count at four chars and it is quite possible that some time in the future I too will be thought wrong. Even now, the success of the Ontario Wendigo program (see page 27) has led scientists to believe that the lake trout and brook trout, used as the basis of this remarkable hybrid, may be so closely related as to be one species that evolved into different forms and ways of life.

Many people insist that the aurora trout is a separate species, but the layman's word is often useless. In Timagami, Ontario, where this fish is supposed to live, I became very excited when an Indian guide told me he would take me into a lake, isolated from all surrounding waters, where we would catch the rare aurora trout. Alas, the aurora trout turned out to be brilliantly colored small lake trout, maturing at about 1½ pounds on a diet of plankton.

So be very careful when people start listing trout under a dozen names, for local variations are legion and game wardens are notoriously lacking in sympathy for the angler who tells them "That's not on my limit of brookies, that's a Screech Island Red trout."

I selected the brown, the rainbow, the brookie and lakers for this chapter because they represent the differences in those salmonids for which most people fish. If you can capture these, then the golden trout, the Gila, the Dolly Varden and arctic char are all fair game to your skills. We are going to examine two true trout and two char.

Trouts

True trout have a Latin name *Salmo,* such as *Salmo trutta* for the brown trout, and *Salmo gairdneri* for the rainbow trout.

Chars

The chars are of the genus *Salvelinus.* The brook trout is named *Salvelinus fontinalis*, and the lake trout is named *Salvelinus namaycush*, a charming mixture of Latin and Indian. The lake trout is so different from the other three that it will be discussed in all its aspects in a separate section towards the end of the chapter. Each of the four species has a number of local names, so I will list the major ones, and hopefully, help to clear away some of the existing identity confusion.

BROWN TROUT (Salmo trutta)

Known also as the *German* brown, the *Loch Leven* brown and sometimes the *European* brown trout, this species started the cult of trout angling, for it was the fish for which the earliest writers cast their crude flies.

The brown is a European fish, as its common names suggest, and was brought to North America in a series of plantings that began around the latter part of the eighteenth century. Although the strains of brown trout that were brought here from Germany and the famous Loch Leven in Scotland must be completely mixed by now, the names persist, at least in literature.

Distribution

Brown trout in Europe are found from the Mediterranean, north to arctic Norway, east to the Black Sea and to Siberia, and west to the northern part of Spain and of course throughout the British Isles.

In North America the brown trout has been planted widely and there are few suitable locations today where this fish is not found. It has been said that it is present in over 40 states, and in Canada it occupies a great deal of the southern area waters which were once the domain of the native brook trout. It lives and prospers in waters that would be too warm, and maybe a bit too impure for the brookie; and thus it is often found in clean streams fairly close to towns where water pollution is not too serious.

Identification

The brown trout is a rather stocky fish with a definite brown, or brown-yellow shading and prominent spots. Young fish have a slight fork to the tail, but adult fish have a beautifully squared-off "rudder." The back is a dark olive-brown, shading to light brown and yellow on the flanks, and to a creamy white on the belly. The flanks have rusty red or orange spots and the large *black* spots with light borders that are found on the dorsal fin, the back and the upper portions of the sides help to distinguish the brown from the brook trout and laker. The brown is distinguished from the rainbow by its almost unspotted tail, whereas every inch of the rainbow seems to be covered, including the whole of the tail.

Size

It has been said that the average size of the brown in eastern streams runs to 1½ pounds, a large average size caused by the very large fish which exist in even the small, clean creeks. The largest reported brown trout was one in Scotland that weighed close to 40 pounds. While this is subject to argument, there are well-substantiated reports of browns in the 20- to 30-pound regions, and fish from 7 to 10 pounds occupy selected holes in thousands of North American waters. The cannibal nature of this fish aids in its growth, but it is more likely that its wily nature allows it to escape capture in many waters and thus grow to a superior size.

In the well-regulated European trout rivers, old cannibal browns are removed by fair means or foul when spotted, in the belief that they are better out than in, since they prey on smaller fish, but still starve. I once watched in strong disapproval as a skilled old river-keeper fished a 10-inch live trout for a marked big brown, in a river that averaged around 7 feet in width. When the lunker pouched the live bait and was dragged in, I was forced to admit that those folks know their business, for this fish weighed 7 pounds, but was lank and lean, with hollow flanks, and a head and jaws as big and as ugly as a mean crocodile. A fish in this state, said to be "going back," bears no relationship to the big, sleek, smallhead browns found in many North American waters.

Spawning

Brown trout spawn in late fall or winter any time from October to February, according to local weather conditions. The fish move into the streams seeking gravel redds and running waters, but lake fish with no access to streams will spawn on coarse rubble near the edge of the lake, in similar habit to the lake trout proper. The number of eggs varies from 450 in a small female to about 3,000 in the larger fish, and the fry hatch by spring.

Feeding Habits

The brown trout eats other fish, this including his own kind, as well as the unfortunate, timid, "taker"-sized rainbows and brook trout dumped in front of his nose from a hatchery truck. However, this trout never gives up the habit of eating aquatic insect life and at some time of the day or night will turn from the juicy crayfish and mollusks, and gorge on all the available insects. Frogs, mice, moths and even small muskrats are taken into the capacious maw of the brown trout and swallowed with one gulp, yet even the largest fish in the stream will forget such gross appetites and begin delicately sipping down tiny insects that float on the surface of the stream. Since food of this size can be of small nourishment value to the biggest fish, it is possibly a habit retained from younger days.

M.G.LOATES

The glorious native eastern brook trout, a most enchanting sports species, today, alas, is being pushed further and further north by the polluting activities of mankind. The brookie is a delicate species, a fish of the purest waters where the depths are chill enough in the summer to support this char. The biggest brook trout are found only in the far northern lands, and even this habitat dwindles year by year.

Beneath a chill falls, an angler fishes delicately for the brook trout feeding in the oxygen-rich waters. In this type of habitation the brook trout does well, and privileged indeed is the angler who hooks and plays this most beautiful of all fish species found in North America.

In lakes, browns tend to occupy deep holes, but, unlike the lake trout, are more apt to cruise and feed, especially in the late evening and early morning when minnows or fly hatches create a feeding period. In rivers, their choice of location is at once wise and hard-nosed, as they choose the best deep hole they can find in a place where there is a sheltering bank for protection and where the current brings down food to their doorstep. In any stream with a population of brown trout the best fish will be in the best pool, the next best fish in the next best pool and so on, for the brown is not in the least reluctant to fight ruthlessly for a preferred habitat. If you take a big brown from a pool, always remember to make a note of it, for within a very short time, there will be a new tenant, almost as big as the original.

Browns are largely night feeders that drift out of their holes to move into the nearby feed zones, but these wary fish are always ready to slip back home and stay there if anything is amiss.

RAINBOW TROUT (Salmo gairdneri)

The rainbow has as many incorrect common names as any fish that ever spawned. Often called Kamloops, steelhead, silver trout, Mountain Kamloops and so on, the proper name of the fish is simply *rainbow* trout. However, those fish that migrate to the sea are properly called steelheads, and while it is not accurate to call the big Great Lakes migratory fish by this name, in my opinion it is harmless and rather romantic. But the common names applied to this fish are nothing more than that. It is a single species.

Distribution

It would take a computer more than a long weekend to list all the waters in the world in which rainbow are to be found today. This native North American fish is held in such high regard that it has been planted in every suitable water in the world. Native to the waters of the coastal regions from Alaska to California, the rainbow, a wanderer in his own right, has been shipped out and planted in New Zealand, Australia, South America, Europe, India and a score of other lands. In North America the species has been spread wide as a simple stream dweller, and the migratory form continues to create an incredible fishery in such large water systems as the Great Lakes and New York's Finger Lakes. Rainbow trout today are where you find them, and that is everywhere that has conditions which suit their wandering needs.

Identification

The rainbow is usually easy to identify on sight, being silvery with a green or green-blue on the back, and with a lovely red or scarlet streak running down the sides of the mature fish. It can be distinguished from the brown by the mass of small black spots that cover every part of the body and fins, except for the belly, and by the fact that these spots extend to the end of the tail. It differs from the brook trout, in that it has no red spots, the belly fins are one color and it lacks the very pretty china-white edging found on the pectoral and anal fins of the brookies. This general coloration can vary a great deal with habitat and feed, so follow the system of observing the spots and it will be impossible to mistake a silvery, sea-run brown trout for a rainbow.

Some fish caught in migration runs in the big fisheries of the eastern inland waters can be puzzling in that they are not silver, but quite dark. The first one I caught I took to be a kelt, in other words, a fish that had spawned and taken on a dull hue, as the Atlantic salmon does. I was surprised to find that the fish was fresh-run and filled with eggs. It had the usual markings of the rainbow, with a slightly duller red stripe down the side, and seemed to be simply a darker form of the standard silvery fish. I have seen many like this since and they match the silvery fish in size, shape and condition. I accept them without question, but would like to know *why* they should be different, whether it is feed or an inherited factor.

Size

The biggest rainbow trout reported to date weighed 52½ pounds, and came from a large lake in British Columbia. This is extreme, but it has been shown that when this species is planted in large bodies of water with suitable feed situations, it has a surprising growth potential. In the smaller streams, populations of prolific rainbows range up to 1½ to 2 pounds, and at this size provide grand sport and are an excellent table fish.

Rainbows were planted in Lake Pend Oreille in Idaho some years ago and thrived to such an extent that they utilized previously planted kokanee salmon as their forage species. On this rich diet, the growth rate of the rainbows was phenomenal. From plantings made in the fall of 1942, two new world-records were caught in 1945 and these were only four-year-old fish. A study of their scales showed that they had grown 15 pounds during their third year. The fish that set the world record in this lake weighed 37 pounds, was 40½ inches long, and 28 inches in girth. Steelhead trout running to the sea reach 20 pounds easily and 30-pound fish are not uncommon. The improving eastern fisheries, such as the Great Lakes waters, may soon compete with these fish. At the time of writing, rainbows of barely 20 pounds have been taken and possibly, in future years a planted kokanee population may allow a growth rate that will match the amazing situation of Lake Pend Oreille.

Spawning

The system used in spawning by rainbows was covered earlier in this chapter, so we will only deal here with some minor points.

Most rainbows spawn in spring, running into the rivers or searching out the streamy redds from March to late May, according to conditions. However, there is always a heavy fall run of migratory rainbows up the rivers from the lakes and a number of these fish are ripe, and do spawn. On the west coast there is a *winter* run of fish steelheads which spawn at any time from December to May.

The fry hatch in the gravel, commence feeding as soon as the egg yolk has been absorbed, and usually stay in the river from two to three years before heading to the wild open waters and the rich feed to be found there. When rainbows spawn in short rivers the fry apparently move in a feeding pattern out of the river and along the edges of the lake, for I know a number of such rivers very well and by midsummer it is obvious that few fish are present.

Feeding Habits

In stream habitats the rainbow has a basic diet of small aquatic life ranging through insects, nymphs, crayfish and little fish, especially such toothsome items as the sculpins. Its feed varies little from that of a brown or brook trout of similar size.

When the rainbow heads into big waters he changes substantially, becoming a purely carnivorous species, harrying the shoals of herring, alewife, perch, whitefish and school minnows. The angler must base his fishing approach on this feed pattern. Most big rainbows are caught on their spawning run though, and it is possible that their reactions at this time are less guided by hunger than instinctive response to stimulation.

Location

The smaller stream-dwelling rainbows are quite easy to locate, as they remain in the flow, which will bring down food and provide a modicum of shelter. These rainbow trout can make better use of water than either the brown or the brook trout, and tend to the more open areas of streams. The gypsy nature of the fish makes him less of a hermit than the brown.

The lake migratory fish are a different tale. Twice each year, in the spring spawning run and the fall run the rainbow steelheads enter well-known rivers and swim up with seeming disregard for the anglers lining the shores. I once saw three large rainbows resting in a smooth fast current just above a minor rapids they had swum, finning contentedly less than 3 feet behind a line of anglers who were casting frantically into the middle of the stream.

It is almost impossible to suggest a regular habitat used by rainbow trout in large waters. They are wanderers, and sometimes make incredibly long journeys in a very short time. But it is known that they follow and prey upon schooling smelts and alewives. About the only reliable method is to fish just offshore near the mouths of creeks and rivers when the rainbows are expected to make their biannual runs. This gives two distinct fishing *seasons* in the year, and makes for first-class fishing.

BROOK TROUT (Salvelinus fontinalis)

This delicate and lovely char, native to northeastern America, has been given a bewildering number of common names, including speckled trout, square tail, Aurora trout, red trout, and even mud trout, (in Newfoundland). Even its proper name, *brook* trout, is a subject of confusion in parts of Canada, especially Ontario, where many anglers believe that the fish is called a *brook* trout only when it is caught in a small river, and that the larger fish taken in wilderness lakes are *speckled* trout.

Less hardy than the brown and the rainbow, the brookie is regarded by thousands of anglers as the most prized quarry of the fisherman. Often naive, always subject to easy destruction from man's constant misuse of the land, the brook trout is still with us — an easy fish to catch, but one that can gladden the hardest heart.

Distribution

Native to northeastern America from Georgia to the Arctic Circle, the brook trout has been planted in other countries with suitable waters, and in many regions of North America which are outside its natural range, including some western areas where it has done poorly because of fierce competition from hardier native species. It prefers the wilderness and does best in isolated areas where there is chill water, cover and little angling pressure.

Since the brook trout is a short-lived fish, and easy to catch when small, it is only in remote districts such as the wilds of Labrador, northern Quebec, Ontario and Manitoba, and the lush and lonely lakes of South America, that it reaches any great size. A four-year-old specimen is rare and the species may attain an age of ten years but only in these places. However, the fish is so popular that there are always men willing to pay to be flown into virgin brook-trout fishing territory. The fame of a wilderness lake or river is spread when triumphant anglers return with deep, brilliantly colored brook trout in the 10-pound class; angling pressure is applied; the limited population of big, old fish is very quickly depleted; and the search moves to the next hotspot and the small population of large but easily caught fish. The only note of hope in this is that as long as a breeding population is left, there is the chance that the wilderness waters will recover. Unfortunately, the big wilderness brook trout is one of the very few species of freshwater fish that can be forced to extinction by fair angling.

Identification

The big wild brook trout in its spawning robes could never be mistaken for any other fish, for it blazes magnificently with deep hues, red predominating. Except for the pallid fish from the hatchery, which arc fed on liver and deprived of natural coloration, the brook trout can normally be recognized by the rich red spots with bluish halos which are on its flanks. The color of mature fish varies tremendously according to the habitat and type of feed, but is standard enough for identification. The color of its back ranges from a near black through brown to green, and there is a distinctive china-white edge on all the lower fins.

Size

The world-record brook trout, which weighed 14½ pounds and was 34 inches long, was taken in 1915 from the Nipigon River in Northern Ontario. Although several very large brook trout are caught each year, they only weigh between 8 and 10 pounds, so it seems likely that the 14½-pound fish is not just exceptional — it may be unique. Still, they say records are made to be broken, and perhaps some time in the future scientific work will produce a race that will grow much larger than this.

In the best brook-trout waters around the fringes of the wilderness, a 4-pound brook trout is a grand catch, a 3-pounder is nothing to sneer at, and fish around 2 pounds arc an excellent standard.

In waters further south, the majority of fish caught weigh quite a bit less than 1 pound, with 4- to 6-*ounce* fish making up a large part of the catch. Once, in an unfished northern river about 3 feet wide I found an overcrowded situation, and fat little brookies hit everything I dropped into the water. I caught a legal dozen of the little fish, none of which was as long as my hand, and while I doubt that any of them weighed more than 3 ounces, no one could produce fish as delicious as they proved to be.

Spawning

The brook trout spawns in the fall at which time the mature fish often wear an almost scarlet cloak. I found this entrancing the first time I saw it. I was walking around the edge of a northern lake in late October when I noticed a great red hue in the shallows ahead. I was enchanted to discover that it was caused by masses of spawning brook trout.

When spawning in streams, brook trout work up into the head-waters, intent on finding a shallow, gravel-bottom stretch with a current that will wash down over the redds. A nest is cleaned out by the female, the eggs dropped, fertilized and covered with gravel. When the fry hatch out they live on the nutrient from the yolk sac, until it has gone and they are forced to come out and participate in the savage life of the stream. The number of eggs laid is small compared to some other species of fish, averaging 100 for a 6-inch female, and about 1,200 for a 14-inch fish.

Feeding Habits

This fish is less of a predator than browns and rainbows, enjoying insect life of all types, as well as crayfish and terrestial creatures that fall into the waters. The larger fish are more predatory and will take a complete range of lures from spinners to fairly large spoons. The bigger fish are particularly fond of the slimy sculpins, which they hunt rapaciously and greedily gobble.

Location

Brook trout can often be found in lakes by simply locating the area with the water at a temperature they prefer. They are unhappy at temperatures above the fifties and will always move in chillier levels if possible. Once, on a lake that was thought to contain no fish, I was dunking a minimum-maximum water-temperature thermometer at regular intervals and found a line of very cold water. I trolled along my discovery and caught a bulging brook trout of 6 pounds 4 ounces.

In very cold northern lakes the fish tend to cruise the waters in search of food. In streams and rivers, brook trout occupy much the same sort of feeding station as browns and rainbows, including under-cut sections of banks; deeper holes and eddies below rapids, log dams, or other stream obstructions; and the edges of fast currents at bends and bridges where there is a wash of feed and a place of concealment.

On a river where all three species are found the skillful angler will tend to fish carefully in all these places and will probably capture all three as he fishes up or down the stream.

"Intelligence" Assessment

It is difficult to realize the gap in "intelligence" which exists between these three similar fish. The brook trout is actually a rather simple fish and the rainbow is little better; yet the brown is cunning and wily enough when mature to contend with the highest skills of the angler. Earlier in this book I stressed the cunning of the carp, but the brown trout in public fishing streams can be one of the hardest fish to take.

Many people resent any criticism of the brook trout, but I write that they are simple-minded because it is a proven fact, not because of any prejudice. The brown is much more capable of protecting himself and has a far greater instinct for survival than the other two fish, and wild strains of brookies have better survival capacities than hatchery-bred strains. We should examine this more closely, as it has a direct bearing on angling needs and, more important, should be considered when restocking programs are suggested.

Some years ago a series of experiments was conducted at Cornell University to study the differences between a strain of wild brook trout from an isolated lake in the Adirondacks, and a strain that had been raised for ninety years in a hatchery. The two groups were raised in troughs set side by side and it was obvious that the wild trout were less comfortable than the domesticated strain. During a growth period of one year, the fish from the wild stock were continually frightened by the sight of humans, while the domestic strain was not. When the fish were compared at the end of the year, the domestic fish had grown to an average of 5.2 inches, while the wild strain averaged 3.6 inches.

Both batches were then released into natural conditions. Just seventy-three days after planting, 80 per cent of the domestic fish had perished, compared to a loss of 67 per cent of the wild stock. During this period it was the wild fish that grew faster. The domestic strain never became wary and the survival capacity was 65 per cent for the wild strain, to 43 per cent for the domestic.

Brown trout seem capable of inheriting wariness and fear of man, for while the heavily fished streams of southern England harbor some of the world's most evasive brown trout, lochs and rivers in isolated areas of Scotland, and especially the Orkney Isles, have great stocks of brown trout that are caught so easily by comparison, that they appear to be a different breed. They are only different in that those in the north are little fished, while those in the south have been heavily fished for at least 2,000 years. I suggest that the existing stocks of browns in the southern streams are made up of fish descended from generation after generation of "smarter" trout that survived because of wariness or some similar factor and bred with other fish possessing similar qualities.

When brown trout brought to North America were taken from heavily fished waters in Germany and Loch Leven, these two wild strains of fish, well-fitted for survival, were mixed to create a highly superior species for planting.

All trout appear to have the ability to inherit wariness and possibly the superior wariness of the brown trout relates directly to the fact that they have been subjected to angling pressure for many more years than brook trout.

When browns are compared to rainbows and brook trout their superior ability to survive is very much in evidence. An experimental stock of browns was planted in an Oregon river with an equal number of a similar strain of rainbows with the end result that *one* brown was taken for every *four* rainbows. In a similar experiment in Maine, the ratio of captures in a brown/brook trout trial was *one* brown trout to every *five* brookies.

Brown trout grow so large on small rivers in North America, because their sharp survival instincts permit them to live longer than the brook trout. The fact that the rainbows go out into the lonely reaches of the big waters is all that prevents them from sharing the small growth and early demise of the native brookie.

Tackle and Techniques

Our basic spinning outfit is excellent for taking stream and lake browns, brookies and rainbows. Used with a slightly heavier line, it also serves well for trolling offshore for the migratory trout heading into the rivers to spawn.

However, for people who prefer special gear, I suggest a medium-action and medium-weight fly outfit, with a hollow glass rod from 7 feet, 6 inches to 8 feet, 3 inches, a single-action reel, and a level line weighed to match the rod. This type of gear is excellent for stream fishing and can be used to fish live bait with a bobber, a small shot leger, or with just a single shot on the leader to roll the live bait down where the fish are feeding. Later, when the angler has gained some knowledge of the habits of trout, he can get a tapered line to match his rod, and enjoy the ritual of fly fishing.

In my long angling apprenticeship, my first trout were taken on live bait, and it wasn't until I was an adult that I took my first brown trout on a dry fly cast to feeding fish. I did not feel deprived because I baitfished for trout, and in fact, I learned a great secret that angling writers have kept from their public for years — you can catch far more and bigger fish on bait, than you can on the fly. The baitfishing I have in mind is not the technique of throwing in a big dew worm and sitting on the bank to wait for a bite. It is a very subtle system of angling.

Without doubt, one of the most effective techniques for taking stream trout is with the minute nymphs and other aquatic creatures on which they regularly feed. A brown or brook trout might spurn the big dew worm trundling down close to the bottom with a big hook sticking out of one end, but when a mayfly nymph, or a caddis grub floats down and twists and flips as it writhes near the bottom, they are very interested.

These are the baits that I use, and because they are small it becomes necessary to use hooks that correspond with their size. I carry a range of size 14's, 16's and 18's, and although most people have never even seen these sizes, I assure you that they are efficient, and hold so well that they are difficult to remove from the jaws of a sizable trout.

To fish these small hooks better and to make the bait seem even more natural, I use tapered leaders on my spinning gear to thin the line to a mere hair at the terminal end of the tackle. Fly outfits are best rigged with the commercial tapered leaders, but the spinfisher can make his own, using the valuable blood knot.

The Tapered Leader

If ultralight spinning tackle is used with a 4-pound-test nylon monofilament line a tapered leader is unnecessary, as this weight is highly suited to fishing with small bait, but lines of 8- to 6-pound test should be reduced to a 4-pound, or in very clear waters, even to a 2-pound tippet.

For example, when using a taper from 9-pound-test spinning line to 4-pound-test tippet, we cut off 3-foot lengths of 6-pound and 4-pound line and start the taper by tying the 6-pound line to the 8-pound line in the following fashion:

The Blood Knot

Cross the two strands leaving 6 inches of spare line and hold the join firmly between your thumb and forefinger. Take one end, (it doesn't matter which) and twist it around the standing part four times, then bring the end back and poke it through the loop formed by the crossed strands. Now shift the knot under the opposite thumb and forefinger and wind the other end four times around the standing part before poking it through the loop so that it comes out the side opposite from the first end.

Next, hold each end firmly between each thumb and forefinger and pull *all* four parts tight. When the knot is neat and taut, snip the ends close to the knot. Then knot the 4-pound-test length to the 6-pound line in the same way and you will finish with a neat 6-foot-long leader that is tapered beautifully from the main line.

This knotting-taper system works properly only when the two ends joined have similar diameters — such as 6-pound to 8-pound; 10 to 12; 17 to 20; or 25 to 30. When the leader is tapered in the opposite direction, that is, from a light line to a heavy tip, it is called a shock leader and is excellent for use with light tackle where big fish are apt to be encountered (see Chapter 4, page 97).

Stream Baits

An ample supply of natural bait can be picked up from the under-side of rocks lying in the shallows of the trout stream and there are dozens of useful live creatures in the water that are easy to catch.

On the underside of the rocks are the strangest little creatures, some of them rather like miniature dragons, all of them fearful in shape and design. These are the larvae of any number of useful aquatic fly species such as the stonefly, cranefly, dragonfly, mayfly and so on. Some are tiny, some are fairly large, but all are outstanding baits when presented on an ultralight tippet with a tiny hook.

One of my favorites is the caddis larva, a strange little insect that at this stage lives in a short stick-like home, or in a cunningly fashioned and superbly camouflaged tube made by gluing together various items of stream debris. Chivvied out of this home, the caddis appears as a fat white maggot-like creature, and even the wisest old brown in the river will move his ponderous bulk over to intercept one of these toothsome tidbits floating downstream.

I fish these on at least a size 16 hook or, better still, a tiny size 18 hook using a fragile bobber to guide the bait into all the likely places. A single shot on the leader can allow these small baits to be trickled down into all the likely places.

The essence of this style is a patient, gentle probing of the holes with a sly and careful approach. Once, on opening day on a public fishing stream, I used this method to take a limit of brown trout up to 2½ pounds, and six wild brook trout to 9 inches long, while anxious, so-called anglers rushed from place to place, throwing hardware, flies, and monster-sized dew worms into every likely pool. All I did was move into each stretch, and try out the pool, let it rest for a while, and then trot down a wiggling miniature larva into the better places, trickling it along the bottom, beneath an accurately weighted slender bobber. I found it rather amusing later when a disgruntled fisherman set up with the finest spinning tackle told me that the stream was fished out. When I showed him my trout he almost choked in disbelief.

At times it is impossible to find a place to pick up these aquatic baits and in such circumstances I have often probed the bank, breaking open rotten logs and filling a small bait-box with the strangest array of natural baits. It doesn't seem to matter what it is, as long as it is alive and well presented on the light gear. I once took a 3-pound brown from a hole with a baby salamander I found under a stone. I've used crickets, wood lice, grasshoppers, slugs, wasp grubs from a nest smoked-out, tiny little white worms, fly maggots, and of course the more normal dew and red worms broken into small pieces to suit the tackle.

All these and more will bring fish to the careful fisherman of the streams, and if the angler baitfishes properly, he will begin to learn the way of the waters and the fish, and be better prepared for the specialist delights of baitfishing for the big browns, or for taking stream trout in the delightful ritual of fly fishing.

Stream Tactics

The above baits and methods will take most brown trout, stream rainbows and brook trout, but larger baits are needed for the real lunkers and a big brown trout is usually made the subject of a campaign that can last a whole season, not just a few minutes sending a bait down into a pool.

The best live baits for the lunkers are large live fish that suit the trout's size and appetite. For a really big trout a 7-inch dace is not too large, with a 3- or 4-inch minnow highly suitable for fish in the 4- or 5-pound range. Once the fish is spotted and the campaign planned, the angler crawls silently into casting range and flips his minnow bait to run down and wander around the home of the trout.

Large brown trout are usually night feeders, and in my favorite areas, where every little creek holds superb brown trout in all the deeper holes, the specialist fishermen seldom venture out until the nights get velvety warm and dark. The rule of thumb with this group is that if you can fish without needing to wear a protective head-net, you are out at the wrong time. So you locate your fish, prepare a big bait, sneak up on the lunker, and prepare yourself for a long campaign.

Very specialized tactics are sometimes brought into play, such as the time my wife, Joy, floated a huge white moth on the surface using a bubble float so the stream would take the struggling moth under a road bridge where she could hear a fish feeding.

Sometimes the brown trout loners grow so large that it is very difficult to land them on ordinary tackle and in this event it again becomes necessary to invent new devices. By far the best example of this that I know of occurred when a friend took a brown that had escaped almost everybody in the area at least twice. I had hooked the beast four times on light tackle and lost it every time in a wild tangle of sunken trees and logs.

My friend went out one night and fastened a small live mouse to a little harness holding a sizeable gang hook. He attached this hook to a 50-pound-test line wound onto a monster reel fixed to a solid 14-foot

English greenheart salmon rod. After dark he swung the mouse out to the centre of the pool and lowered it in. As it swam vigorously towards shore, old brownie sipped it in with joy. At that point my friend leaned into the fish, kept up the rod point and walked backwards into the shallows while the furious brown trout beat the pool into a sea of foam. It weighed 14 pounds, 12 ounces, which is not bad in a river that averages 12 feet in width, with its biggest pool less that 20 feet across and filled with snags.

Lake Tactics

I find lake fishing for browns, brookies and standard rainbows less fun than stream work, mainly because it seems more of a chuck-it-and-chance-it affair, with little of the subtle work required in stream fishing.

Live bait is much less useful and the most generally accepted technique is to cast the shorelines and select areas with a range of artificials ranging from Mepps spinners to flies. One of the most effective flies is a slim streamer resembling a small fish, which can be thrown by fly gear or by spinning tackle with a pair of split shot added to the leader to provide casting weight.

Special attention should always be given to the shoreline upon which the wind is blowing, especially if there is a hatch of insects about, but I like to fish this windward shore at anytime, because the movement set up by the lapping waves has a powerful pull for the small fish which draw predators. When the wind is blowing the length of the lake it is best to take the boat to the right casting distance from the shore and drift down before the wind while lures or flies are carefully thrown into the shallows and retrieved.

I once sat on a lonely lake without taking a fish, until I began rowing gently back and forth across the edge of the shallows with my leader, equipped with three flies and two shot, kept well back from the boat. Then I caught a dozen fish. This is a variation of trolling, which the British call *whiffing*. Straightforward trolling is also a good tactic. It consists of simply trailing a lure behind a slow-moving boat regulating the depth by the length of line released, with or without one or more sinkers on the leader. This lazy method is often the best way to catch big migratory fish as they feed offshore near a river before coming in to make their run, so I will treat it more thoroughly with respect to steelheads in the next section.

Migratory Trout Tactics

Western anglers who fish the great rivers on the Pacific side of the Rockies would be horrified to see the tremendous crowds that gather at the inland fishing locations to enjoy a run of rainbows from a big lake or impoundment waters. Yet in the midst of that crowd some extremely good fishing is possible as long as the angler doesn't expect to be able to use the fly, in which case all that he would catch would be the second line-up of men on the bank. If I seem to be relegating fly fishing to a secondary role, please remember that I do not say that you shouldn't use flies. I am merely telling what happens, not describing some dream world where the trout streams are empty except for the solitary figure of a lone angler. If you wish to fish for the big migratory rainbows on their biannual runs anywhere but in the extreme west-coast steelhead waters, you will have to use either bait or lures in very confined quarters.

Although illegal in some areas, rainbow spawn is the best bait for a big rainbow. Even salmon spawn is inferior unless it is very fresh and tied up in a little bag with the oil oozing in globules from each individual egg.

Worms are excellent baits when used by truly skilled fishermen, by which I mean those people who work along the river before the fish run and select the places where a fish will rest for a while. They return when the season opens and the fish are moving, place a dew worm in the exact spot, sit back and eventually collect some of the biggest rainbows caught during the run.

Spinners such as the Mepps No. 2 and No. 3 are excellent as long as it is possible to bring them back across the stream, letting them tap over the stones on the bottom as they curve in towards the angler. If used well, this is most effective, although it is apt to be expensive because of lures lost through snagging. It is best done in those smooth, fast places *above* a rapids, which is the sort of water where the steelheads stop to take a breather, even if it is pouring through as from a massive firehose.

For the newcomer who wants to catch a rainbow on its run, there is nothing better than a little sack of spawn made by tying up roe in a square of nylon stocking to form a small sack about the size of a man's little finger to the first joint. Slip this onto a size 8 or 6 hook, with a suitable weight of sinker set a couple of feet up on the line, cast it out and allow it to wash around in a selected spot. When a running rainbow meets with it he will take it in one swift bite.

Typical places to fish a worm or a sack of spawn are: at the junction of two currents at the bottom end of an island; at the bottom of a long, smooth flat above rapids; at the edge of broken and smooth water, in an open stretch; just below a jam of logs or a dam that breaks the current flow and provides a resting place for a running fish. You will learn to tell them by experience, and will also learn that when a big rainbow takes off downstream you must follow until you get below the fish and by putting on pressure, make him fight the force of the stream and the urgent pull of the rod. For rainbows are not really hard to catch, being neither shy nor smart. But you should know that there are very few freshwater fish that can fight as hard. When they feel the prick of the hook they fly wild-eyed into the air, land and take off downstream, determined to get back safely into big water, even if it is twenty miles away.

Offshore trolling for the steelheads brings in many big fish each year in all large freshwater lakes where they are found. It is usually necessary to keep moving back and forth over a reef that forms a gathering place for the fish, or to work lures along a line that intercepts the route taken by the fish as they head up river. The lures used vary according to the locale and the type of feed, with small, wobbling spoons being the most common. Standard spinning gear, 8-pound-test line, a lot of patience and plenty of gas for the outboard motor are the major needs — plus the determination to keep fishing hard for the very worthy rewards.

LAKE TROUT (Salvelinus namaycush)

The lake trout has been left until last not only because it is the largest of the four chosen trout, but also because it is more limited in distribution, has a specialized habitat and, for angling purposes, requires an approach altogether different from that given to the others dealt with previously in this chapter.

Known also as the gray trout, togue, mackinaw trout, mountain trout and salmon trout, the laker is the largest char and an important species both for sport and as a commercial catch. It is strictly confined to the northern locales of the North American continent.

They are fairly easy to catch, once the special techniques are mastered, and anglers who have only caught lakers of moderate size are often unaware of how formidable they can be when they weigh 18 pounds or more. The medium and large fish are powerful, showy fighters, even though they don't jump. Their jaws are very strong and Indian guides that are used to both lake trout and pike appear to have a great deal more respect for the well-toothed mouth of the lake trout than for that of the biggest pike.

Distribution

Lakers are found in cold, deep lakes throughout Canada and Alaska. they extend north to Hudson Bay, east to Labrador, west to the Yukon and Alaska and south to those northern regions of the United States where there are chill, deep, oxygen-rich lakes. Having such a restricted habitat, the fish does not take well to stocking, and although it is found in a few mountain lakes outside its range, the lunker fish remain well north.

This is a distinctive feature of the lake trout, for most species appear, on the average, to do less well in the more northern waters. The person seeking a monster fish must go up to the north country, and since the old axiom of *big water, big fish* is definitely true, he should seek it in one of the great waters, such as Great Slave, Great Bear, or Athabaska Lakes.

Identification

The lake trout is a distinctive fish with a large head, a deeply forked tail and a mass of wormlike spots that cover back and sides, cheeks, gill covers, dorsal and tail fins. These lighter coloured spots stand out well against a darker coloration of the back and sides that varies from light grey through green to almost black. Generally the larger waters harbor the lighter fish, the smaller lakes tend to produce a darker variation.

Where lake trout are locked into a small lake and have developed plankton feeding habits, the smaller fish produced tend to be brighter in color. It is not uncommon to find the fish in these places with an almost rainbow sheen on their flanks, but the large head, the forked tail and the mass of lighter coloured spots allow for a positive identification.

In numerous places around the Great Lakes, where the lake trout-brook trout hybrid — the Ontario Wendigo — has been planted, anglers will find a certain amount of difficulty in setting them apart from true lake trout. The Wendigo — or splake — however, retains the square tail of the brookie and this is the clue. At a glance, the Wendigo and lake trout appear identical in color and shape, except that the tail is different.

Size

Although the laker is a big fish, the average size of those which are caught is probably somewhere between 3 and 5 pounds but fish of 20 and even 30 pounds are common even in the southern part of the range, and rod-caught fish of 40 pounds cause little excitement if taken in the northern areas. Even these are small, compared to those caught every year by commercial nets men, who regularly land lake trout weighing around 100 pounds. At the time of writing, the biggest laker caught was a 102-pound monster from Lake Athabaska in 1961. This fish (see picture, page 29) was an oddity, gross in comparison to other large lake trout, and lacking sexual gonads, it had never spawned. More normal fish of approximate weights have been recorded regularly and there seems to be no reason why a keen angler, who is prepared to spend some time in the arctic lakes, could not catch one of these massive trout.

Spawning

As the waters begin to cool in fall, lake trout move out of the deep, chill waters that they have occupied all summer and seek out the spawning beds around October and November. The beds are usually broken-rock rubble or rocky shoals, but the fish will use clay bottom or even a bottom on which large boulders are scattered. The depth may vary from 1 foot to 60 feet, and some rivers may be run for a short distance. The area is swept rather carelessly and the eggs are dropped and fertilized, with none of the nest-building fury of the other trouts.

The nest is left unprotected and about the only eggs that will be safe are those that fall into cracks and inaccessible crannies between stones. The period of incubation varies from about 160 days at 37° to 50 days at 50°. The fry move from the shallow-water redds into deep water almost at once and it has been found that when kept in shallow water with direct sunshine, as in the average hatchery setup, the baby fish have a tendency to develop cataracts.

Feeding Habits

Lake trout are carnivorous and feed on school fish such as herrings, ciscoes and whitefish. Big fish will hit quite large baits and indeed it is not uncommon to hook a medium-sized laker and have it attacked by a bigger fish.

In some smaller waters lacking suitable forage-school-species, lake trout often become plankton eaters and because of this diet seldom exceed 3 pounds. These fish usually go on a feeding spree in the shallows in the spring, when fry and minnows are bunched into schools and at this time, these small but hard-fighting little lakers can be taken on a full range of lures scaled down to their size.

In the early growth stages, lake trout feed on all manner of aquatic insects, and while this does not carry over into adult feed patterns a big hatch of juicy insects such as mayflies will bring the smaller trout scuttling up for a feed at the surface.

Location

Lake trout can be found more easily during the summer months than any other freshwater fish, for their physical needs move them directly into deep channels, cuts and holes. From a swift look at the water, the angler can usually tell where the deep water is (obviously not close to a low marshy shoreline) and then quickly plumb the depths with spinning gear, which will soon disclose the presence or absence of lakers.

More careful investigation is sometimes necessary. I was once at a Canadian lodge where little fishing was done for lakers and was told that the channel near the lodge was at least 80 to 90 feet deep and very cold. This was the local conviction, but I found it puzzling, as the banks each side were low in contour, so I checked the main channel with a minimum-maximum thermometer and found that the water was, in fact, less than 20 feet deep and only 64° at its coldest point. Worse still, it had a mucky bottom, consisting of a light silt in which no self-respecting lake trout would dream of living. However, in the broader portion of the lake there was a sheer cliff running into clear, green water, that was 85 feet deep, at a temperature of 46°, so I ran a troll the length of the cliff, scant yards out from the rock and caught two lakers of about 3½ pounds each. Local knowledge is usually more reliable and the guides at fishing lodges have the best spots pinpointed with accuracy.

In the early days of spring just after the ice has moved out, lake trout feed on the surface and also roam along certain shorelines hunting food, and it is best to fish around islands and to troll along shorelines close to the deep. But even then, a deep troll in the known channels will always catch fish, and casting is best reserved for places that have proven to be havens for fish at this period of the year. This will be discussed in more detail in the section on fishing techniques.

Laker Tackle

While our standard spinning outfit is useful in fishing for lake trout at certain times, the angler who is going to pursue these fish in a serious manner must buy special gear. Most angling for this fish is done by trolling and there is no better way to learn the good spots in unfamiliar waters. This means probing as deep as 80 to 100 feet and we will need a pretty large trolling spoon, which we can only get down efficiently by weighting the line.

People who have never attempted this form of angling regard it as a terribly coarse way of fishing and as a dull and heavy style. This is because, instead of nylon or some form of fiber line, we use either a single-strand metal line in steel or monel metal, or a very thick braided line with a heavy lead core. People fishing this way for the first time usually refuse to use a metal line, and insist on putting out a nylon line with a heavy load of sinkers to take it down. What they fail to realize is that the metal line is not only heavy, but is vibrant and sensitive, thus allowing the angler to feel the difference between a lure scraping over a clay bottom and one scraping a sand bottom. A length of nylon line that is long enough to take a big spoon deep becomes elastic even when sinkers are used. This rubbery effect, further softened through hundreds of feet of water, soaks out all contact with the lure.

A friend was fishing with me one day and he swore the mightiest oath that he would never use "that unsporting metal line." He found it necessary to put out 260 *yards* of his 15-pound-test nylon trolling-line, and when we reeled in to move on, after I had walked three small lakers to the boat on my metal line, he sheepishly wound out a 4-pound lake trout — dead. He hadn't felt the fish hit and had spent an hour or more

Even the most inexpensive trolling tackle can take good fish, such as this fine lake trout from Lake Timagami in Ontario. This basic outfit consists of a stubby steel rod with a spring coil tip to prevent line kink, a reel of large diameter for swift retrieve, plus a long narrow Williams Whitefish wobbling spoon.

dragging the poor thing around until it drowned. He moved onto metal line.

The standard gear used in metal-line deep trolling consists of a solid or hollow glass rod of 7 feet, with a wooden butt, a big reel with star drag and free spool, metal line of different tests and the normal lake-trout spoons. These items are moderately priced, costing far less than the better spinning or casting tackle simply because you don't cast when trolling and therefore the rods and reels are less complex.

Rod

Lake-trout trolling rods should be powerful sticks of 6 feet. You should be able to swing a good rod violently in a solid *whamp* and feel a confident surge of power through the entire length of the rod. This important test will reveal any weak spot where the glass joins the wooden handle and any rod giving evidence of working at this joining should be at once rejected. Wire trolling involves a lot of weight and any flaw in the rod will be considerably enlarged once there is several hundred feet of line out behind the boat combining with the drag of water resistance to curve the trolling rod into its working bend.

I once snapped three design models that I had been asked to try out on a fishing trip and told the makers that the glass tip/wooden handle join was inferior. At a show a year later, I was shown the newest design, and snapped one model by flexing the rod with a surge of power. An examination of the broken half (conducted, I might add

This successful lake trout fisher-man has landed his fish on basic metal-line trolling tackle. His rod is short but powerful, with the hollow glass stick seated well into a plain two-handed wooden butt. His reel, a level-wind star drag ocean model, is securely clamped into the reel seating.

behind the tackle stand away from the eyes of the public) showed that the designers still did not realize what was needed, for they had only set the solid glass tip 2 inches into the wooden butt, then glued it in place and finished off with some fancy silk wrapping. Trolling rods with the glass joined to the wood by ferrules are very strong, but this glued joint was useless, so I suggested that they simply lengthen the solid glass sticks and build the butt handle over the glass, to give strength and avoid using a ferrule. They did this and produced a rod that was worth a great deal more than the moderate $15 price that they set.

Select a stick with action in the top third, for the metal line is rigid and the lures must be worked the whole time they are being fished. Check that the line guides are strong and well made, choosing carbides rather than most other materials, and roller guide tips rather than the rigid ones. The rod should also have a pretty stiff butt and a heavy-duty reel seat with solid screw-fittings.

This fishing is done mainly with lines of 20- to 30-pound test and most of the rods offered in sporting goods stores will be correctly balanced for these lines. Lighter lines such as 15- and 12-pound test require lighter rods and the ultralight metal lines are used with standard angling tackle.

Reels

The best reels for basic wire trolling are the standard saltwater models with star drag and free-spool fittings. I strongly recommend the superb Mariner series by Penn. These reels have narrow spools, but a large capacity and I have three slightly different models that have served me well for many years and which I also use when I go light-tackle big-game fishing in saltwater. But even the moderate cost saltwater reels are great for this work and in the lighter weights it is a good idea to get one with a level-wind system so the line goes on evenly.

The important features for wire trolling reels are fast retrieve, to get the long line in quickly; power in action, because trolling can be rough work; and especially a non-reverse spool to avoid overruns and kinked lines, for fighting a jammed, kinked wire line out of a big reel is a painful process.

Trolling Lines

Deep-water trolling lines are made either of a single wire of copper, steel or monel metal, or of a braided material covering a heavy lead core. Neither type is pleasant to use but the single wire lines have a number of valuable features. Core lines are softer and less liable to kink than single wire lines, but are also thicker, sink more slowly, and offer more water resistance in relation to their test weight. Most dedicated laker anglers put up with the difficulties of fishing with steel or monel line because it is a sensitive contact with the terminal tackle. As he gains experience, the angler can use the line as an extension of his sense of touch, for the taut line is an accurate conductor and the skilled fisherman can tell the difference between mud, clay, sand and marl, just through the feel of the rod tip and line as the lure hits bottom. This is felt through as much as 300 to 400 feet of line strumming tight behind the boat and falling in a great shallow curve.

Some lines come with beads set at 50-foot intervals, with a number code of beads at the 100-foot marks, which makes it possible to tell how much line is out. This can be extremely valuable if a fish is hit over an underwater reef, for there are probably more fish at the same depth. Once, while trolling over such a place with 350 feet of line trailing behind the boat, I caught a good fish, and caught five more fish in six runs by putting out the same amount of line, with the boat moving at the same speed.

But nothing can be of more value than the sensitivity of the line groping down in the green depths to give the angler an exact indication of what form the ground takes. It is the one feature that turns lake trout deep-water trolling into a craft rather than a dreary matter of luck.

The amount of line needed varies according to depth and in the deep Great Lakes region is usually 500 to 600 feet of monel or steel wire attached to a solid base of strong nylon monofilament line. Since the largest lake trout are formidable fighters, it pays to have a good backing line beneath the wire and on my reels there is a minimum of 200 *yards* of nylon, beneath 500 feet of wire, which brings the line well up on the spool to allow for a faster haul in. Care must be taken that the wire line has full clearance at all times, even in the excitement of a battle, for careless work might result in a high build-up one side of the spool, and the angler should make it a habit to run the line back and forth across the spool when winding in, so that it does not build up in one place.

Leaders

I never use a leader as such for lake trout fishing although I do use a length of nylon monofilament that I suppose could be termed an "action leader." Although lake trout usually chomp down hard on lures and get the hooks square in their mouths, I like to add to the lively dance of my spoon, by using a 6-foot length of 20-pound-test nylon at the end of the steel wire line, tying a snap to the end of the nylon so that I can change lures without having to change the nylon. This prevents spending time making knots.

Lures

Lake trout prey on all the shoal fish they find at their preferred level, so this is the basis for a choice of lures, which should include a fair range of wobbling spoons. They must be slim so that they will sink fast, thus aiding our metal line; they must be in a range of sizes that will imitate whitefish, herrings, ciscoes and whatever else might be around; and most important of all, they must be designed to send a brilliant series of vibrations through the waters to attract the predator to the bait. See Chapter Five, page 108 for information on how to make them work properly, and Chapter One, page 19 for an illustration of the need to add fish scent to the trolling lure.

I carry the following basic lures: first, the big, long, slim spoons such as the Dominion Canoe Spoon and the largest size Williams White-fish, and Williams Wablers; next, what I term the medium spoons, around 6 inches long, including the Lucky Strike Spoons and the Williams Whitefish and Wablers; and finally, the strangely shaped Gibbs Popeye, the Dominion Spoon 177, the Fullwave and Halfwave Spoons by A L & W, and two handfuls of Williams spoons in every shape and size. I have them in gold and silver, but don't think that color matters one bit. I have often used the opposite color to that which the guide has suggested, and still come home with a limit, which makes the point for the younger guides, but which convinces some of the older ones only that I happen to be lucky. In that dark, green world where the lakers feed, *action* counts more than color.

Trolling Techniques

A Word About Guides

In lake trout fishing more than any other form of angling, a guide is a decided asset. When deep trolling however, he is more — he is a part of the game. The guide locates the best spots, handles the boat and the chores and gaffs or nets the fish. It is possible for an experienced angler to deep troll with wire gear *and* run the boat, but it is not something I would recommend to the beginner.

The guide can make the day, but he can also ruin it and it is up to the angler to establish a proper relationship right at the start. I always tell guides that I want to be kept in the picture and that no moves to new locations are to be made without discussion. I also insist that in matters of angling, my word is final. I wouldn't dream of attempting to tell a guide if a rapids is safe to run, or a section of windswept lake is safe to cross — that's their business. But I am well aware that few guides have my general experience in angling and I make it clear from the start that if I yell for the boat to be stopped when I hook a fish, it must be stopped immediately.

It is not necessary to be arrogant about this, but it is necessary to be firm. Since I am paying the expenses, I insist that the angling be carried out my way, and if the guide doesn't like that, he may look elsewhere for a client. Actually, friction between angler and guide is infrequent, but if there is going to be any, it's just as well to get it over with on the shore rather than out in the boat when a big fish is on the hook.

I enjoy the company of guides and have the utmost respect for their ability and character. Mutual respect is the proper attitude and it makes for peaceful, enjoyable fishing.

Trolling

In deep-water wire trolling the first important element is the choice of the fishing location, the second is the handling of the tricky tackle, and the third is the stamina to persevere until a fish is hooked.

Wire line must be kept taut at all times on the reel spool. The reel must always be on anti-reverse except when paying out line, and then, the spool must be firmly controlled by pressure with both thumbs. If the line gets away and makes an overrun, it will wind back and jam the spool. Worse still, if this happens the line usually gets dangerously kinked.

As I near the reef, I prepare the 6-foot length of 20-pound-test nylon joining it to the end of my 20-pound-test monel wire line. I don't like direct nylon to wire connections so I fix a simple, strong snap to the end of the wire, and join the nylon to the snap with a clinch knot.

The wire is easily rigged by bending it into a loop at the end, slipping the snap into the bend and twisting the doubled wire to make a neat join. I clip off the sharp end with pliers, crimping it down so it won't tear my fingers if I grasp the joint. Then I join another snap to the end of the six-foot nylon "action leader," for easy replacement of lures.

I usually begin with the biggest spoon, a Dominion Canoe Spoon about 10 inches long, with a fish head mounted on the gang hook, as suggested and described on page 19. I rub the spoon with cod-liver oil to remove the man-scent, make sure the rod, reel, wire, line, snaps, spoon and fish head are all in good shape, and then lay the line out over the side and start feeling for bottom. This is the part that calls for 90 per cent of the required skills.

The amount of line to go out depends on the weight of the wire and the spoon, the speed of the boat, and the depth of the water. Every time the deep-water troller moves into a new location, he has to deal with a new and highly complex problem.

Generally about 350 feet is needed to fish an average depth at average speed, so it is usually safe to let out a long length of line right at the start. The best way to do this is to approach the chosen trolling location from some distance away. Put the spoon over the side with heavy thumb-pressure on the spool, and have the guide crack open the throttle to lance the boat forward. This slashes line off the reel viciously, far more efficiently than if the boat crept along at basic trolling speed. The spool purrs away while your thumbs almost blister, and when there is a good long length of line out, have the boat slowed to regular trolling speed and stop the reel so that the line can sink to its proper level.

Chances are that the spoon will be running along quite a distance from the bottom, so when the line has adjusted to the boat's speed, start letting off more line in dribs and drabs, carefully feeling all the time for bottom. I cannot emphasize too strongly that this must be done firmly, but under control. If your lure is not close to the bottom it is not fishing and you are wasting precious trolling time. On the other hand, if you allow the line to run unchecked, the spoon may drop into broken rocks, which can mean the loss of a great deal of gear. The best lake trout angling is over such rocky beds which are a constant threat to spoons when the angler is probing for bottom.

The best technique that I have found is to let about six turns of line run off the spool, stop, work the lure with the rod to allow the extra line to sink, and repeat this until the bottom is felt. The moment there is a touch on the bottom of the tackle, I lift the rod high, turn the reel swiftly and swing the lure up through the water. Rock registers as a series of shocks along the line that the angler feels like a dental drill boring deep; sand and small gravel actually grate on the spoon and can be felt on the rod point; clay or a solid bed of heavy mud catches and releases the spoon in smooth but irregular pulls; and muck or marl cause a woozy feel as the lure sloshes through a mix of leaves, sticks, weed and thin mud.

Mud or marl is not laker ground, but is often hit on the approaches to a good reef. This is one reason why I use lures that vibrate sharply, such as the Dominion Canoe Spoon, the Williams Wablers or the Williams Whitefish, for if weed or a stick get caught on these clean-working spoons, the resulting loss of their sharp vibration on the line warns the angler that he is fouled and he will not spend time trolling ineffectually.

Working the Lure

Once the lure is accurately positioned close to the bottom the hard work begins. The boat's speed is carefully set to just work the lures and maintain depth, and the angler hauls back on the line, releases it, and makes his lure dance, jig, and flutter down in the green depths. This is essential and is very hard work with the heavier lines. If there are two people fishing identical rigs from the same boat, and both their lures are down to the correct depth, *but only one is working his spoon,* he will be the one who will get all the strikes. People who know this are the ones who consistently come back with good fish.

The necessity of working the rod back and forth all the time raises a problem. A sharp kink in the single wire lines is dangerous, and must be carefully smoothed out, but they often form at the extreme end of the rod tip when the rod is moved back and forth to work the lure. Some trolling rods are built with a spring end that prevents this by curving with the line, but all other types of rods require the angler to move the line up and down, so that a different spot on the line is subject to the sharp angle at the rod tip. I always suggest that beginners and youngsters give the rod a maximum of twenty strokes, let out a couple of feet of line, give twenty more strokes, take in a couple of turns and continue this throughout the day. If this is not done, and the line is kept in one spot too long, it will fatigue and snap and the startled angler will watch in anguish as several dollars worth of line disappears into the lake.

Snags

Getting snagged is an unavoidable part of deep-wire trolling techniques, because if your lure doesn't hit bottom now and then, it means that you are probably not fishing the right depth, and a bump on the bottom, while reassuring, sometimes results in the lure getting hung up. When this happens the rod whips down swiftly and line is pulled steadily off the reel against the drag (heaven help you if the drag isn't set when this happens). When experienced trollers feel this solid grab, they push the rod quickly towards the stern and bring it back, sending a bounce down the slackened line. About 85 per cent of the time this jag creates a curve in the line that will whip the lure free, and the troller can spend more time fishing, and less time freeing his lure from snags.

If the bounce back doesn't free the lure, the boat is brought to a halt and the other trollers swiftly wind in their lines. The boat is backed up, following the snagged line, while the angler winds in the slack and keeps the line taut so it can be followed back. The boat is stopped over the lure and the angler, using his limber tip, gives some swift jags on the line from the opposite direction of the lure's entry. This will usually free the lure, which should then be inspected for blunted hooks, but if it remains stuck, the line is given a smooth lift by hand. When doing this, the angler should try to avoid kinking and should protect his hand with a rag or glove.

Strikes

In this form of angling the fish hit so hard against the unyielding line that they almost always set the hook themselves, but lake trout have iron-hard mouths, and the moment a pull is felt the rod should be brought up sharply in a strike. Very big fish have the nasty habit of swimming up, grabbing the lure and swimming away with it clamped between their jaws. If there is no attempt to set the hook, they only need to open their mouths to get rid of it. But if this happens and the angler strikes, the slim, smooth spoon will slide through the jaw and plant the gang hook in the outside of the mouth, where it takes hold firmly. So, everytime there is a tap, a bump or even a slow steady pull, hit fast, and if nothing happens, work the lure more actively still, for lake trout will hit and miss, come again and miss again, and come back a third time and be caught. But don't get the impression that this fish is easily fooled. I once had one pick three minnows off my gang hook, one at a time, so neatly that it was obviously darting in and nipping them off, ignoring the wobbling spoon. I now use a fish head on the *shank* of the hook, so that if any fish wants it, he has got to throw an open mouth over the gang hook first.

Playing Lakers

The beginning angler will probably be disappointed by the lack of fight put up by a small or medium-sized laker on wire trolling tackle. When you hook fish to 4½ to 5 pounds on 20- to 30-pound wire, you simply wind them in to the boat. Many fish of this size are lost each year because an angler has stopped winding when he could no longer feel the fish. This is when the laker usually manages to throw the hook. On heavy tackle such small fish give no more than a couple of kicks and a wiggle. But lake trout are not poor fighters: they are simply overcome by the weight of the gear. Bigger fish will make strong runs against the heavy tackle and lunkers of 25 pounds and more will try just about every trick known.

They should be played in the same way as any other game species. When they run, allow them to take line against the drag of the reel and when they stop, raise the rod and pump the fish. It is smart to keep a really big fish out to one side of the boat, or it will surely get the line caught in the propeller, and here's where a top-grade guide is worth his weight in gold.

The finest system for getting most of them into the boat is with the largest landing net possible, and since I find that many guide's nets are unsatisfactory, I always take my own. The largest trout are best handled with a gaff, planted firmly into the area back of the gills. Then the fish is brought in smoothly, but only after the hold has been tested and found firm.

Spinning and Other Lake Trout Gear

Light-tackle fishermen usually take on the lake trout in very early spring, at ice-out time, when the water temperature is low through all levels of the lake. In some regions this period heralds the spawning runs of certain species, and when conditions are right, the lake trout come inshore to shallow waters, preying on the shoals of spawning fish that are attempting to reach the redds. In some areas of the Great Lakes the prey is the smelt, and in numerous other places it is the various species of suckers.

Most of the activity is near the mouths of streams and rivers used by spawning bait fish, and the early spring conditions present hazards, such as floating ice and limited open water.

Stillfishing with a live minnow is one of the favored methods for this very short upper-surface lake trout season, but I have observed that the anglers who cast a lure in the pattern of the spawning fish, get more and bigger lake trout. The trout are roaming throughout the depths and the greater coverage available with a lure seems to be more effective.

Many people believe that this short period at ice-out is the only time when basic spinning and casting tackle can be used, and they eagerly head north as early as possible to join battle with lakers before warm weather sends the fish into deeper waters. However, I have found that lake trout are not as rigid in this respect as most people think they are, and I take a number of lake trout on my standard spinning outfits every year, trolling those places where they are known to live with my lure a short distance beneath the surface.

I discovered this technique in a most unusual way. I was staying at a Canadian lodge early one summer to gather filmed material for a television series and took a day off to fly to a wilderness lake for brook trout. The camera crew decided to go fishing, and being rank amateurs, shied away from the wire-line trolling rigs I offered them. "Not me," said my producer frankly. "All I want to do is wander around the islands trolling with some light tackle. I don't care if I catch anything or not."

The camera and sound men agreed, so I rigged them all with medium-weight spinning outfits, put medium-sized lake trout spoons on the end of the lines, and clinched a 1-ounce sinker on each outfit, about 3 feet up from the lure. They took off from the dock, dropped lures over the side as they cleared the boats, and started trolling lazily around Chimo Island, which was our base. My plane came along, the gear was loaded and as we turned out to taxi into smooth water for our take-off, I asked the pilot to make a run over my friends so I could give them a wave. When we did this, I spotted my producer standing up in the boat with a deep bend in my powerful steelhead rod. I nearly fell out of the plane when I spotted a fish beneath the surface, violently fighting the hook. It was obviously going to be a long fight and since time was limited, we shot off for my rendezvous with the wilderness brook trout.

All day the image of that big fish beneath the surface stayed in my mind, and when I got back I was not at all surprised to find that it was a superb lake trout of 19 pounds. Confident that this light-tackle fishing was the real sport, my crew took every opportunity to use the spinning gear rigged as before, and in the odd times that they had for fishing during the remaining two days, those rods racked up seven fish, four of them over 10 pounds.

It worked again when I tried it out on my next trip and ever since then I spend a portion of every lake-trout trip lazily trolling around the edge of the islands over deepish water. Over the years I have learned that this system will take fish in even the warmest weather, either late in the evening or early in the morning. In the northern waters, where the water is frigid and the air cool, the method works any time of day, and any angler who gives this easy form of lake fishing a good try, will sooner or later thrill to the walloping belt and glorious fight of a lake trout on light sporting tackle.

13 🐟 Panfish Delights

~~~~~~

The word panfish describes a group of fish species that are considered too small to be called game fish, but fit nicely into a frying pan. Some anglers use the term with a sneer, implying that panfishes are beneath the dignity of the angler. I disagree. I enjoy a session fishing for white bass or yellow perch and there is a lot of so-called game fishing that I'd pass up for the chance to spend the dawn hours fishing for bluegills in a southern swamp.

Panfish are found in wilderness lakes and in ponds located within major cities. The fish are all eager biters and first-rate quarry for youngsters. They are not hard to catch and are usually excellent table fish, toothsome and dainty.

Panfish helped make one of my family vacations almost dreamlike. We rented a furnished cottage on a wild sand-bar island with a clean blue lake out front, and a wide, slow-moving river on one side of the property. We caught bass, pike, and channel catfish at the mouth of the river, but the real fun began when I found that a row of sunken trees along one side of the river held very large, hungry crappies. Every evening I drifted my boat down the smooth river, casting little bugs into the tangle of branches, catching fiery, slab sided crappies that tore the calm waters to a white froth in their fury.

I have often worked my way at dawn down a wild southern swamp, casting flimsy little bugs into the edge of the rich undergrowth,

268

Panfish are a delight for all to catch, but for a youngster, catching a big bag of jumbo perch on light and simple tackle is sheer bliss.

to hook the heroic little bluegill, or bream. In spring, when the spawning runs start, I find it great fun to take a group of youngsters to some local river with a high run-off, where the yellow perch are swarming. The squeal of a treble voice signals a child's thrill at hauling out a fat-bellied little perch.

The fisherman who sneers at panfish has gone too far in specialization. He has become like the purist who at first fishes only for trout, next, only for trout on artificial lures, and then only for trout on the dry fly, until finally he hunts the hatches to find flies at a specific stage of development. The purist ends up turning to entomology — he stops fishing and starts chasing butterflies.

YELLOW PERCH (Perca flavescens)

I have never heard a perch called anything but a perch. There are all kinds of funny names put down by angling writers, but I have never heard them used, and I will not trouble the reader with them. This is one of the most widely distributed panfish and a species highly appreciated by millions of anglers who flock to the rivers and lakes when the perch are running in the spring. It is an eager biter, a dogged fighter for its size, and one of the finest food fishes found in freshwater.

The perch's habit of snapping at the tails of prey fish is superbly illustrated by this small yellow perch that hit the tail treble hook of a lure almost as big as itself. It also shows how predators will attack a large lure, for this is the largest Cisco Kid pike and muskie plug, which was being cast for giant pike in Saskatchewan's Lac La Ronge. (Note the over-sized diving vane on the nose of the plug, which makes it run deep.)

Description

The yellow perch, a member of the family *Percidae*, is a close relative of the yellow walleye. It is a deep-bodied fish with a humped back with a tall back fin, bristling with sharp spines. The scales are rough to the touch, and there are sharp serrations on the gill covers. This is definitely a prickly customer. Color varies slightly according to habitat, but the fish are generally olive on the back with bright yellow flanks and a sheer white belly. The sides are barred with six to eight dark stripes. There is little chance of mistaking this species, as there is none other like it.

Size

The yellow perch is a much smaller fish than its husky walleye relatives. The average size caught varies from 4 to 10 ounces. Fish of 1 pound are common, but are nonetheless called *jumbos,* 2-pound individuals are caught fairly regularly and the top weight is around 4 pounds. Since perch are a school species, capturing one usually means that others will be taken, usually all the same size, since they tend to gather according to size. This can sometimes mean a great catch either of big fish or of small ones, but not invariably, for perch roam a great deal when feeding and the schools tend to wander back and forth, so that more than one school may be encountered.

Distribution

This is the most widely distributed member of the family, and its range has been extended by stocking in a number of western states. The yellow perch is found throughout Southeastern Canada, and extends south to Kansas, Missouri, Illinois, Indiana and Ohio. In the Atlantic drainage system, it runs from Nova Scotia to South Carolina. It is present throughout the Great Lakes drainage basin in great numbers and the commercial market catch of this species in Ontario alone reaches 9 million pounds per year, with a value of close to $2 million.

Habitat and Habits

Perch will live and prosper in rivers and streams, but appear to have a decided preference for lakes, small and large, especially where there are cool waters and bottoms of sand, gravel or rock, with clean sparse weed beds where the fish can hide or hunt for food.

It is a predator with an appetite out of proportion to its size, and is known to hit plugs and lures bigger than itself. The perch is often hooked, because of its style of predation. It is a sight hunter that corners shoal minnows against an obstruction and then charges in to pursue them. Perch follow every twist and turn of the fleeing bait fish, constantly snapping at the tail in an effort to slow the prey fish or put it off stroke long enough to make it an easier catch. Very large old perch often are caught with ragged tails, for the tail-snapping technique is so ingrained in the perch that they can't resist taking a nip at any tail crossing their field of vision (see illustration, opposite).

Spawning takes place in the spring, when the fish often ascend rivers and create an exciting run for the cane-pole set. They usually spawn at night, over weed or brush, sticking the ribbon-like egg mass on to vegetation where it clings and is sometimes exposed when spring water-levels drop. No protection is offered by the parents and the fry hatch out in approximately three weeks.

Tackle and Techniques

The perch is a relatively small fish, so special tackle is needed. As with many of the panfish, there are times when a cane-pole outfit with a bobber is by far the best rig. When I take youngsters out to a nearby river for the spring run, I rig them all up with 9-foot light bamboo poles, 8-foot lengths of 12-pound-test line, bobbers the size of walnuts, three split shot for weights, and size 6 hooks. With minnows on the hooks — or even better, snippets of dew worm — the kids fling their gear out, let it float down in the current and, when a perch pulls the float

Panfish Delights 271

away with that peculiar bob-bob-bob action, lift the pole to set the hook and to swing the perch out all in one motion. It is simple gear for simple fishing and our catches are always better than on those parties where the kids are working with reels and other unnecessary gismos.

When boat fishing where the jumbos are gathered, any light spinning outfit or baitcasting rig will suffice. A float may be used if the water is not too deep — and it seldom is — or better still, a rigid leger is made up, with a small sinker tied to the end of the line and two single hook-links fastened to loops made further up the line. This style of terminal tackle is called a paternoster and allows the angler to cover two depths at once.

Perch will hit all small spinners and plugs, as well as streamer and wet flies, but most dedicated anglers feel that they are best caught on bait. They will take any small minnow or worm and will even bite freely on a segment of flesh removed from one of their own kind.

Edible Qualities

Outside its commercial value, which is considerable, the yellow perch brings sport to millions of people. It is a superb table fish — white, delicate and delicious. In northern regions it is a popular ice-fishing catch as it bites freely, even in sub-zero temperatures. About its only drawback is its tendancy to get into waters where it is not wanted and overbreed to the point where the sports value of the water is greatly reduced. For this reason it should never be used as a bait minnow, or carried into waters outside its regular habitat.

WHITE PERCH (Roccus americanus)

Sometimes called "the silver perch" and often mistaken for the white bass, the white perch is a very small member of the family *Serranidae* and is a relative to the striped bass and the giant sea basses. This is a popular panfish which unfortunately matures at a small size. Because it lives as long as 12 or even 17 years, it is highly prolific and in some waters we find overcrowded populations of small and stunted fish. This is of less account in large fertile waters where there is room for the fish to expand. Given such good conditions, the white perch can provide rich sport for the light tackle panfish devotee.

Description

The white perch doesn't look at all like the yellow perch, being compressed to a deeper and thinner body. It has a spiny dorsal fin and joined to the rear of this is a second soft dorsal. There is a sort of thin soft membrane joining the two back fins and this provides a major point of distinction between this fish and the white bass. The back is olive green to dark brown, shading to silver or silvery-green on the flanks. Fish taken in salt or brackish waters tend to be brighter in color, having a silvery tone.

Size

The average size of white perch is from 8 to 10 inches, at a weight of 1 pound. Fish of 15 inches at 2 pounds are taken in some fertile waters, and the top weight for this species is about 3 pounds.

Distribution

As might be expected with a descendant of the sea basses, the white perch is found in the coastal regions from Nova Scotia to South Carolina, where it occupies salt, brackish and fresh waters. It is beginning to spread through some parts of the lower Great Lakes.

Habitat and Habits

The white perch eats a great deal of insect life which it grubs from the bottom, so it is usually found in areas where a firm mud bottom encourages insect growth. Saltwater and estuarial schools feed on fry and the larger species in freshwater pursue yellow perch fry of prey-preference size. The white perch runs into rivers to spawn in spring, depositing the eggs in the shallows where they adhere to marine growth — rather as the yellow perch does. The eggs are left and the mature fish move off in schools to search for food. Their pattern of feeding dictates the angling techniques for taking them.

The white perch is a predatory school fish, and one would think, since it is a school fish, and thus subject to severe competition, that it would hit quickly and at times unwisely. But this is not necessarily the case, for they are selective feeders. In early spring the fish grub food from the bottom, gradually turning to the larger insects which emerge as the waters warm, after which they hunt growing crustaceans and the schools of growing fry. By fall, when most of the small fish present have grown too big for the predation of the white perch, they feed on insects once again. The best fun for anglers is in the evenings during the warmer months, when the schools come to the surface to feed on hatching insects. At this time they can be caught on small flies, poppers and slow-sinking artifical nymphs or natural nymphs. Light tackle is a must as they are often shy and selective.

Tackle and Techniques

The best tackle for these fish is fairly light spinning or fly fishing gear. The fish are small and there is little need for powerhouse rigs. Ultralight spinning gear with 2-pound-test line, a round clear plastic bubble float and a collection of live or artificial flies and nymphs form superb tackle for evening-rising fish. At other times, the best bet is ultralight spinning gear with a midget spinner, trolled or worked close to the bottom, in areas where there is water 15 to 30 feet deep, with the firm mud bottom in which white perch typically find their food. Worms and small live minnows can also be used. Try fishing first on bottom; then test the depths by taking line in with a couple of turns of the reel handles at a time keeping track of the number of turns. When the fish are found, the bait should be lowered to the bottom and then swiftly raised to the right level for the school by turning the reel handles the same number of times.

Small hooks should be used for this little fellow, ranging from size 8 to size 12, according to the size of bait used. A big part of the sport is finding the fish and testing depths and techniques until the correct formula is found. The time and trouble will be well spent, for this fish can put up a spirited fight against ultralight gear.

Edible Qualities

The white perch, from salt, brackish or fresh waters, is one of the finest of all the panfish when prepared in a chowder or fried in a skillet. They may be small, but half a dozen topped and tailed fish form a grand breakfast for an angler with a large appetite.

WHITE BASS (Roccus chrysops)

The white bass, often called silver bass in the Great Lakes region, is a freshwater member of the sea bass family. Although found only in limited distribution around the turn of the century, it earned a place of distinction as a valuable sporting and commercial species and because of this has been planted in many regions outside its natural range.

This species bites freely on live bait, lures and flies, and is a determined fighter. Since it is a school species it is common during runs for double-figure catches to be taken by skilled anglers.

Description

The white bass is compressed from side to side, which gives it an upright tin plate effect, and it has a pronounced humping of the shoulders, a spiny first dorsal and a second soft-rayed dorsal that is not attached to the first. This separation of the dorsal fins distinguishes the white bass from the white perch, with further differences that include bright silver flanks with ten or so stripes or unbroken lines running the length of the body and a typically sea-bass like mouth, in which the lower jaw projects past the upper.

Size

As with other school species, white bass catches tend to run towards fish all of one size. If the angler is taking ¾-pound fish and then starts to haul out fish of 1½ pounds, it means that a new school has moved in. I have found that this does not happen too frequently and it is usual to catch forty or sixty fish and find them all of the same size, even though they might have been taken through the whole of one day.

Where I do most of my fishing for white bass a fish of 1 pound is about average and specimens of 2 pounds are considered large fish. But this standard varies and in other places white bass to 2 pounds are considered average, 3-pound fish are known to be caught, and even 4-to 5-pound monsters are taken. In many years of fishing my own area, I have seen just one fish of 3 pounds landed, and compared to the rest of the fish, it was a monster. Maximum size for white bass is probably around 6 pounds.

Distribution

The original range of the white bass was from around the Great Lakes to Missouri, Arkansas, Kansas and the general area of the Mississippi river system. However, since the turn of the century this useful and appreciated panfish has been regularly planted in those areas where there are large, clean waters that best permit the species to prosper. The establishment of major reservoir systems throughout the south and southwest has provided suitable waters for planting and the fish tend to do rather well in these waters, providing first rate sport for many thousands of anglers.

Habitat and Habits

Strictly a freshwater fish, the white bass does best in large rivers and lakes where the waters are clean and clear and where there are large areas of deep waters. It has been suggested that the species does poorly in any water of less than 300 acres.

Spawning may occur anytime during spring, from late April even to July, depending on location and prevailing weather and water conditions. The fish school into stream or river inlets where they swarm in great numbers creating a run which becomes a source of sport for anglers, who often gather in great numbers. The fish spawn in water of a moderate 6- to 7-foot depth, over clean rock, and if conditions are not absolutely perfect, the spawning may fail and a whole generation will be lost. It is said that the white bass usually fail to spawn successfully three out of four times, which accounts for alternate years of plenty and of scarcity. The poor standard in spawning is partially compensated for by the large number of eggs dropped by the female — 25,000 to 1,000,000 according to her size.

On a successful spawning year the fry hatch in two or three days and the little fish form giant, dense schools that are a target for every predator in the waters. The survivors will have reached 5 inches in northern waters and 7½ inches in southern waters by the end of the summer, at which time growth ceases as temperatures drop and the fish stop feeding earnestly.

White bass tend to stay in fairly deep water and to come up at dusk to feed, but when a school gets a shoal of minnows trapped, the fish come boiling up to the surface to attack the minnows, no matter what the time of day. It is a particularly thrilling spectacle. A whole series of rigid fins cut through the smooth surface and create a great boil as they hit the minnows. In such circumstances, white bass will hit any moving lure that is of the right size for their rather small mouths.

At other times, when the white bass are schooling they tend to travel slowly through deep water and are usually caught by deep-fished bait, such as minnows, that are run in front of the school. With the exception of places known to be favored, such as the white water below the power stations on the Niagara River, white bass are, in my opinion too chancy to pursue when running deep. Like most anglers, I confine my angling to well-known hotspots, especially during the times in spring when the schools will be running those particular locations. But any time a school surfaces on feed, it is standard procedure to grab a fly or spinning rod and start fishing.

Tackle and Techniques

Any basic tackle will take white bass and the only point to be made is the use of gear that will be light enough to draw out the sporting capacity of this exciting little game fish. Hooks must be small, for the white bass has a surprisingly small mouth and will think nothing of nipping in, snapping at a minnow and whipping it off the larger hooks. I keep my single hook down to size 8 at the most and find size 10 better still. The size of streamer flies should also be small. Spinners are effective but must likewise be small; size 1 Mepps is quite good for catching this fish, but the smaller size 0 gives an even better chance of success, especially with a short snippet of hair or bucktail on the treble hook.

In ordinary circumstances, I have found it best to fish along the bottom when there is no activity on the surface, using a small live minnow bait. This is best worked beneath a slider float as I find the fish may be in waters as deep as 18 to 20 feet, even on a cool spring day. Below white-water dams or power plants, the small lead-headed jigs are by far the best bait. These are thrown out across the current and allowed to bounce downstream and curve in an arc back to the bank. This form of angling has double value; first, because the non-snagging nature of the jig saves tackle, and second, because its weight and fishing characteristics take it bumping along the bottom where the fish are seeking food. Heddon's Fin jig works extremely well in very fast waters and even the largest size takes good fish. But any good jig with effective bottom-bumping action will do.

In spring, the spin fisherman should throw size 0 Mepps or a similar bright, fast, vibrating spinner, trying different depths until the fish are located. I have found that it pays to vary the depth as at this time of year the schools appear to run far closer to the surface and even in the daylight hours will suddenly boil to the surface. Streamer flies used on either spinning gear of fly tackle are excellent lures and indeed the fly fisherman can enjoy great sport when the fish come up to harass a pack of minnows.

Edible Qualities

Not only is the white bass fun to catch, it makes an excellent meal, and since this short-lived species has a high rate of reproduction, no one should feel guilty about taking home a large catch. It has a certain value as a commercial catch in parts of the Great Lakes and sells at a good price as fresh fish. White bass fillets, lovely, delicate and almost transparent, are perfect for frying and baking.

WHITE & BLACK CRAPPIE
(Pomoxis annularis and Pomoxis nigromaculatus)

These two large members of the sunfish family look so much alike that in most places where they are found together, people seldom bother to set them apart. I am including them under the same heading for this reason, and also because it will make it easier to compare them.

Both fish are called *Croppie* in a number of areas, evidently to avoid saying their proper name. (This always reminds me of the Victorian hostess who, unwilling to mention the indelicate word "leg" to a Minister of the Gospel, asked him if he could eat another limb of chicken.) Other common names for the black crappie include: crappie, calico bass, Oswego bass, strawberry bass and speckled bass. The white crappie is also known as crappie, silver bass and white bass.

Description

Both fish are deep-bodied and are flattened from side to side into dinner-plate shapes, but apart from this the two species differ considerably.

The *black crappie* has seven to eight sharp spines in the dorsal fin, and has a distinctive forehead depression. The color is dark green to black on the back, with silvery sides on which are scattered a thick speckling of dark green or black blotches. The dorsal, anal and tail fins are thickly covered with dark green speckles.

The *white crappie* has six sharp spines in the dorsal fin and also has the distinct forehead depression, but is longer and less chunky in shape than the black crappie and other sunfish. The back is dark green to black, shading down to silver on the flanks, with dark green or black blotches arranged in vertical stripes on the sides of the fish. These stripe formations are more common in young fish and the surest way to distinguish between the two species is to count the sharp spines in the dorsal fin.

Both fish have soft, thin mouths (which has earned them the descriptive name "papermouth") and a hook will pull through if any attempt is made to strike, so the accepted means of putting the hook into a crappie is to simply tighten the line, gently but firmly.

Size

These are among the largest species of panfish. Both are known to exceed 5 pounds, but the average size of a crappie depends very much on where it is caught. I am thrilled to catch a 1-pound white crappie or a 2-pound black crappie in cool Canadian waters, but think nothing of taking much larger fish from warm waters, such as South Carolina's Santee-Cooper water impoundment system.

Distribution

The natural ranges of the two species overlap and both have been planted so extensively that it is difficult to establish exactly where each originated. However, this is less important than the knowledge of where they are now. The white crappie is found from southern Ontario to Nebraska and then south through the Ohio and Mississippi Rivers to Texas and Alabama and north from there up the coastal plain to North Carolina. The black crappie is more widely distributed in Canada, being found in Quebec, Ontario and in the northern reaches of the Great

Lakes as far as southern Manitoba. It is spread through the Mississippi River system to Texas and northern Florida. So it cannot be suggested as the northern form of the white crappie, as some people insist, since the two cover an almost similar range. Extensive planting has moved both fish into western regions, and some crappie were planted in California as early as 1891.

Habitat and Habits

The black crappies prefer clear weedy lakes and rivers, while the white will accept more muddy waters and habitat, probably because the white crappie is not a bottom dweller. I have caught them both on big lakes by drifting down a fairly deep channel, bumping a live fish fairly close to the bottom. I have also taken them off the end of lake points and islands and, as I mentioned earlier, from among the sunken branches of trees lining the eroded bank of a fairly big river. Generally the crappie is a fish that seeks shelter, and because of this the angler should look for them in brush conditions by the weed beds close to deeper waters, in and under sunken trees and even under overhanging banks. The urge in these fish to seek shelter is so strong that in many places giant brush piles are moored out in the lake to form a shelter situation, the idea being that if you lack natural brush piles, adding them will improve the chances of sport.

As the summer heat begins, crappies head into deeper waters, but still seek shelter, and any angler wishing to catch them must locate every brush pile in the lake. This is a very sure method and eliminates any dependency on luck.

Both fish follow the sunfish spawning pattern of building nests and guarding them from predators, but the crappies differ in that they tend to nest in much deeper water than the other species. Spawning time depends on water temperature and therefore varies according to locale.

Tackle and Techniques

Both species of crappies are simple fish to catch, once the trick is learned of tightening the tackle to avoid tearing those paper-thin mouths. The major part of the angling technique lies in locating the preferred hiding places of brush and weed shelter. Once these are found it is only necessary to send down a live minnow on a slider bobber, drop down a small lead-headed jig, or work various small lures over and around the hotspot.

One of the most delightful systems I have seen is the cane-pole-drift technique used on Santee-Cooper in South Carolina. Here a couple or more anglers make themselves comfortable in a flat-bottom boat, put long cane poles out with just the right length of line to reach the fish, arm the hook with a live minnow, and let the boat drift through good fishing waters. The tips of the poles shiver down when a crappie bites, the fisherman lifts with a smooth take to set the hook, an exciting battle ensues and the chunky, slab-sided catch is taken aboard. If there is not enough wind, or if it is blowing in the wrong direction for a good drift, the fishermen *slow-troll,* with the motor down to its lowest possible speed, drawing live minnows past the underwater brush homes. When the crappies take they are fought out on those long but delicate cane poles. It's a pity that this method is so limited in use, for it could be enjoyed in many more areas.

Edible Qualities

I would as soon sit down to a meal of crappies, as to one of almost any other fish you could put in front of me. The flesh is white, delicate and sweet, and that's all I ask in an eating fish. Since both species overbreed and become stunted because there's not enough food to go around, you do no harm if you take home as many as the limit allows. You will enjoy some very fine eating.

BLUEGILL (Lepomis macrochirus)

Known as sun perch, blue sunfish, copper belly and, most important of all, bream (pronounced 'brim'), the bluegill is a most important

Panfishing delights continue through the winter with anglers using tip-up rigs and hand jigs, ice-fishing for everything from lakers to the ever-welcome small school fish. Here, a successful ice fisherman adds a nice fat bluegill to his catch.

panfish. It is a beautiful fish and makes a delightful meal, but most important, it is a valuable sports species, capable of providing recreation in waters ranging from clear lakes to farm ponds. On one pleasant winter trip to the glorious Fripp Island in South Carolina, when it was difficult to get out after stripers, spot and other fish in the estuaries, I spent an enjoyable day with a long, light pole fishing for bluegills in one of the water hazards on a golf course. I used a light bobber and some salmon eggs on a tiny gold hook and caught a fine string of fish that provided me with a top grade breakfast the next day.

Description

The bluegill is often highly colored and there can be a tremendous color variation from place to place. Usually the back is blue-green, or olive-green (even shades from yellow to dark blue occur). The sides are lighter, often with a vivid orange shade at the throat and there are vertical bars on the sides. The fish is short, chunky and compressed from side to side. The mouth is tiny and requires small baits, small lures and small hooks.

Size

The average bluegill throughout the range is a very small fish indeed, for this popular cane-pole fish overbreeds in many waters to produce stunted races that delight young anglers, since they bite freely and are often caught in great numbers. However, the species is capable of surprising growth in rich habitation. It may reach 15 inches and 4 to 4½ pounds, and even in the cooler waters of Ontario is reported to grow to lengths of 10 or even 12 inches.

Distribution

The bluegill is found throughout the Great Lakes, east to Quebec, west to Minnesota and south from there to Georgia and Arkansas. It has been heavily stocked, both as a sports species and as an excellent sports-forage species with bass, (that is the two predate on each other, thus mutually limiting population and providing bigger sporting fish of both species). Thus, this fish thrives over a very large part of the North American continent.

Habitat and Habits

The bluegill loves the quiet, weedy places where it can hide and feed. In small ponds, stunted and crowded populations give a false impression of the fish, since the constantly hungry hordes swarm into every spot where food might be found. Where there is rich feed and room to spread out, bluegills tend to hide away, and the largest fish often spend the daylight hours in deeper waters, venturing into the shallows to feed only at dawn and dusk. These are the conditions that provides what is for me, the essence of bluegill angling — the soft paddling down a southern marsh while the night birds fly by, the cast into the velvet black edge of the brush, the gentle kiss of a fish taking the lure, the swift strike and the raging battle as a chunky bluegill charges in fury across the surface.

The bluegill spawns when the water temperatures reach beyond 60°, which can occur from late May to early August, according to the region. The parent fish scoop out saucer-like nests in the sand and gravel and when the eggs are dropped and fertilized the male vigorously protects them for the two to six days it takes them to hatch, after which it busily looks after the young fish for a few days and then leaves them to fend for themselves in an extremely hostile world.

The adult fish mainly eat insects and any of the smaller forms of aquatic life. Small snippets of worm, fly maggots, salmon eggs or any small lively bait brings results, but the bluegill is a true sporting fish in that it will strike savagely at flies and spinners of the correct size.

Tackle and Techniques

For the most part, bluegill angling is a cane-pole game, using worms, a bobber and a small hook. No one should sneer at this method of taking these hardy scrappers, for it can be not only productive, but tremendous fun. However, the bluegill provide fine sport when fly tackle is used and few would argue that the most enjoyable way of taking them is with a carefully planted small surface bug dropped lightly into the edgings in the early or late evening. Unlike other fish that take bugs, the bluegill prefers the quiet ones, so that instead of cracking the bug to make it spit fury, the wise angler moves it just a fraction at a time, trying for a gentle swirl.

Finally, a word to the bug fisherman and pole-and-can angler alike: when the bluegill takes, set the hook swiftly. This sunfish may only have a small mouth, but few species can be as fast in spitting out something that has suddenly become suspicious. It takes a while to get the knack of it, but fast reflexes are very much a part of this game.

Edible Qualities

About the best comment I can make on the edible qualities of the bluegill is this: my *favorite* breakfast consists of pan fried bluegills surrounded by crisp golden brown home fried potatoes.

There are a number of other fish that properly fit into the category of panfish. Some, such as the yellow bass, are popular locally, others, such as the rock fish, are regarded as pests when they take the bait intended for bigger quarry.

I have dealt with the important species, and any that have been left out can fit into one of the categories I have presented. The punkinseed and the longear, the yellowbelly and the green sunfish, can all be caught in one of the ways I have described. They are smaller fish to be sure, but are important nonetheless. They are often the thrilling start of a life of enchantment for some child who hauls out a brilliantly colored little fish and, with a sense of awe and delight, starts the life-long pursuit of fish.

One of the great delights of angling is a shoreline lunch of freshly caught fish. Here, the author, hundreds of miles into the northern Canadian wilderness, enjoys a plate of golden crisp panfish fillets and beans — food for the Gods and honest fishermen.

In Conclusion

There is so much delight in angling — so much to learn, so much to teach, so much to discuss and to debate. The joy of it is that it lasts throughout the angler's life.

But a book must come to an end and we have reached that point. We started with a discussion of what a fish is; we have looked at tackle; and, in dealing with the major species of fish, we have covered techniques and styles.

Some readers may be disappointed that there is not more of this or that, or that fly fishing has not been given greater coverage. But what I have done is to introduce the reader to the *art* of angling. The deeply based sense of what to do — and when and how to do it — is of far greater importance than the discussion of a particular style. I have given less emphasis to fly fishing partly because of the large number of excellent books on the subject. Also, I happen to know that while this style is the most talked about, most anglers fish with spinning, baitcasting and live-bait rigs — and at that, not necessarily in an efficient manner.

I feel that in the preceding pages we have broken new ground in treating the styles, techniques and ideas that, while not revolutionary, are part of the basic art of the angler.

The art of angling will never be complete as long as there are anglers willing to experiment with new ideas, and with tackle designs resulting from advancing technology.

The scope of the sport is broad and while most people will stay in the pleasant general field, there will always be those who burn with the desire to specialize, to catch the biggest fish in the waters, or to take the largest brown trout, or even to see how light a set of tackle can be used to capture some bruising carp.

All these ideals are what I hope to stimulate by this book. But there is more to it than that. In a world in which commercialism in every field has become the standard of value, I hope that I have communicated some of the joy of a sport that gives personal enchantment of the soul.

So may I, in conclusion, pray that your path down by the waters is a sweet route without sidetracks into purist faiths that deny the very spirit of the recreation. There is a joy in catching every fish from the brightly colored little bluegill, to the lavender-hued leaping rainbow. We are all brothers and sisters of the angle, and all of us should understand what Father Izaak Walton meant when he wrote: "I envy nobody but him, and him only, that catches more fish than I do."

Glossary

Angler: One who catches fish with rod and line for sport, as opposed to the fisherman who catches fish for food and/or profit.

Angling: The art of the angler, the sport of fishing for pleasure.

Artificial: In angling, a bait or lure manufactured to imitate a natural item of fish food, i.e., a fly is an *artificial* when it is tied from silk and feather or hair; a captured mayfly impaled on a hook is a natural.

Bait: A substance used on the hook to induce a fish to bite. Live bait includes live fish, worms and frogs; artificial bait includes lures, flies and such things as doughballs, shelled corn, bread and even macaroni.

Bass Bug: An artificial lure of cork, plastic or hair, fished on the surface, usually on fly tackle, to catch bass. Some large bugs are built for use on spinning gear.

Bass Bugging: The art of fishing a bass bug.

Bite: When a fish takes hold of a bait such as a worm, minnow or doughball fished in a static manner it is correct to say that this is a bite. *See also* Strike, *and* Take.

Bobber: A bite indicator (plastic ball, bird quill, etc.) that sits on the surface and suspends tackle to present bait to the fish. The bob under gives visible warning of a bite. A secondary use is for working the hook bait into a suitable location by controlling its path in a flowing stream. *See also* Float.

Bottom Tackle: The gear at the end of the line, including sinkers and hook systems, used in still fishing rather than casting.

Bottom Fishing: Fishing on the bottom in a static manner as in the presentation of a doughball to feeding carp.

Butt: The lower end of the rod, carrying the reel, usually covered with a non-slip material, and thickened to comfortably fit the hand.

Cannibal: Used to describe a big trout, usually a brown, that through excessive predation of a section of stream, has created an imbalance in the sports fish population. The term should be used strictly in this sense, as the majority of predatory fish habitually eat their own kind.

Cast: The act of throwing bait or lure with the rod and reel or, in the case of a cane pole, by swishing the pole forward and propelling the terminal gear towards the fishing spot. Used also in Britain, to describe a gut or nylon leader.

Chum: Edible or attractive material thrown into the water to draw fish close to the bait. Chum can be simply waste bread or, in the case of pike, whole, dead fish. Chum for some catfish consists of stink material such as blood or oily fish left to rot.

Chumming: The act of putting out chum.

Coarse: The description given to fish not regarded as useful sports-fishing species. An over-used word, often applied to some species of definite value.

Creel: A wicker basket carried on a strap over the shoulder and used to contain the catch of a wading angler. Plastic creels exist, but being poorly ventilated, are decidedly inferior in keeping fish fresh.

Doughball: A ball of bait made from bread or grain materials, either cooked, or kneaded. Often made more attractive by the addition of some scented oil such as aniseed.

Drag: A mechanism built into many reels. Adjustable at will, it allows for the setting of tension on the line to aid in tiring a fighting fish. A secondary use is to assist in preventing overruns of the reel in the event of a fish striking while trolling.

Ferrule: A male and female socket-and-plug system used on the end of rod joints to allow easily transported short lengths to be fitted together to make a long rod. Made mostly of light metal to date, a built-in system utilizing fibreglass has proven to be superior.

Float: Another word for bobber but also used to describe a fishing trip down a stretch of river in a drifting boat.

Gaff: A curved metal hook fitted to the end of a pole that is fastened into big fish so they can be hauled aboard with no strain on the tackle.

This can be done in such a way that the fish is not harmed. There are spring-loaded gaffs that clamp into the fish when triggered, but these are inefficient and in many places illegal.

Groundbaiting: Another term for chumming.

Guide: Usually a professional who takes out an angler, runs the boat, lands the fish, cooks the food, and hopefully turns out to be a congenial companion.

Guides: Rings of hardened metal attached to the rod that carry the line and, through their distribution on the stick, allow an even strain to be exerted on the rod during the playing of a fish. They are functional in casting and in developing the correct fighting curve.

Holt: The resting place of a fish, from which it often darts out to intercept food; used mainly for trout, pike and muskies.

Landing Net: A landing device for bringing fish ashore or into the boat and thus avoiding a strain on the tackle. Most are of net twine suspended from a hoop on the end of a pole.

Leader: The terminal end of the line. Metal leaders protect the line from sharp-toothed predators and some tapered nylon leaders perform the same task, while others, tapering off to fine ends, are used as a means of delicately presenting a small fly as well as offering less visible evidence that might scare a shy fish.

Leger: A bottom-fishing rig consisting of a hook-length passed through the eye of a sinker that is fixed in place to allow a cast, yet allows the line to slide through without a check when a fish bites. This results in an extremely light and delicate unit for sensing bites without warning off a shy fish — yet the sinker can weigh as much as two or three ounces if a powerful stream flow demands it. Not well known in North America, and seldom practiced, the word comes from the Old French *legier* — light, delicate.

Level Line: The basic line used in fly fishing, denoting a casting line of plastic or woven nylon that is level along its length. *See also* Tapered Line.

Level Wind: A mechanism fitted to baitcasting reels. It runs back and forth across the spool when the reel handles are turned and spreads the returning line evenly across the full width of the spool. The term is not applicable to spinning reels which spool line evenly using a different action.

Line Guides: *See* Guides.

Lunker: Popular term for a large fish according to species weight. A 5-pound pike is not a lunker — a 5-pound chain pickerel is.

Lure: A manufactured bait in the form of a decoy of just about any material that, when pulled through the water, will bring about the strike of a predatory fish. A worm is not a lure when fished static, but is when added to a spinning vane. This comes from the Old French *loerre* — bait, decoy used, as feathers on a leather bag swung around the head to bring a trained falcon back to the handler.

Lure Dressing: Feather, fur or nylon hair used in the decoration of a lure or as the raw material in making flies.

Minimum-Maximum Thermometer: A precise form of thermometer that registers low and high scale. Used to record the temperature of different layers in deep water. Anglers are now better served by inexpensive simple thermometers that have a bulb container at the base that takes in water at the chosen depth and keeps the reading static long enough for it to be hauled to the surface and read.

Minnow: Properly, a fish of the family *Cyprinidae*. In angling terms it means any small fish sold, caught, or used alive or dead as bait.

Multiplier: A term that has fallen into disuse today but was previously used to describe reels of the baitcasting variety with gearing built in so that one turn of the reel handles results in multiple turns of the reel spool.

Nibble: A small nudge given the bait either by small fish, or by big ones that have not made up their mind to take. They should be ignored.

Paternoster: A bottom fishing rig of a sinker fastened to the end of the line, with two or three hooks on short leaders stuck out at right-angles from the main line. Especially useful for fishing for perch and sunfish, this rig aids in covering different depths to efficiently intercept school fish swimming through varying levels. The word is very old in angling, coming from the Latin *our father*, and based upon the fact that the rig closely resembles a rosary used in prayer.

Plug: Wooden or plastic lure commonly used in bass fishing, but available in a range of sizes suitable for all predatory fish. Muskie plugs may be as large as 14 inches long.

Popper: A hollow-headed plug or bug surface lure that, when given a nudge, tips down sharply against the surface of the water and makes a range of noises from gulps to pops. Invaluable in bass fishing, but often extremely effective for members of the pike family.

Pound Test: The breaking test of line rated upon the snapping point when wet and stretched to exhaustion on a specific testing machine.

Predator: Fish that basically prey on other fish and living creatures as compared to those that feed on minute plankton, vegetable matter or insect life. Omnivorous fish that do eat other fish are not termed predators.

Priest: Any blunt instrument used to kill a fish – it administers the last rites.

Pump: Correct working of the rod in playing a fighting fish. The tip is lowered towards the fish on a tight line, raised up, and the slack obtained is reeled swiftly in as the rod is lowered, again on a taut line. This removes strain from the reel and leaves the angler better prepared to handle any sudden rush made by the fish.

Redd: The spawning place of the migratory and stream-dwelling members of the trout and salmon family; the area cleared in the gravel bed of the stream, to form the spawning nest.

Rod Joint: One section of a rod that comes apart and fits together again with the aid of ferrules.

Rod Point: The extreme top end of the rod where the tip ring is fitted.

Rod Tip: The section at the top end of the rod that develops the major action curve.

Rough: Another form used to describe so-called coarse fish.

School Fish: Fish that normally congregate, swim and feed in groups.

Setting the Hook: Rearing back with the rod to fix the hook into the mouth of a biting or striking fish. *See also* Strike.

Shot: Small round lead sinkers usually split across the face so they can be crimped onto the line.

Shot Leger: A sliding sinker bottom rig built up from split shot. *See* Leger.

Shotting: Fastening the required number of split shot to a rig to balance the tackle system to the desired weight.

Sinker: Any weighted object, usually made of lead, that helps to balance tackle, provide an anchor to the bottom, or add casting weight.

Slider Float: A float or bobber so rigged on the line that the line can slide down through attachments and set the bait at depths greater than the length of the rod. When the desired depth is reached, the hook bait is arrested by a stop fixed to the line above the float. On hooking a fish the line slips easily through the float and enables the fish to be brought within the angler's reach.

Slipping Clutch: Another name for the drag unit on spinning reels (*see* Drag). It allows light line to be used for big fish, because any time the fish runs, a clutch slips and line is released.

Spinner: A lure that revolves around a central spindle, usually sending out a series of vibrations that attract fish. This is an excellent type for casting but has a tendency to put tangles in the line when trolled.

Spinning: The art of using spinning tackle with a fixed-spool reel on which a line flier revolves around the spool to replace the line during the retrieve. In Britain, where spinning was first evolved, this style of fishing is known as fixed-spool angling. The term spinning is used there to describe a special form of baitcasting.

Split Bamboo: A rod material made by splitting special kinds of bamboo into accurately measured splines, fitting them together again with the hard outer layer on the outside, and gluing the whole together with special compounds. A delightful, but expensive rod material.

Split Cane: Another term for split bamboo.

Spoon: Lures shaped like spoons, usually made of metal but embracing many materials and a host of shapes. The best send out powerful vibrations on retrieve and most are top lures for many predatory fish.

Star Drag: A star-shaped mechanism used for setting the drag on many reels, including the modern range of baitcasting reels. The spokes of this mechanism radiate from the centre core of the reel handles, and the drag can be altered by a nudge with the finger while a fish is being played.

Stick: General term used to describe the entire length of the rod but not including any part of the butt if the rod material does not penetrate this fitting. In a rod with a separate butt, the part that fits into the butt is properly the stick.

Still Fishing: Static angling with a bait suspended in the water or resting on the bottom, as opposed to systems in which the bait is cast and retrieved to provide action.

Strike: The act of a fish hitting the lure, and also the setting of the hook by the angler.

Take: Another term for the acceptance by a fish of either a lure or bait — generally used in stillfishing or static situations.

Tackle: Sports fishing gear from rod to reel to the smallest accessory. The equipment of angling in general.

Tackle Up: The act of setting up a fishing outfit.

Tapered Line: The specially tapered, balanced line used in fly fishing. Since it is the line that provides casting weight in fly fishing, various tapers are built in to provide for various needs. *See also* Level Line.

Tippet: The fine replaceable end of a leader. Being the lightest part and the one most likely to become worn, it should be carefully inspected at regular intervals. *See also* Leader.

Trolling: The act of trailing a lure behind a boat at a speed that will create proper lure action and hopefully provoke the strike of a predatory fish.

Trot: The act of working a bait on a float or bobber rig downstream so that the bait passes over places where fish are suspected to be feeding.